FEMINISM, FEMININITY
and POPULAR CULTURE

FEMINISM, FEMININITY and POPULAR CULTURE

Joanne Hollows

Manchester University Press

Manchester and New York

distributed exclusively in the USA by Palgrave

Published by Manchester University Press
Oxford Road, Manchester M13 9NR, UK
and Room 400, 175 Fifth Avenue, New York, NY 10010, USA
www.manchesteruniversitypress.co.uk

Distributed exclusively in the USA by
Palgrave, 175 Fifth Avenue, New York NY 10010, USA

Distributed exclusively in Canada by
UBC Press, University of British Columbia, 2029 West Mall,
Vancouver, BC, Canada V6T 1Z2

British Library Cataloguing-in-Publication Data
A catalogue record for this book is available from the British Library

Library of Congress Cataloging-in-Publication Data
A catalog record for this book is available from the Library of Congress

ISBN 978 0 7190 4394 9 *hardback*
ISBN 978 0 7190 4395 6 *paperback*

First published by Manchester University Press 2000

First digital paperback edition published 2012

Printed by Lightning Source

Contents

Acknowledgements

I am grateful to the Faculty of Humanities at Nottingham Trent University for granting me the sabbatical leave which made completing this book possible. I would like to thank the students at Trinity and All Saints College, the University of North London and at Nottingham Trent: I have learned a great deal from their observations, insights and arguments. In particular, students on 'Post-War Women and Cultural Production' helped me work through many of the ideas in this book. I am also grateful for all colleagues who make Nottingham Trent a rewarding and friendly place to work and, in particular, Bob Ashley, Steve Jones, Ben Taylor and Dave Woods in Media and Cultural Studies.

Books do not get written without all sorts of support. For their emotional and material support over the years, I would like to thank: Al, Chris, Joanne G., Karen, Roma, Sara and, especially, Joyce and Dave Hollows. For their friendship and intellectual support, I would like to offer special thanks to Jo Entwistle, Ruth Furlong, Bev Skeggs, Lisa Taylor, Andy Willis and Maggie Wykes. I am very grateful to Michael Hoar for reading through the manuscript when he had far better things to do with his time. I would also like to take this opportunity to thank Mac at Trinity and All Saints College for giving me a break and then devoting so much time to trying to convince me I deserved one. I am indebted to Kathy and Matthew at Manchester University Press for their support and patience. Last, but not least, I would like to thank Mark Jancovich who is probably even more glad that this book is finished than I am: he devoted vast amounts of time to convincing me I could write this and tolerated my tantrums when I didn't believe him. His ideas, editing, and enthusiasm have improved this book immeasurably and his support has been fundamental to the writing process. Unfortunately, the numerous problems that remain are all mine.

Part I

INTRODUCTION

1

Second-wave feminism and femininity

This chapter examines how some of the key ideas introduced in this book have their roots in what has become known as 'second-wave feminism', the ideas and practices associated with the women's movements of the 1960s and 1970s. While it might seem unnecessary to turn back to this period of feminist struggle, there are a number of important reasons for doing so. First, for many students of feminism today, myself included, second-wave feminism is seen as a product of the past. Therefore, this chapter aims to give, albeit sketchily, a history of some of the ideas, activities and struggles that informed second-wave feminism. Second, a major concern of this book is the ways in which popular culture and femininities need to be studied historically. For this reason it is also necessary to understand feminist identities as the product of specific historical contexts. Third, debates about popular culture within feminist cultural studies often engage with the concepts and ideas generated by second-wave feminism. Therefore, an introduction to the debates of the past offers a context for understanding the debates of the present. Finally, feminism today is sometimes seen as something that happened in the past and is redundant in the present. While this debate is explored in the final chapter, it is only possible to think of what role feminisms might play in the present if we reflect on their, sometimes troubled, past.

This chapter also begins to develop some the major themes of the book as a whole. It examines the different ways in which femininity was constituted as a 'problem' in second-wave feminism. For many feminists, feminine values and behaviour were seen as a major cause of women's oppression. In this way, the chapter explores how second-wave feminism, and the identity 'feminist', was predicated on a rejection of femininity.

The politics of second-wave feminism

There is a wide range of forms of feminist activity and thinking that predates what is known as the second-wave feminism of the 1960s and 1970s. However, it is out of this second wave of feminism that contemporary debates and theories have been produced and feminism has entered academic life. Any definition of feminism is notoriously difficult as it was never a uniform set of ideas: the aims and character of feminist struggles were hotly contested from the outset. However, it is generally accepted that feminism is a form of politics which aims to intervene in, and transform, the unequal power relations between men and women. Expanding on this, Caroline Ramazanoglu has offered a tentative definition of feminism as 'various social theories which explain the relations between the sexes in society, and the differences between women's and men's experiences', theories 'which are also a political practice' (1989, 8). Feminisms of the 1960s and 1970s – and, arguably, of the present – did not simply seek to explain the inequalities between men and women but to use this as a basis for change. However, there were significant differences in the explanations they produced and the forms of political practice they adopted.

To be involved in the women's movement in the 1960s and 1970s was, for many women, to engage in a new and vital practice. Many accounts stress how women 'began to value each other and be proud to be women'. As one of them later recalled, 'It was like that old cliché of the light bulb going on over my head' (Coote and Campbell 1987, 5). For women of later generations, it is often difficult to imagine the sheer sense of energy, optimism and empowerment which participation in feminist struggles produced. For example, Lynne Segal recalls the feeling that 'as women we could change our lives and those of others once we saw through "male lies". Many feminists were eagerly attempting to change every aspect of their lives; how we lived with and related to other adults and children, how we worked and developed new skills, how we saw ourselves. Even cutting one's hair off could give feminists a sense of freedom then' (1987, 69).

Feminisms differed in their form and character in different geographical contexts. However, if we take the cases of the UK and US, we can see some similarities in feminist concerns, despite the crucial differences between the forms of feminism which were created. Feminists in these countries struggled for equal pay, equal access to education and equal job opportunities; they fought for free contraception and the right to abortion; they campaigned about unpaid domestic labour, the need for free child-care provision and for both economic and legal independence; they claimed women's right to define their own sexuality; and they protested against domestic and sexual violence against women (Gelb 1987, 269; Jordan and Weedon 1995, 182). However, there were also crucial differences between the two national contexts. In the US, the National Organisation for Women (NOW), which was founded by Betty Friedan in 1966, fought for legal reform in order to give women the same rights and opportunities as men. In addition, by the late 1960s, women in the US who had been brought together through their involvement in student politics and the counter-culture would claim that an end to women's oppression required not reform, but a radical transformation of society: the overthrow of patriarchy. In the UK, however, while feminists also called for a radical transformation of society, feminism developed in relation to a much stronger tradition of socialist and Marxist politics. As a result, British feminists were much more likely than their US counterparts to argue that the fight for women's liberation required them to tackle both patriarchy *and* capitalism.

Although such a portrait over-simplifies the differences between different types of feminism, there were also common concerns and modes of organisation which underpinned feminist activism in the period. Consciousness-raising groups were a crucial forum in which feminist ideas and identities were formed. In these small groups, women set out collectively to reassess their lives and who they were (Freeman 1978). Whereas the political agenda in left-wing political groups had been primarily set by men, women began to share feelings and ideas and define their own agendas (Evans 1980, 204). The women's movement, therefore, 'started *from* consciousness' by challenging those aspects of women's lives which appeared as 'natural' but were revealed to be 'ideological' (Brunsdon 1978, 19).

Central to second-wave feminism in general, and the consciousness-raising groups in particular, was the idea that 'the personal is political': what appeared to be individual, private problems that women endured in isolation were, it was quickly recognised, common problems experienced by all women in the groups. Whereas other forms of politics had often distinguished between the 'public' realm of politics and the 'private' realm of the family, feminists came to see the family as a key source of their oppression and, therefore, political. As Elizabeth Fox Genovese argues, 'Feminism has led the way in demystifying personal relations, forcefully insisting they are political to the core' (1991, 11). Once women began to recognise common problems and experiences, they used these insights to challenge existing ways of understanding the world which did not fit with their experience of it. As well as producing new 'feminist' theories which sought to challenge 'man-made' knowledge, these theories also aimed to produce 'strategies for transforming existing institutions and practices' (Weedon 1987, 5). However, while the emphasis on the personal as political was also crucial in socialist and Marxist feminisms in the UK, the 'desire to change personal life [also] coexisted with a strong pull towards public political action' (Rowbotham 1996, 7).

As feminists recounted their experiences as women, and found a compelling commonality in these experiences, the idea of 'sisterhood' became increasingly important. Whereas women had previously seen themselves as not only isolated from other women but also as being in competition with them, they began 'to assert their identification with one another' (Mitchell and Oakley 1976, 10) and claim through the notion of 'sisterhood' a collective strength, embodied in the claim that 'Sisterhood is Powerful'. The idea of sisterhood affirmed 'the similarity and solidarity of all women' (Fox Genovese 1991, 13) and their common experience of oppression. As the Redstocking of New York in their manifesto of women's liberation claimed: 'Women are an oppressed class' (Coote and Campbell 1987, 6). Many feminists were no longer concerned with simply expressing their experiences but tried to explain these experiences and 'present a coordinated account of What Was Really Going On' (Knight 1997, 46).

For many feminists, the most useful concept in explaining women's oppression was patriarchy, a system of male domination. As Ramazanoglu argues, 'theories of patriarchy are, implicitly or explicitly, theories which explain the creation and maintenance of men's social, ideological, sexual, political and economic dominance' (1989, 33). While feminists disagreed about the causes and characteristics of patriarchy, many shared the idea that the cornerstone of all women's oppression was a patriarchal system. Many women felt their experiences were marginalised in Left politics and the Black Power movements of the 1960s, where class and race, respectively, had been the organising concepts in understanding inequality, rather than sex and gender. Patriarchy put unequal gender relations at the centre of any political analysis. While Marxist feminists in the UK did not believe that patriarchy alone could explain women's oppression and considered the ways in which capitalism and patriarchy worked together to oppress women, many still believed that the concept of patriarchy was needed to explain what seemed to be the universal oppression of women (Beechey 1987; Stacey 1993).

Second-wave feminism and the politics of difference

If younger readers of this book may feel marginalised or excluded from the concerns of second-wave feminism, so did many women during the period. Many critics have pointed to the ways in which the feminist 'sisterhood' was not as all-inclusive as it claimed to be. Indeed, by the late 1970s, the women's movement fragmented as the idea of 'sisterhood' was contested by the recognition of crucial differences in the experiences of women and the sources of their oppression (Ramazanoglu 1989, 3). The recognition of differences between women calls into question many of the central assumptions which underpinned second-wave feminism. Not only was second-wave feminism 'a cultural product of a particular historical period', but it also became increasingly clear that it offered theories of oppression which in many ways were produced from 'a position of privilege and power' (Ramazanoglu 1989, 22).

The experiences recounted in consciousness-raising groups which were used as a basis for theorising the universal oppression of all women were, in fact, largely the experiences of middle-class white women. As Fox Genovese argues, 'the middle-class spokeswomen for the new women's movement, without fully recognising what they were doing, established their own autobiographies as the benchmark of experience of all women' (1991, 29).[1] While these women felt the primary source of their oppression by men was a result of the sexual division of labour, and while they sometimes fought to 'lend a hand' to their less privileged 'sisters', by generalising from their own experience to the experience of all women they alienated many black and working-class women who did not see gender as the central site of their oppression. As US feminist bell hooks remembers, 'white feminists lamented the absence of large numbers of non-white participants but were unwilling to change the movement's focus so it would better address the needs of women from all classes and races' (1982, 188). As it became increasingly clear that all women did not share the same experiences and were subject to different forms of oppression, the idea of 'sisterhood' and a common cause of women's oppression were undermined. However, they were even more forcefully undermined when it was claimed that white middle-class 'sisters' were, at the end of the day, simply fighting for equality with their men within the very system they claimed to criticise (p. 189). Furthermore, by fighting for equality with middle-class men, middle-class women often strengthened 'class lines by pushing lower-class and minority women, singly or together with their men, further down the socioeconomic scale' (Fox Genovese 1991, 22). This reproduces a history in which 'white women have benefited fundamentally from the oppression of black women' (Amos and Parmar 1997, 55).

If these insights challenge some of our preconceptions about the feminist politics of the 1960s and early 1970s, they also challenge some of the fundamental assumptions of many feminist theories of the period. These theories saw women as a common group rather than recognising the way that gender intersects with other identities: as Judith Butler puts it, 'If one "is" a woman, that is surely not all one is' (1990, 3). Indeed, this problem is highlighted by the claims that women are a class or share the same situation as blacks. For example, the 'Chicago Women Form Liberation Group' in 1967 proclaimed, 'Women must not make the same mistake as blacks did at first of allowing others (whites in their case, men in ours) to define our issues, methods and goals' (cited in Evans 1980, 200). This form of thinking demonstrates how the universal group of women was conceptualised in such a way as to reflect the identities of the white middle-class women who produced the ideas. As hooks (1982) argues, to make an analogy between the position of women and blacks depends on the idea that black women are excluded from the category of 'women' because it would be redundant and indeed meaningless to claim that black *women* share the same social status as *black* women!

Once a common cause of women's oppression was questioned, so was the concept of patriarchy. Patriarchy, in the way in which it is formulated by many radical feminists, is an inflexible structure offering no room for resistance or change and implies a universal form of oppression based on biological differences between men and women. Thinking about women as a monolithic category offered little scope for thinking about difference and the complexities and subtleties of different women's oppression in different historical and geographical contexts (Rowbotham 1981). Even when Marxist and socialist feminists tried to theorise capitalism and patriarchy together to explore the relations between class and gender inequalities, they have still dealt in 'abstract generalities' rather than 'the contradictions of historical developments' (Ramazanoglu 1989, 39). However, despite these problems the concept of patriarchy has not been displaced from feminist theorising. For many feminists, patriarchy may not be a perfect concept but it remains the best tool for understanding women's subordinate position (Alexander and Taylor 1981). For this reason, many contemporary feminists have continued to use the concept of patriarchy. Within feminist cultural studies, the concept is often taken for granted: a system of male domination is assumed to exist and used to identify and explain different instances of women's oppression. However, explanations of the nature, form and operation of patriarchy are often side-stepped (this is less true of the feminist psychoanalysis discussed later). In this way, notions of 'patriarchal culture' are commonplace within feminist cultural studies – indeed, they are often a 'commonsense' of feminist cultural studies – but patriarchy is rarely examined or explained: too often things are simply referred to as 'patriarchal' or as 'an effect of patriarchy'. For this reason patriarchy has remained a largely ahistorical concept, despite the fact that it is now acknowledged to cut across, and be cross-cut by, other forms of inequality and power.

While the concept of sisterhood is far less central in much contemporary feminism, it is still influential in many forms of popular feminism. The emphasis on a 'familial' bond between women acting collectively to support each other is one feature of the ways in which feminist concerns have entered into 'mainstream' popular forms – for example, the 'sisterhoods' in films such as *Steel Magnolias* (1989), *A League of their Own* (1992), *Waiting to Exhale* (1995) and *The First Wives Club* (1996).[2] Indeed, while in many ways affirming that 'sisterhood' might be powerful or at least empowering, *A League of their Own* also suggests the limitations of sisterhood by highlighting that the fight for 'equal opportunities' with men in professional baseball, was an opportunity only open to white women (Taylor 1995). The concept of 'sisterhood', however, has continued to be important in some academic and popular forms of black feminism. The emphasis here is less on the universal and abstract notion of sisterhood inherited from second-wave feminism and more on a grounded sense of sisterhood which emphasises how 'mutual support' is necessary to black women's (and men's) survival (Bobo and Seiter 1997, 178).

The idea that the 'personal is political' and the importance of experience still retain an important place in some contemporary feminist thought. Indeed, although not always acknowledged, many critics in cultural studies – feminist and otherwise – have produced a 'politics' from a reflection on their own experience (McRobbie 1991; Skeggs 1997). Indeed, many seemingly 'trivial' experiences of being positioned as 'stupid' or in a state of 'false consciousness' because of my own investments in 'feminine' popular culture undoubtedly shaped the focus of this book. However, experience cannot simply be thought of as a source of knowledge (Skeggs 1997): experience is not self-evident and an explanation of how things are but is itself a construction, 'Experience is at once already an interpretation *and* in need of an interpretation' (Scott 1992, 37).

This section has explored some themes in the history of second-wave feminism and has inevitably sacrificed complexity in the interests of brevity by placing greater emphasis on feminisms in the US. While I have begun to identify some of the problems with second-wave feminism, and shall continue to do so in the next section, it is also worth remembering what these feminisms have achieved. While a radical transformation of gender roles has not occurred, legal reforms have made a real difference to many women's lives, although they may not have benefited all women equally.[3] Furthermore, this 'progress' can never be assumed but is still a site of struggle, and rights which have been won are not guaranteed.

Feminism and the critique of femininity (1): femininity and masculinity

The following two sections examine why femininity has been seen as a problem by feminists. As there is not space here to survey a wide range of feminist criticism, some 'canonical' feminist texts have been selected to act as case studies.[4] These case studies are used to highlight the ways in which feminist critiques of femininity are often dependent on creating an opposition between 'bad' feminine identities and 'good' feminist identities. However, feminists have often disagreed about what qualities these feminist identities embody. This section examines one form of feminism

which sees femininity as inferior to masculinity: that is, that
equality between men and women might be achieved if women
rejected feminine values and behaviour in favour of masculine
values and behaviour. The following section explores a different
opposition, that between femininity and femaleness, a position
which equates women's liberation with throwing off the 'false'
mask of femininity to reveal the 'real' female values which lie
beneath.

For many second-wave feminists, femininity was seen as
fundamental to understanding women's oppression. Girls, it was
often claimed, were socialised into feminine values and behaviour
which were associated with passivity, submissiveness and dependence. For many feminists, in becoming feminine, women were
'colonised' by patriarchy and became implicated in their own
oppression. (For example, Millett 1977 and Rowbotham 1973.)
The distinction between sex and gender was crucial in understanding this process. Culturally produced masculine and
feminine gender roles, it was argued, were mapped on to biological differences between males and females making them appear
to be part of men's and women's biological 'nature' rather than
cultural constructions. For example, it was argued, while biological differences between men and women did mean that women
were biologically destined to give birth to children, it did not
necessarily follow that women naturally had feminine, 'maternal'
instincts which made them essentially more supportive, nurturing
and caring than men. For radical feminists such as Kate Millett,
the production of ideological consent to patriarchy, through
socialisation into masculine and feminine roles, was 'based on the
needs and values of the dominant group [men] and dictated by
what its members cherish in themselves and find convenient in
subordinates: aggression, intelligence, force, and efficacy in the
male; passivity, ignorance, docility, "virtue", and ineffectuality in
the female' (1977, 26). For these reasons, many feminists saw the
rejection of feminine identities as crucial in producing a feminist
identity and consciousness. However, as will become clear in the
next section, this has not stopped some feminists returning to the
notion of biological differences in asserting women's superiority
over men.

For many second-wave feminists, femininity was self-
evidently problematic. However, Betty Friedan's *The Feminine
Mystique*, a foundational text of second-wave feminism, produced
a developed critique of femininity. Often using the form of a

crime thriller (Bowlby 1992; Knight 1997), Friedan set out to investigate the lot of US women in the 1950s, an era in which it was claimed women's involvement in the public sphere declined as they succumbed to 'the feminine mystique' which defined women as 'healthy, beautiful, educated [up to a point], concerned only with her husband, her children and her home' (1963, 13). The feminine mystique claimed 'the highest value and the only commitment for women is the fulfilment of their own femininity' (p. 37). Striving to fulfil their 'feminine potential' produced a common range of symptoms – feelings of failure, of nothingness, of 'is this all there is?' These were symptoms, Friedan claimed, of 'the problem with no name', a problem of epidemic proportions in US women.

Attempting to conform to the feminine ideal promoted by media forms such as women's magazines and advertising, it was argued, caused these Stepford Wives of the 1950s incredible psychological harm by making them deny their minds. Household drudgery caused a fragmentation and a loss of concentration and led to fatigue and breakdown. Women no longer had a sense of their own identity because they were encouraged to see themselves only as someone's wife or mother. Friedan (over)dramatises her point by comparing the loss of identity experienced by the American housewife to that of the prisoner in the Nazi concentration camp. Both housewife and prisoner are dehumanised; both are taught to behave like children and be dependent and passive; and eventually, both become prisoners of their own minds, consenting to their position because they can no longer conceive of having any other place in the world. The feminine mystique produced the housewife who

> stunts her intelligence to become childlike, turns away from individual identity to become an anonymous biological robot in a docile mass. She becomes less than human, preyed upon by outside pressures, and herself preying on her husband and children. And the longer she conforms, the less she feels as if she really exists. She looks for security in things . . . she lives a vicarious life through mass daydreams and through her husband and children. (Friedan 1963, 296–7)

Although Friedan's work has been subject to rigorous criticism, I want to concentrate here on three key problems in *The Feminine Mystique* which would be reproduced in some later feminist thought. First, Friedan argues that feminine ideas and values are

a problem which, although not produced by women, are reproduced by women, an idea which would become part of the
'common-sense' of much second-wave feminism. However, while
many feminists also would be critical of masculine behaviour and
values, Friedan sees the traits associated with masculinity as
preferable, and more 'human', than those associated with femininity. Friedan's solution to the problem with no name was for
women to stop conforming to the feminine mystique, pursue
higher education and get a career – to fulfil their human potential, women needed to 'get a life' and make a commitment to the
masculine world of work. Furthermore, Friedan links the idea of
the 'waste' of women's 'human potential' with a wider concern
about 'national waste' (Bowlby 1992, 82) – the feminine
mystique isn't just a problem for women but for the very family
women were meant to be supporting. The obsessive mother, she
claimed, stopped her children developing full adult identities,
producing sons who were juvenile delinquents or homosexuals!
The 'happy housewife heroine' with no sense of identity is
revealed to nag more and be worse in bed than the educated
superwoman who combines career and home.

Second, if Friedan reproduces a masculine value system
which sees feminine qualities as inferior qualities, she also
presents the character and experience of being feminine in the
1950s as monolithic. Friedan presents the 1950s as a period of
'conservatism and constraints', but this hides the complexity of
the era and portrays women simply as victims, rather than considering how they might have transformed and resisted dominant
notions of femininity (Meyerowitz 1994). This idea that femininity is a monolithic entity ignores the ways in which femininity is
cross-cut by class and race. The sense of despair that the feminine
mystique was meant to have produced in women across America
was in fact one that may mainly have been experienced by women
isolated in white middle-class suburbia. However, if confinement
within the domestic sphere caused these women problems, the
ideal of being a full-time suburban wife and mom seemed like an
impossible dream to many working-class women (hooks, 1982).
The class position of Friedan's women suffering from the feminine
mystique becomes clear when she castigates them for their lack of
commitment to the public world of work: 'For fear of that
commitment, hundreds of able educated suburban housewives
today fool themselves about the writer or actress they might have
been . . . or apply for jobs as receptionists or saleswomen, jobs well

below their actual abilities' (Friedan 1963, 334). Many working-class women may, of course, have found a position as a receptionist a step up in the job market. Friedan equates women's liberation with women having the same rights and entitlements as men, but this begs the question, 'which men?'

Third, if Friedan's conceptualisation of femininity is one-dimensional, there are also major problems with her understanding of culture. Friedan finds much of the evidence for the existence of the feminine mystique in women's magazines, which seemed to promote a unified picture of a feminine ideal. However, this evidence is challenged by Meyerowitz (1994) who identifies far more complex and contradictory constructions of femininity in the period.[5] Friedan implies that this feminine ideal portrayed by the media is absorbed by an anonymous passive mass of consumers – for example when she conceives of the housewife as 'an anonymous biological robot in a docile mass'. In this way, she draws on the assumptions of mass culture theory which presents consumers as 'cultural dopes', who are 'living in a permanent state of false consciousness' (Hall 1981, 231). However, these assumptions have been challenged by work in media and cultural studies which shows that audiences make active engagements with media texts to produce different readings based on the knowledge and experience that is a product of the social and cultural groups to which they belong. (These issues are discussed in much greater detail in the following chapters.) In contrast, Friedan assumed that messages from magazines are simply injected into a passive audience who absorb them uncritically.

Friedan is not the only feminist whose work is underpinned by the assumptions of mass culture theory. Radical feminists in the 1970s would often reproduce a conspiratorial version of mass culture theory. For example, Alice Embree claimed that the mass media 'shaped people into one-dimensional receivers of communication – people who were more easily channelled into the roles of unprotesting consumers' (1970, 196). Indeed, 'psychological warfare was declared on the domestic consumer' (p. 197).[6] In the process, it is argued, the media reinforces the position of women as both passive and as 'emotional nonintellectuals' (p. 201). Feminist activism has also been underpinned by similar assumptions: protesters against the 1968 Miss America Pageant claimed that the event exercised 'thought control' ('No More Miss America' in Morgan, 1970, 588).[7] Underpinning these feminist variations on a mass culture theme is a circular argument: the media produces passivity in the female audience, female audiences are passive and therefore they accept the content of the media.

The privileging of 'masculine' over 'feminine' qualities seen in Friedan, while not as explicit, haunts a range of feminist positions. For example, in another 'foundational' text, *The Female Eunuch*, Germaine Greer constantly aligns herself as feminist critic with masculine values. 'Feminine parasites' (Greer, 1970, 22) are not included in Greer's 'sisterhood': she urges women to stop 'cajoling and manipulating' and instead to claim 'the masculine virtues of magnanimity and generosity and courage' (p. 330). In the process, Greer's feminist credentials are established by distancing herself from both femininity and feminine 'other women' (Morris 1988a, 29).

Feminism and the critique of femininity (2): femininity and femaleness

Not all second-wave feminist work celebrated masculine over feminine values. For example, Kate Millett in *Sexual Politics* sees femininity as a form of 'interior colonisation' (1977, 25) and, like Friedan, argues that in becoming feminine women are infantalised and left with no sources of dignity and self-respect (p. 54). However, for Millett, femininity cannot be simply shrugged off for, in a patriarchal society, women who resist the 'feminine' role are met with force in order to reproduce the status quo. The solution for Millett is the abolition of gender altogether: she criticises both masculinity and femininity and instead advocates androgyny. However, this raises the question of what the androgynous person would be like, what traits they would combine from those previously separated into masculine and feminine (Tong 1992, 98). It also raises the question of what values, and whose values, the 'androgynous' human would reflect.

Androgyny is, however, no solution for the radical feminist, Mary Daly, who believes it sounds like 'John Travolta and Farrah Fawcett-Majors scotch-taped together' (1979, xi), nor does she have any desire to have anything to do with masculine values. Instead, Daly privileges 'real' femaleness over 'false' femininity, distinguishing between 'real' females – whom she approvingly describes as witches, nags and hags – and 'plastic', 'mutant', feminine, 'painted birds' – 'man-made' women. In Daly's

universe, men have colonised everything, even 'the final frontier':
'Patriarchy appears to be "everywhere". Even outer space and the
future have been colonised' (p. 1). Patriarchy has invaded
women's heads making most of us deny the 'Wild Woman
within': 'If the terms *feminine* and *masochist* are used synony-
mously, this has nothing to do with the deep reality of the female
self, but with patriarchally imposed, self-denying masks' (p. 27).
While Daly urges us to free 'the Hag within' (p. 15), most
women, it is claimed, are not up to the task because 'patriarchy is
everywhere'. Furthermore, those brave enough to become 'wild
women' are not only threatened by men but also by feminine
'painted birds' who are after them: the wild woman 'who sheds
the paint and manifests her Original Moving Self . . . is attacked
by the mutants of her own kind, the man-made women' (p. 334).
Indeed, patriarchy has even colonised feminism, producing in its
place 'plastic' or 'man-made pseudofeminism' (1988, 217). Daly
claims that these plastic feminists – 'reformist roboticized tokens'
(1979, xv) – are simply out to double-cross their sisters. With
more paranoia than *The X-Files*, Mary Daly makes it clear that
most women aren't to be trusted and aren't to be let into the
'Nag-nation' (1988, 147). Only the chosen few can save the
planet: 'it becomes clear that there are women, including some
who will describe themselves as "feminists", with whom I do not
feel enough identification to warrant the pronoun *we*' (1979, 25).

While it is easy to dismiss Daly's work as deeply paranoid,
many of the underlying assumptions of her work would be reproduced by some radical feminists in the 1980s and 1990s. For this
reason, it is necessary to tease out some of the implications of her
work. First, Daly's feminism has given up on most women, her
'journey to the "Otherworld" of the Race of Women is for the
chosen few' (Segal 1987, 20). As Morris puts it, Daly is a 'political elitist' who distinguishes 'the elect-in-a-state-of-grace from
those beyond the pale' (1988a, 37–8). Second, if 'patriarchy is
everywhere', it is difficult to see how anybody, Daly included,
could see through patriarchy to find the real woman within (Tong
1992). Third, Daly is arguing that men and women are *naturally*
different. This reinstates the biological determinism that most
feminisms have sought to challenge, indeed her work is 'a celebration of "natural" differences' (Barrett 1988, 73). As Segal
argues, 'A feminism which emphasises only the dangers to
women from men, which insists upon the essential differences
between women's and men's inner being, between women's and

men's natural urges and experience of the world, leaves little or no scope for transforming the relations between men and women' (1987, 37).

A further problem is raised by the ways in which Daly conceptualises language and culture. Daly's use of 'weird' words isn't whimsy but a central part of her project to 'dis-spell the language of phallocracy' (1979, 4). She argues that wild women must dismantle patriarchal language and claim language as their own. For Daly, patriarchal language changes its meaning when it is 'pronounced' by wild women. For example, whereas, from Daly's perspective, Friedan uses 'nag' within 'a patriarchal context' when she claims that the 'feminine' woman makes her husband's life a misery, when a wild woman pronounces that she is a 'Nag', it is used with 'pride and defiance' (Daly 1988, 37). Daly then issues a challenge to patriarchal language which has 'allowed expression only under male control' (p. 8). However, as Morris has argued, this conceptualisation of language is problematic. Daly believes that words structure reality and, therefore, by changing the words, we can change reality. By replacing 'false' words with 'true' words, Daly claims, we can subvert patriarchal language (Morris 1988a, 31). However, this ignores the way that words – or signs – do not have an inherent meaning: meanings are produced only when 'words work together in discourse or *language in use*' (p. 30).

If Daly privileges women's 'natural' 'virtues' over men's violence and greed for power, she is not alone in doing so, although she obviously has her own unique take on the idea. As Lynne Segal has argued, the 1970s and 1980s saw a trend towards this kind of thinking within some feminisms. Indeed, it has become something of a common-sense in some feminist circles – popular and academic – and ends up reinforcing rather than challenging notions of gender differences. Women and men, it is proclaimed, are simply different. For example, critics such as Susan Brownmiller (1977), Andrea Dworkin (1981) and Susan Griffin (1981), writing on sexual violence and pornography, continually reaffirm men's inherent evil and women's 'natural virtue'. Similarly, Segal identifies a 'maternal revivalism' (1987, 145) in writers such as Carol Gilligan, who assert that 'women's moral development is distinctly different from that of men ... They display greater compassion and empathy' (p. 146). However, as Segal points out, these are the same notions of women's moral virtue which underpinned Victorian conceptions of gender. Differences between men and women are universalised so that women become characterised by 'maternal' behaviour (p. 148). Such a view extracts women from the social and cultural relations in which mothering takes place: as Segal neatly asserts, 'Mothering is not determined by consciousness, but consciousness by mothering' (p. 149).

In conclusion, we can see how it was not only men and systematic male domination which were constituted as a problem in second-wave feminism but also women's investments in 'femininity' which, it was claimed, blocked the development of a feminist consciousness. Femininity remains largely untheorised and self-evident in these works. Some feminists did acknowledge how femininities changed over time (for example, Friedan 1963; Rowbotham 1973), but little attention was paid to the different modes of feminine identity, not only between historical and geographical contexts, but also within them. The idea that femininity was a cultural product was central for many second-wave feminist critics, but few actually outlined what they meant by culture. Furthermore, as we have seen, some feminists wanted to have their cake and eat it: they distinguished a 'false' culturally produced femininity from females' 'true' nature which presumably lay in their biology, a 'deep' 'femaleness' which was waiting to be released once the 'surface' trappings of femininity had been thrown off.

However, what is decisively produced across most work from this period is an opposition between feminist and feminine identities. Morris draws on Le Doeuff to argue that 'certain philosophical discourses produce their own identity by projecting an image of an Other who lacks the same identity (thus *creating* that Other in the process)' (1988a, 43). This raises questions about whether the feminine 'other woman' was a necessary fiction in order to produce an 'oppositional' feminist identity. A central theme in the chapters that follow is the extent to which this opposition between the feminine anti-heroine – the 'ordinary woman' – and the feminist heroine has been reproduced, reworked or resisted in feminist media and cultural studies (Brunsdon 1991).

Notes

1 It remains the case that the experience of white, middle-class, heterosexual women still acts as a presumed 'norm' against which other identities and experiences are classified (Mirza 1997, 13): for example, the languages of

feminism still often work to portray the experiences of black women as an 'exception' (Aziz 1997, 71). Furthermore, Aziz argues, this can often work to make it appear that black women are *homogeneously oppressed in almost every politically significant way* (p. 73).

2 For a useful discussion of female friendship in contemporary Hollywood movies see Tasker (1998, 137–60).

3 For example, feminist campaigns for women's right to legal abortions failed to acknowledge that 'many black women's reproductive struggles were around the right to keep and realise their fertility. For these women, abortions, sterilisations and [the contraceptive] Depo Provera were all too easily available, and were often administered without adequate consultation and/or under the shadow of poverty' (Aziz 1997, 70).

4 For example, both de Beauvoir (1972) and Mitchell (1974) contain extended discussions of femininity. De Beauvoir's *The Second Sex* was highly influential but predates second-wave feminism, being first published in 1949. Mitchell's *Feminism and Psychoanalysis* examines the implications of appropriating psychoanalysis as a tool for understanding women's oppression. The influence of this move can be seen in the psychoanalytic film criticism discussed in Chapter 3.

5 Indeed, Friedan's assertions are not only contradicted by her own evidence of problems women were facing taken from magazines but also by the fact that her own work appeared in these magazines (Meyerowitz 1994).

6 These kinds of ideas have not disappeared from feminist writings: for example, Naomi Wolf's *The Beauty Myth* (1990) not only claims to act as *The Feminine Mystique* of the 1990s, but Wolf also sees women as powerless in the face of the 'hard sell' of the beauty industry.

7 The protest took the form of throwing 'woman-garbage' such as 'bras, girdles, curlers, false eyelashes, wigs and representative issues of *Cosmopolitan, Ladies Home Journal, Family Circle,* etc.' into 'a huge Freedom Trash Can' (Morgan 1970, 585).

Further reading

Mirza, H. S., ed., *Black British Feminism: A Reader* (London, Routledge, 1997)

Segal, L. *Is the Future Female? Troubled Thoughts on Contemporary Feminism* (London, Virago, 1987)

Tong, R. *Feminist Thought: A Comprehensive Introduction* (London, Routledge, 1992)

2

Feminism, cultural studies
and popular culture

This chapter explores the movement of feminism into academic life in general and the study of popular culture in particular. Given that the women involved in feminist struggles in the US, and to a slightly lesser extent in the UK, were often highly educated, middle-class women, it is perhaps not surprising that feminist concerns made inroads into academic disciplines relatively quickly. However, this was not a straightforward process: feminism's impact on different disciplines was uneven and feminist perspectives did not encounter existing bodies of knowledge without resistance. Feminists not only tried to challenge the gender-blindness and sexism of existing forms of knowledge, but also often tried to produce new forms of knowledge which would provide the basis for political action.

Feminism also made an impact on academic life through the institutionalisation of Women's Studies courses and options. For example, as the *Women Take Issue* Editorial Group have argued, feminists working in Women's Studies often drew on their experiences of the women's movement and brought them into their academic practices by 'organising together both to share experiences, and work together towards a knowledge of them, and to interrogate and appropriate "knowledge" and skills which exclude or ignore women' (1978, 8). Although there would be great variation between Women's Studies courses, they were often linked to a process of consciousness-raising while also situating women's 'personal experience and their subjectively registered responses to them in a sociological and historical context' (p. 9). Women's Studies was also distinguished from other academic fields by the insistence on taking women as the starting point; by providing 'a critique of sexism and chauvinism in existing theories, texts and courses'; and by attempting to develop new conceptual tools to do feminist analysis (pp. 9–10). A key problem which was quickly recognised by many feminists was what became known as 'women and ...' syndrome: questions about women were made an 'addition' to existing forms of knowledge rather than used radically to reformulate those existing forms of knowledge by making questions about gender central to them (p. 11).

Assumptions about the effects of popular culture on women had been a commonsense of second-wave feminism: for example, it was common for feminists to claim that a whole range of popular forms and practices – from romance-reading to dressing up – locked women into feminine identities which made them blind to, and collude in, their own oppression. However, by the mid-1970s, questions about how gendered identities were culturally produced and reproduced became the topic of much more in-depth feminist research and discussion. This chapter explores two main ways in which feminist research into popular culture entered academic life. First, it examines the 'images of women' debate. By the mid-1970s, feminists working in the social sciences had begun to generate a body of research into how men and women were represented in the content of the media and the effects this had on media audiences. This research into 'images of women' was increasingly criticised by feminists drawing on other theoretical sources such as structuralism and psychoanalysis and produced widespread debate about questions of representation. The critiques of the 'images of women' tradition lead to the development of one key focus of feminist media, film and cultural studies: how the processes and practices of representation worked to produce ideas about what it means to be a woman (explored in depth in Chapters 3, 4 and 5).

Second, feminist cultural studies has not simply equated the significance of popular culture with questions of representation and textual analysis. Feminist cultural analysis also informed, and was informed by, wider debates about how to analyse and theorise culture, in particular work at the Centre for Contemporary Cultural Studies in Birmingham. Cultural studies explores the complex relations between cultural institutions, industries, texts and practices and, therefore, while questions about representation have been central, they are not the only concern of cultural studies. As Angela McRobbie (1997a; 1997b) has argued, feminist cultural studies' preoccupation with questions of representation should not make us ignore feminist contributions to questions about the political economy of culture, cultural policy and 'lived experience'. While cultural studies is not just about the study of popular culture, questions about what is at stake in studying popular culture have been central in cultural studies. These debates inform much of the feminist work discussed in this book and, for this reason, they are introduced in the second section. Furthermore, 'cultural studies involves an active engagement with the social creation of "standards", "values" and "taste"' (Morris 1997, 43). This has been a crucial dimension of much feminist cultural analysis which has explored how judgements about value have often been gendered.

The 'images of women' debate

By the mid-1970s, the study of women and popular culture across a range of disciplines often centred on questions about 'images of women'. In the US much of this research continued the project started in *The Feminine Mystique* and examined how the media played a role in socialising women into restrictive notions of femininity. This work was influenced by the dominant modes of communications research in the period which carried out research into the 'content' of media output and the 'effects' of media messages. The relationship between this research paradigm and a post-Friedan feminist agenda can be seen in Gaye Tuchman's reasoning: 'Suppose for a moment that children's television primarily presents adult women as housewives, nonparticipants in the paid labour force. Also, suppose that girls in the television audience "model" their behaviour and expectations on that of television women' (1978, 6). Research into the content of the media seemed to prove Tuchman's first supposition to be the case. For example, research into television showed that not only were women far less likely to be shown in employment outside the home than men but they were also heavily under-represented in general. Tuchman called this process 'symbolic annihilation' (pp. 10–13). Furthermore, she claimed that media images had not kept up with changes in society, especially the 'transformation' of gender roles brought about by the women's movement. For Tuchman, therefore, the media were even more sexist than society and 'misrepresented' reality. Tuchman's second supposition also appeared to be substantiated by research into media 'effects'. The media messages which presented stereotypical images of women, it was claimed, not only socialised children into 'traditional sex roles'' but also taught them that they 'should direct their hearts towards hearth and home' (p. 37). The conclusions which were drawn from the research are very similar to those of Friedan: to prevent people internalising 'negative' images from the media, they should be replaced with 'positive' images of working women. Like Friedan, this research tended to share 'the liberal feminist objective of integrating women into the present system on an equal basis with men. The characteristics associated with "maleness" in media images are those which have been defined implicitly as the goal for women in media images' (Janus 1996, 8).

However, this was not the only problem with this kind of research. Although the critiques are wide-ranging, I want to highlight three main issues: the relationship between the media and reality; the problems with content analysis; and the problems with effects research. First, the relationship between the media and reality within this research paradigm rests on the assumption that the media acts as a 'window on the world', that media images are, *or should be*, a reflection or representation of society. The problem that researchers found with images of women was that media images were not keeping up with 'real' social changes – there was a 'culture lag' – and therefore, the media was *mis*representing how women *really* are and worked to reinforce 'traditional' images of women. This produces problems: if the media are meant to be showing 'real' women, this assumes we can agree on what a 'real' model of womanhood looks like and assumes that the media can simply show her as she is (Walters 1995, 40). As Charlotte Brunsdon states, 'Arguing for more realistic images is always an argument for the representation of "your" version of reality' (cited in van Zoonen 1994, 31). Furthermore, this research assumes that what it means to be a man or a woman is straightforward, self-evident, unchanging and ignores the ways that gendered identities are cross-cut by other forms of cultural identity such as race and class. As many critics have since argued, the media do not represent or misrepresent gendered identities but work to construct and structure the meaning of gender. Media forms therefore work to construct what it means to be a woman in specific historical and geographical contexts, meanings that are often 'contradictory and contested' (van Zoonen 1994, 34). This argument that 'representations were not expressive of some prior reality, but instead were actively constitutive of reality' (McRobbie 1997a, 172) would inform a wide range of feminist work in feminist film, media and cultural studies, as the debates surveyed later in this book demonstrate (for a more detailed discussion of the impact of structuralism and psychoanalysis, see Chapter 3).

Second, these problems with 'images of women' research are also related to the problems with content analysis which concentrated on '*what* the media showed' rather than '*how* they produced meaning' (MacDonald 1995, 15). The researcher using content analysis aimed to measure the content of the media by taking a sample of media texts and isolating the features of the texts they want to measure. For example, in a sample of adverts, content analysis might aim to 'count' the numbers of men and women in employment outside the home in order to assess whether the number of working women in these adverts reflected the number of working women in 'reality' (Tuchman 1978). This has the advantage of being able to deal with a fairly large sample of texts and, through comparative studies, document evidence of change over time. It would, in this way, seek to reveal the extent to which 'stereotypes' of women existed in TV programming. However, by treating women as a homogeneous category this would tell us nothing about the differences between how different types of men and women were portrayed. Furthermore, not only does this treat the content of media texts as if it were transparent and not subject to different interpretations, but it also ignores the way in which meaning is organised within the text. For example, a series of advertisements in the UK for the household cleaner Flash Excel has portrayed the male partner doing a range of domestic duties: cleaning the bath, the top of the cooker and the kitchen floor. If this was included within a content analysis, it might signify 'progress' – evidence of men's responsibility for domestic labour. In this way, it would totally ignore the way in which the adverts work to confirm the 'exceptional' nature of men's involvement in these tasks, and the way the male character is presented as doing a favour for his wife by helping out in order to get in her good books, thereby confirming the notion that it is *normal* for women to be responsible for domestic labour. Taking the meaning of images as self-evident and extracting them from both the context of the text in which they appear, and a wider cultural context in which they are produced and consumed is highly problematic. As Michele Barrett points out, if a Martian looked at photographs of British royalty, 'they might be forgiven for concluding, from all those pictures of the Queen reviewing regiments, opening Parliament, enthroning archbishops and so on, that she controlled all the repressive and ideological state apparatuses' (1988, 107–8).

The idea that media messages are self-evident and transparent relates to the third problem with 'images of women' analysis: this type of research assumes that media messages have direct effects upon their audience. By attempting to measure changes in the behaviour and the attitudes of audiences which are exposed to particular types of material, researchers often came to conclusions such as 'Watching lots of television leads children and adolescents to believe in traditional sex roles' (Tuchman 1978, 37). However, the meaning of the text cannot be assumed. All texts are inherently 'polysemic' – that is, capable of generating multiple meanings – and, as a result, although a text might have a 'preferred reading', it does not follow that it will be decoded in the same way by everyone (Hall 1980). To assume all people interpret the same text in the same way is to assume either that the text is all-powerful and the audience totally passive (that they are 'cultural dopes') or that every member of the audience shares an identical cultural background and have identical resources at their disposal. As a result, it is necessary to consider how 'The meaning of the text will be constructed differently according to the discourses (knowledges, prejudices, resistances, etc.) brought to bear on the text by the reader' (Morley 1992, 57). For example, the media images that the white, middle-class, professional Betty Friedan interpreted as damaging to women in the 1950s, were the very same images of femininity which some working-class women may have found 'liberating'.

Cultural studies and popular culture

While a range of disciplinary and interdisciplinary areas have analysed aspects of popular culture, it is in the field of cultural studies that questions about how to define and analyse 'the popular' have been central and, from the outset, cultural studies has demanded an interdisciplinary approach. As Nelson et al. have pointed out, cultural studies 'draws from whatever fields are necessary to produce the knowledge required for a particular project', and makes use of whatever resources are needed to, in Stuart Hall's words, 'enable people to understand what [was] going on' (Nelson et al. 1992, 2). As Richard Johnson has argued, one discipline is insufficient to 'grasp the study of culture as a whole' (1986, 279) and, for this reason, many people working within 'disciplinary' areas – for example, design history or film studies – are increasingly using interdisciplinary approaches in their work (p. 278), often producing work that is best characterised as cultural studies (for example, the work of the design historian Judy Attfield discussed in Chapter 6).

It is not within the scope of this book to replicate or rewrite the histories of cultural studies, nor do I want to offer a definition, although I do have a fondness for Raymond Williams' description of it as a 'baggy monster'.[1] To set out to narrate or define cultural studies always involves a process of selection, in which one neglects the ways in which cultural studies 'is a whole set of formations; it has its own different conjunctures and moments in the past' (Hall 1992, 278). However, the people involved in making these histories of cultural studies have not simply been working to produce a 'rag-bag' of a field which might mean anything, there has been 'a determination to stake out some positions within it and argue for them' (*ibid.*). Furthermore, Hall argues, 'there is something *at stake*' in doing cultural studies: the project of cultural studies is a political project which focuses on the way in which cultural industries, institutions, forms and practices are bound up 'with, and within, relations of power' (Bennett cited in Nelson *et al.* 1992, 3).

As a result, feminism and cultural studies (in their different forms) have common concerns. As Franklin *et al.* argue, both have close relations with radical political activism and both 'focus on the analysis of forms of power and oppression, and on the politics of the production of knowledge within the academy, as well as elsewhere in society' (1991, 1–2). Both cultural studies and feminism have explored connections between experience and theory (p. 2). Not only do feminism and cultural studies have overlapping concerns but, as Stuart Hall has argued, feminism also transformed cultural studies. The idea that 'the personal is political' opened up the range of areas studied in cultural studies and forced critics not only to reflect on how they conceptualised power relations but also on how these power relations were bound up with issues of gender and sexuality. Furthermore, feminism put questions about identity back on the agenda of cultural studies (Hall 1992, 282). None the less, some critics have claimed that feminist concerns have remained marginalised and are not central to the agendas of cultural studies (see below).

Cultural studies has often been dominated by questions of how 'popular culture' has been defined. The ways in which the 'popular' is conceptualised shapes the ways it is studied and analysed, and, in turn, shapes different ideas about cultural politics. The following section draws on Stuart Hall's discussion of

the four different ways in which 'the popular' has been conceptualised. The following section explores the ways in which each
conception of 'the popular' implies a different notion of feminist
cultural politics.

First, there is a conception of popular culture which claims
that it is something imposed on 'the people' from outside and is
therefore an 'inauthentic' form of culture, a 'totally administered
culture "for the people"' (Bennett 1986b, 19). These ideas are
often associated with mass culture theorists who equate popular
culture with a mass culture which is imposed on a passive mass
of 'cultural dopes'. From such a perspective not only is commercially-produced popular culture debased, but also 'the people
who consume and enjoy them must be debased by these activities
or else living in a permanent state of "false consciousness"' (Hall
1981, 232). This type of thinking, as demonstrated in the previous chapter, haunts the work of Friedan, as well as some radical
feminists (and, as I discuss below, some forms of feminist cultural
studies are not immune from these assumptions). However, a
definition of popular culture which presents the majority of
women simply as the passive victims of mass culture assigns an
intelligence to 'the feminist' which the 'ordinary woman' is
presumed to lack. Furthermore, it offers no way of understanding the activities of these 'ordinary women' as they engage in
meaning-making practices; the pleasures involved in these practices; or the potential for resistance which might be present in the
use of mass-produced commodities.

The second way in which 'the popular' has been used,
according to Hall, is more celebratory and often equates popular
culture with folk culture, something both produced by and
consumed by 'the people'. This meaning of popular culture is
often used in left-wing criticism to refer to 'a pure and sponta-
neously oppositional culture "of the people"', such as workers'
songs (Bennett 1986b, 19). In feminist criticism, this understanding of popular culture is often used when critics try to
identify an authentic tradition of women's arts: for examples,
quilt-making or a 'lost tradition' of women's writing. However, it
is worth pointing out that if the first sense of the 'popular'
equates popular culture with mass culture, then this second sense
of the popular distinguishes an 'authentic' popular culture from
'inauthentic' mass-produced popular forms such as TV and film
produced 'for the people' but not by them. For Hall, this definition is problematic because it assumes that there is a 'whole,

authentic, autonomous "popular culture" which lies outside of
... the relations of cultural power and domination' (1981, 232).
When used by feminists, this often implies that a 'women's
culture' exists somehow 'outside' of 'patriarchy'.

The third conception of 'the popular' that Hall discusses is
the 'descriptive'. In this definition 'the popular' is simply equated
with 'all the things that "the people" do and have done' (Hall
1981, 234). Indeed, a similar point could be made about the ways
in which the 'feminine' is used to designate all the things that
'women' do and have done. The problem here is that it simply
provides an inventory: listing 'popular' forms and practices
ignores how 'the real analytic distinction' between 'the people'
and those who are 'not the people' is made (*ibid.*). For Hall, most
approaches simply present the distinction between 'popular' and
'non-popular' forms as a 'condition' of specific texts and activities, rather than as the product of the ways in which these texts
and activities are appropriated by, or become associated with,
specific social groups. In this way, Hall argues that 'the popular'
is simply part of the process by which texts are classified and, as
a result, no text or practice is inherently popular or elite in character, but may well move between the two as historical conditions
change.

For this reason, critics like Hall and Bennett offer an alternative way of conceptualising popular culture: popular culture
should not be seen simply as either the means by which dominant
groups impose their ideas on subordinate groups, or the way in
which subordinate groups resist domination. Instead, Hall
defines popular culture as a site of struggle, a place where
conflicts between dominant and subordinate groups are played
out, and distinctions between the cultures of these groups are
continually constructed and reconstructed (Hall 1981; Bennett
1986a, 1986b, Hollows and Jancovich 1995). Such an approach
makes central three key ideas: that the analysis of popular culture
is always the analysis of power relations; that these struggles, and
what is at stake in them, must always be studied historically; and
that subjectivity – or our sense of who we are – must also be
studied historically. This understanding of popular culture has
been central to many feminists whose work has been informed by
cultural studies, as the rest of the book hopes to demonstrate.
Gendered identities and cultural forms are produced, reproduced, and negotiated in specific historical contexts within
specific and shifting forms of power relations.

Feminism, popular culture and cultural politics

Each of the ways of understanding popular culture discussed above raise questions about different forms of feminist cultural politics. Although the conceptions of the popular that Hall discusses tend to be more closely aligned with socialist politics, it is possible to find parallels within feminism. First, the idea of popular culture as mass culture not only underpins a variety of feminist criticism, but also forms of feminist activism. For example, in some forms of feminism, a distinction is drawn between a 'bad' patriarchal popular or mass culture and a feminist avant-garde culture: a clear case of this is to be found in some forms of feminist film criticism and film-making. Avant-gardist tendencies within feminist film criticism and film-making create an opposition between avant-garde, feminist 'non-narrative, difficult, even boring, oppositional cinema' and its degraded 'other' popular, patriarchal 'realist, narrative, mainstream cinema' (Williamson 1993, 313). As Judith Williamson goes on to argue, not only are these avant-garde films the very ones which are valued by the bourgeois culture which they are meant to oppose, but also avant-garde film exists precisely through its opposition to 'mainstream' cinema and therefore depends on the very practice it seeks to undermine (Jameson 1979, 134). This also raises the question of for whom avant-garde feminist film is made, not to mention avant-garde feminist theatre and art or 'radical' feminist poetry. For example, Chantal Akerman's *Jeanne Dielman* (1975), is shot in 'real-time', and for most of the film shows a housewife going about her domestic duties. The pleasure of the film is (allegedly) constructed through the film's formal features (de Lauretis 1988) rather than, for example, the narrative. The central question this raises is *who* finds this pleasurable and *why*? Does someone who has spent a week performing domestic labour (unpaid for her own family or paid for a feminist film-maker's family) really want to go out for the evening and watch a film which is over three hours long and shows a woman doing domestic labour? And if she does go, will she have the incredibly rare, class-based cultural competences which will allow her to share in the aesthetic experience produced by the film's formal features? As Barrett argues, feminists might be slightly more successful in trying to reach a wider audience if they reject this kind of 'moralistic purism' (1982, 55). This kind of feminist 'alternative' is doomed to remain marginal because its appeal is not so much based on a recognition of gendered experience and competences but more on the possession of cultural codes and competences which are the product of a particularly privileged class position. In the process, the audience for such films not only feel legitimate in their feminist identity, but also legitimate in their cultural preferences which enable them to identify 'what is worthy of being seen and the right way to see it' (Bourdieu 1984, 28).

In feminist versions of cultural politics which are related to the second definition of the popular, we are left with what we might call 'folk' feminism. Here 'authentic' feminine cultural forms and practices are privileged over commercially-produced popular culture and an attempt is made to unearth a women's cultural tradition which has been hidden, marginalised or trivialised by a masculine cultural tradition and/or an 'inauthentic' women's culture. This takes a variety of forms: it is seen in the valorisation of traditional women's skills such as quilt-making and it is evident in a nostalgia for more 'traditional', 'preindustrial' forms of cultural production such as woodcuts and folk singers. 'Folk' feminism searches for an authentic women's culture as if it could 'exist isolated like some deep-frozen essence in the freezer of male culture' (Parker and Pollock cited in Bennett 1986a, xii). This form of feminism is underpinned by what Redhead and Street (1989) call 'folk ideology' in which political legitimacy, integrity and authenticity are conveyed through the idea of autonomy and a connection to some form of 'roots'. A common strand of folk ideology is that it appeals to a more 'intelligent' audience who are not 'dupes' of the culture industries. While the preference for avant-garde forms is a product of one class position – that of an intellectual elite who wield their cultural power – the preference for 'folk' forms is fuelled by a 'populist nostalgia' and is 'a basic element in the relationship of the petite bourgeoisie to the working or peasant classes and their traditions' (Bourdieu 1984, 58). Again, feminist cultural politics can be seen to have a class basis which undercuts the claims for a common gendered experience or aesthetic. Furthermore, this 'populist nostalgia' not only leads to the fetishisation of white peasant and working-class 'popular' traditions in the US and UK, but also the fetishisation of an 'ethnic Other woman' whose cultural traditions are deemed to be more in tune with 'nature'. This can be seen in the penchant for 'ethnic' handicrafts and face-creams that are based on age-old recipes from women in the Amazon rain-forest.

It is worth noting that public funding for feminist cultural production tends to be directed towards projects drawing on either avant-garde or folk feminist conceptions of cultural politics. In terms of public policy, these two versions of feminist cultural politics are often deemed more legitimate, precisely because of their claims to deal with an identifiable gendered experience and their opposition to the products of the culture industries.[2] However, as I have suggested, the audiences for these forms of cultural production tend to be from specific social classes. In this way, alternatives to market provision – for example, state funding of the arts – tend 'either simply to subsidise the existing tastes and habits of the better-off or to create a new form of public culture which has no popular audience' (Garnham 1987, 34).

The third conception of popular culture as an 'inventory' leaves little space for any notion of cultural politics. As Hall argues, specific cultural forms and practices are not inherently 'popular' or 'not popular': instead, it is necessary to explore how specific texts come to be classified in specific historical conditions as such. For example, Douglas Sirk's melodramas which had been criticised as cheap, sentimental and feminine forms of popular culture were reclassified by film critics in the 1960s and 1970s who claimed that they shared many characteristics with (masculine) avant-garde art. For this reason, the idea of an 'inventory' or descriptive approach is not just problematic as a way of defining 'the popular', but also as a way of defining 'the feminine'. If 'feminine' cultural forms and practices are simply identified with all the things that women do and have done, this ignores the processes by which cultural forms come to be classified as 'masculine' and 'feminine', and the ways in which these classifications may change over time. Most of the fields of feminist cultural criticism discussed in this book, as the individual chapters make clear, were motivated in some way by a critique of the ways in which those forms which had been or were classified as 'feminine' were often also classified as 'rubbish' and 'unworthy' of analysis. These critiques became the basis for the serious analysis of those popular forms and practices that had been dismissed as 'feminine rubbish'. In the process, large bodies of feminist research were produced on 'feminine' areas such as soap operas, romantic fiction and girls' magazines. However, in the process, this produced an 'inventory' of 'feminine' areas within feminist cultural studies, an 'inventory' around which this book is structured. As Charlotte Brunsdon has argued, feminist criticism often ends up with claims such as 'Women like these texts because they (both the texts and the women) have feminine concerns. The categories of gender, constituted as pure as if persons are "just" gendered, also begins to function in a theoretical short-circuit as explanatory' (1991, 373).

However, feminist theories of, and research into, the relationship between femininity and popular culture has not been structured simply by a concern to analyse 'women's things' but has also been underpinned by the fourth conception of popular culture which Hall discusses. This sense of 'the popular' as a site of struggle has much to offer feminists. For example, from such a perspective, masculinity and femininity are not fixed cultural categories and identities. Instead, the meanings of masculinity and femininity are made and remade in specific historical conditions. Furthermore, Hall not only forces us to think about how gendered identities are both produced by, and produced in, specific power relations but also how gendered identities (within, and between, historical contexts) are cross-cut by other forms of cultural identity which are themselves structured by relations of power. As a result, femininity is not only made to mean different things over time, but also within any historical moment, there will be struggles over the meaning of femininity. For example, white middle-class femininity has not only been privileged over other forms of feminine identities, but only gets its meaning through its difference to forms of feminine identity which have been labelled as 'deviant' or 'dangerous', identities which have usually been identified with black and white working-class women (see, for example, Skeggs 1997; Young 1996). However, the characteristics ascribed to these different forms of femininity, and their relationships to each other, are not fixed but are instead transformed in specific historical contexts. Furthermore, even the meaning of white middle-class femininity is not unitary and stable but is subject to contestation within a historical period.

Many of the feminist cultural critics discussed in this book exemplify these themes in their work. However, in order to clarify how these ideas have been used in practice by feminists, and how they can generate a different sense of feminist cultural politics, I want to turn to one example: the teenage, single mother who has been the subject of a minor 'moral panic' since the early 1980s. In her analysis of both 'representations' of, and the 'experience' of being, a young single mother, Angela McRobbie (1991;

1997a) has examined how this specific category of feminine identity has been both 'created', and become the subject of, struggle and contestation so that a range of different interest groups have made young, single motherhood *mean* different things. This may seem like a specific feminine identity but because it is made to mean differently, 'there is no "single" single mother, but instead many "single mothers"' (McRobbie, 1997a, 180). The 'single mother' is 'envisaged' in a number of ways: in right-wing tabloids she is often 'presented as dependent on the state, overweight, unkempt, unattractive, unhealthy, a heavy smoker' while pressure groups and feminists often present her as 'a female body struggling against poverty but marked by pride, respectability, determination and the desire to work' (*ibid.*). Furthermore, it is important to remember that the figure of 'the single mother' is also 'envisaged' in relation to other modes of feminine identity: for example, the married mother in a heterosexual relationship, and the lesbian couple with children. McRobbie's work, therefore, provides one good example of what is at stake in feminist cultural studies: by analysing the ways in which different forms of feminine identity are *made to mean*, and also by exploring how these representations are *lived*, a different notion of feminist cultural studies becomes possible, one which can make an intervention *within 'the popular'*. This offers a way of understanding how feminist cultural studies is itself engaged in a struggle over representation and can intervene in policies which have 'real' effects.

However, before leaving this discussion of the popular it is also crucial to point to the 'lack of overlap' between feminism and cultural studies (Franklin *et al.* 1991). While Hall is right to acknowledge the impact of feminism on cultural studies, many feminists working in cultural studies have pointed to the difficulties in making gender a central dimension in a form of analysis which makes class *the* central dimension. As Morag Shiach argues, '"Popular culture" as an institutional space, and as a political concept, embodies definitions of class identity, historical change and political struggle which are often blind to questions of feminism' (1994, 331). As the editors of *Women Take Issue* note about their experience of working in the field of cultural studies in the mid-1970s, they were faced with two alternatives if they wanted to think about gender. On the one hand, they noted that in order to make a feminist intervention into cultural studies, which by necessity involved engaging with a range of disciplines, they would have to conquer the field 'and *then* make a feminist critique of it' (1978, 10). On the other hand, they could concentrate on what for them were central research questions and 'thus risk our concerns remaining gender specific – our own little concerns: the "woman question" claimed by, and relegated to, the women' (*ibid.*). I think it is not surprising that the authors chose to opt for the second strategy: it is a strategy that has been reproduced by many feminists working within cultural studies, and is undoubtedly reproduced by this book. In some ways, this has produced a 'feminine' or 'feminist' ghetto within cultural studies where the women talk about 'women's things': 'for feminist critics, all roads within cultural studies lead to consumption, pleasure and femininity, with only brief detours via hegemony, production, and class' (Shiach 1994, 337). While some male critics have tried to colonise questions about pleasure and consumption for themselves (see Chapter 6), for Shiach, feminists have been unable to develop a 'sustained critique of the dominant paradigms of cultural studies' (*ibid.*). This issue has also been taken up by Celia Lury who argues that conceptions of culture remain largely ungendered, obscuring 'the ways in which culture itself is constituted in relation to gender and other social and political categories' (1995a, 33).

Themes and issues

This book explores some of the key issues, debates, achievements and problems in feminist interventions in discussions of popular culture. One of the key achievements within this field has been the legitimation of femininity as an area of study. Work within feminist cultural studies has challenged the idea that the 'feminine' is inherently worthless, trivial, and politically conservative. For example, the work on 'women's genres' discussed in Part II raises crucial theoretical issues about 'the (historical) understanding of femininity, feminine cultures and gender identity, and the articulation of these identities and cultures with ideas of power' (Brunsdon 1991, 364). However, it is important to note Brunsdon's bracketing of the 'historical' in this quote, a sign which can be read as a gentle reminder that while analysing femininity we should always see it as historical – we are, after all, women in specific historical formations – this has not always been the case. One of the main arguments and themes throughout this book, as I have already suggested, is that what it means to be a

woman is not something fixed for all time but is subject to transformation, contestation and change. While it is as important to be
aware of continuity as well as change, this does not mean that
there is an abstract feminine identity or condition which transcends history. Put bluntly, what it meant to be a woman in the
1920s is different to what it meant to be a woman in the 1940s,
the 1960s or the 1980s.

Furthermore, as I have already suggested, even within
specific historical contexts, there is no single feminine identity,
but multiple feminine identities. As I noted earlier: one is not just
a woman: feminine identities are also cross-cut by class, sexual,
'racial', ethnic, generational and regional identities, and even this
list does not exhaust 'who we are'. It is crucial to not only analyse
the production of different femininities but also explore the ways
in which these femininities are classified, evaluated and ranked
(Foucault 1977). Indeed, questions about cultural difference
have become central in contemporary feminist debates through
the interventions by, for example, black feminisms and lesbian
theorists. However, in the process, despite the ways in which
class has been central in cultural studies as a whole, the ways in
which gender and class differences intersect has been marginalised within feminist cultural studies. Likewise, despite the
initial importance of research into 'lived experience' in cultural
studies, this has been one of 'the most noticeable gaps and omis-
sions in feminist cultural studies' (McRobbie 1997a, 170). It may
be for this reason that many introductory texts have focused on
feminist media and film studies, and on questions about representation, rather than on wider questions about 'lived
experience'. As a result, throughout this book I highlight work
which emphasises questions about class identities, and about
cultural practices and 'lived experience', where appropriate, in an
attempt to make these areas visible once again.

I am aware that in producing the histories of particular feminisms in this way I am running the risk of constructing a narrative
of 'progress' in which the 'mistaken analyses' of the past are
shown to be naive and unsophisticated in the light of present
theorising (Knight 1997; see also Barrett and Phillips 1992;
Gallop 1992), a narrative that is doubly attractive when it is a
past you don't share. However, while I admit my guilt on this
charge, the continuities between feminisms' pasts and presents
are important because the 'mistakes' of the past that have been
assumed to be 'corrected' often reappear in another guise. What

particularly concerns me in this book is the way in which feminist critics have aimed to analyse power relations by examining the ways in which gender inequalities are produced and reproduced while at the same time reproducing other forms of power relations. For example, this was seen clearly in the discussion of the right of white, middle-class women to speak for the situation of all women. Equally, it is seen in the ways in which feminist critics produced distinctions between 'good' feminist identities and 'bad' feminine identities. However, while an acknowledgement of, and an urge to correct, these past mistakes has assumed the status of a 'truth' in much contemporary feminism, this has not necessarily eradicated these problems. This problem constitutes a third major theme of this book: the extent to which feminist cultural criticism still operates around a notion of a 'politically correct feminist identity which constructs other feminine identities as somehow "invalid"' (Brunsdon 1991, 379). What Brunsdon identifies, along with other feminist critics such as Ien Ang and Angela McRobbie, is the continuing idea that a feminist vanguard will teach 'ordinary women' the error of their ways (p. 380), a notion of the feminist intellectual as 'trained, educated and committed to raise the consciousness of others, and to redeem ordinary people from what she ... sees as their ideological servitude' (Ross 1989, 193).

This opposition between feminists and the feminine 'other woman' is related to another key theme of this book: feminist approaches to 'the popular' are examined to see how they relate to questions about taste. To appropriate Dick Hebdige's terms from a discussion in a different context, the book explores the ways in which the distinction between the feminist engaged in rigorous intellectual critique and the feminine 'other woman' immersed in the popular also come to represent 'good' and 'bad' tastes respectively (1988, 59). Drawing on the work of Pierre Bourdieu, Andrew Ross has argued that 'Cultural power does not inhere in the contents of categories of taste. On the contrary, it is exercised through the capacity to draw the line between and round categories of taste' (Ross 1989, 61). In this way, the cultural power of the feminist intellectual comes from her power 'to designate what is legitimate, on the one hand, and what can then be governed and policed as illegitimate or inadequate or even deviant, on the other' (*ibid.*). What concerns me here, then, are the ways in which feminist cultural studies makes distinctions between the 'good' and the 'bad' and not only classifies things but the people who have a taste for them. In this way, we not only need to consider feminist cultural politics, and the ways in which it seeks to transform power relations between men and women, but also the cultural politics of feminism and the extent to which they reproduce other modes of power relations between women. The politics of feminist cultural criticisms, therefore, needs to be understood not only in relation to the ways in which masculinities and femininities are bound up with power relations in different historical contexts, but also in relation to the ways in which different feminine identities (including feminist identities) are bound up with power relations in different historical contexts.

The final aim of this book, however, is perhaps the most important: to offer an accessible introduction to a range of debates about feminism, femininity and popular culture. This is obviously not an exhaustive account and I have selected some areas of debate and some cultural forms and practices and geographical and historical locations (primarily the UK and US in the post-war period) over others.

Notes

1 For examples, see Brantlinger (1990); Grossberg (1993); McGuigan (1992); and Turner (1990).
2 These claims are not always about the appeal to a universal gendered experience but sometimes to the experience of a particular constituency: for example, black women or lesbian women.

Further reading

Barrett, M. Feminism and the Definition of Cultural Politics, in R. Brunt and C. Rowan, eds, *Feminism, Culture and Politics* (London, Lawrence and Wishart, 1982)
Brunsdon, C. Pedagogies of the Feminine: Feminist Teaching and Women's Genres, *Screen*, 32(4), 1991 (reprinted in C. Brunsdon, *Screen Tastes: Soap Opera to Satellite Dishes*, London, Routledge, 1997)
Franklin, S., Lury, C. and Stacey, J., eds, *Off-Centre: Feminism and Cultural Studies* (London, HarperCollins Academic, 1991)
McRobbie, A. The Es and the Anti-Es: New Questions for Feminism and Cultural Studies, in M. Ferguson and P. Golding, eds, *Cultural Studies in Question* (London, Sage, 1997)
Shiach, M. Feminism and Popular Culture, in J. Storey, ed., *Cultural Theory and Popular Culture: A Reader* (Hemel Hempstead, Harvester Wheatsheaf, 1994)
Turner, G. *British Cultural Studies: An Introduction* (London, Unwin Hyman, 1990)
van Zoonen, L. *Feminist Media Studies* (London, Sage, 1994)

Part II

WOMEN'S GENRES: TEXTS and AUDIENCES

Film studies
and the woman's film

Whereas the early stage of feminist research into the media looked at 'images *of* women', from the mid-1970s onwards, many feminists working within film, media and cultural studies turned their attention to 'images *for* women' (Brunsdon 1991, 365). With this shift, a new series of feminist debates emerged which centred on 'women's genres' across a range of cultural forms. This part of the book introduces some of the main themes in feminist analysis of women's genres by exploring the terms of the debate about the woman's film in film studies, about romantic fiction in literary and cultural studies, and about soap opera in media and cultural studies. These debates have overlapping themes but the approaches that feminists took to their subject matter were often shaped by the assumptions of the different academic fields within which they were working.

Studies of 'women's genres' were often motivated by two initial concerns. First, feminist critics tried to demonstrate that cultural forms which had been classified as 'feminine' and associated with a female audience were worth taking seriously. By appropriating women's genres for feminism, feminist critics have, therefore, made them 'assume different identities and cultural functions' (Klinger 1994, xvii), often challenging the cultural hierarchies which deemed 'feminine' forms as 'unworthy' and demonstrating that a feminist of understanding of these forms allows us to see them in a new light. In the process, feminist debates about women's genres have not only created what Charlotte Brunsdon (1991) has called 'canons of femininity', but may tell us as much about feminism as they do the objects of their analysis. Second, feminist critics tried to explain what sets these 'genres apart from representations which possess a less gender-specific mass appeal' (Kuhn 1984, 18) or an appeal to men. Although on a commonsense level, 'women's genres' were forms aimed at a female audience, as Kuhn argues, it was necessary to clarify what 'aimed at a female audience' actually meant (p. 24). As should become clear in the following chapters, very different approaches emerged to address this question, approaches that were shaped by the theoretical frameworks which feminists imported from their own fields of study.

While critics have commonly thought of romantic fiction and soap opera as genres which share common codes and conventions, the same is not true of the woman's film. While the melodrama has been the subject of genre criticism, albeit problematically, and while many feminist discussions of the woman's film have concentrated on melodrama, the category of the woman's film may also include films from other genres such as romantic comedy and even film noir. However, the woman's film has been a meaningful category within the film industry in its attempt to target women as an audience, a strategy most often associated with 'classical' Hollywood cinema in the 1930s, 1940s and 1950s. For this reason, it is the films from this period that have attracted the most attention from feminist critics. Despite the fact the woman's film as a category cuts across a range of genres, it is still possible to identify a number of key characteristics that give the category some sense of coherence. For example, Maria LaPlace has argued that

> The woman's film is distinguished by its female protagonist, female point of view and its narrative which most often revolves around the traditional realism of women's experience: the familial, the domestic, the romantic – those arenas where love, emotion and experience take precedence over action and events. One of the most important aspects of the genre is the prominent place it accords to relationships between women. (1987, 139)

Feminists were drawn to these films because they seemed to privilege what have traditionally been seen as 'feminine' concerns (features which many earlier critics had taken to be evidence of their 'awfulness') and attempted to identify whether they had something to offer 'women' and/or 'feminists'. However, the ways in which they approached these films were shaped by theoretical debates within film studies which determined *how* the woman's film could be seen as significant. As Patricia White argues, the woman's film linked 'the focus on "depictions of women" in sociological criticism with cinefeminists concern with "the figure of the woman"' (1998, 122). For this reason, the first two sections of this chapter introduce these two theoretical frameworks and they deal first with criticism which looks at 'images of women' and second with criticism which focuses on 'woman as image'. The following sections go on to explore the questions of what is meant by 'films *for* women'. Section three, for example, examines debates about whether the organisation of the film text in the woman's film creates opportunities for female spectatorship, while section four moves beyond a concentration on the film text to examine the pleasures that the woman's film may have offered female audiences. Section five examines the work of feminist critics who have problematised some of the assumptions in debates about 'images of women', 'woman as image' and 'images *for* women', critics who highlight how the figure of woman in the cinema, the female spectator and the woman in the audience have largely been conceptualised as both white and heterosexual.

In the process, the aim of the chapter is to offer not only an introduction to thinking about the woman's film, but also to introduce some of the key themes of feminist film theories. These theories should be understood in relation to both second-wave feminist activism – especially against what were seen as 'negative' and 'damaging' images of women in the media and cinema – and to feminist film-making (Thornham 1997, x). As a result, in the 1970s, feminist critics not only sought to identify how cinema was organised around the needs and desires of men, they also aimed to use this knowledge in order to transform film practice to serve the needs of feminism. For this reason, in the first two sections, I briefly discuss how the different theoretical models used by feminist critics have implications for different forms of feminist film practice. However, as Sue Thornham notes, as feminist film theory has become institutionalised, it has tended to become detached from its relationship to film-making. Furthermore, the context of feminist film-making has changed. For example, Michelle Citron has noted how the decline of funding for feminist film-making in the US, combined with the decline of a feminist infrastructure for distributing and exhibiting these films, has made it more of a necessity for feminists to enter 'the mainstream'. Furthermore, this process has been part of 'a larger mainstreaming of feminism' (Citron 1988, 56).

This chapter explores how, for feminists, an intervention into the ways in which films were produced, analysed and consumed is a political act. However, in making political distinctions between different forms of film-making practice, film texts and modes of consumption, feminist critics have also ascribed partic-ular meanings and identities to categories of films and categories of audiences (Klinger 1994). In the process, they have also drawn distinctions between 'films for men', 'films for women' and 'films for feminists'. Furthermore, feminist critics have produced different positions on the relationship between 'feminist films' and 'popular cinema' which are underpinned by different notions of cultural politics. Finally, the chapter also examines how notions of 'the feminine' and 'femininity' have been mobilised in feminist debates about film.

'Images of women' in film

In the early-to-mid-1970s, in the US, film was largely discussed as part of the 'images of women' debate outlined in the previous chapter. Despite the fact that this kind of approach formed the common-sense of much second-wave feminism, Molly Haskell and Marjorie Rosen elaborated on this position in relation to film in the mid-1970s, drawing on some of the assumptions of Friedan's work. These critics took a sociological and historical approach to the changing images of women in film. For Rosen, films both 'reflect the changing societal image of women' and present a distorted image of women: 'the Cinema Woman is a Popcorn Venus, a delectable but insubstantial hybrid of cultural distortions' (Rosen 1975, 13). She claimed that these 'false' feminine images filled the (empty) heads of female audiences. Similarly, Haskell argues that film not only reflects 'society's accepted role definitions' but also reinforces these narrow definitions of femininity (1987, 4): 'film is a rich field for the mining of female stereotypes . . . If we see stereotypes in film, it is because stereotypes existed in society' (p. 30). However, while the movies of the past had reflected societal attitudes, and even occasionally offered innovations on them, by the 1950s films displayed a 'credibility gap' and became more sexist than society (p. 37). Worse still, as a projection of male values (p. 39), films of the 1960s responded to women's demands for equality with a back-lash: cinema became both more violent towards women and 'truly monolithic in its sexism' (p. 370).

However, in the women's films of the 1940s, Haskell finds a more contradictory picture of women and seeks to counter the ways in which these films, through their association with women, have been trivialised. Just as Rosen notes the celebration of women's strength in some of these films, so Haskell recognises that they not only place a woman 'at the centre of the universe'

(1987, 155) but also show that the private sphere and personal relationships are important rather than trivial. In this way, they validate women's experiences. However, this position is somewhat undercut by Haskell's claim that 'At the lowest level, as soap opera, the "woman's film" fills a masturbatory need, it is soft-core emotional porn for the frustrated housewife … women spectators are moved … by self-pity and tears to accept, rather than reject, their lot' (pp. 154–5). Like Friedan, Haskell draws a distinction between the feminist critic who can see through 'the big lie', as she calls it, and the 'housewife' who cannot.

Both Rosen and Haskell also reproduce some other assumptions present in Friedan's work. For Rosen, the 'effects' of the movies was so great that *even* middle- and upper-class women 'reordered values by Hollywood standards' (1975, 103). This not only implies that a threat to middle-class women is of more significance than one to working-class women, but also that working-class women are inherently gullible. She compounds this classism by noting in her discussion of the 1920s how Hollywood was at fault for mainly showing women working in blue-collar jobs, and failing to reflect women in 'jobs requiring skill, aggressiveness, education' (p. 79). Some classes of women it appears are more 'real' and more 'positive' than others. Both critics have also been criticised for their heterosexism, Rosen for claiming that Katherine Hepburn and Spencer Tracey had 'an ideal relationship' (p. 199) and Haskell 'for reducing the history of women and film to the (failed) history of heterosexual romance in contemporary American cinema and culture' (Petro 1994, 70).

The more general problems with 'images of women' criticism were outlined in the last chapter and the feminist film criticism that followed tended to problematise the idea that texts could, or should, reflect reality. Whereas for Haskell and Rosen 'meanings are regarded as preexisting their transmission via film', most later feminists would argue that meanings are 'produced in and through the operations of the film texts themselves' (Kuhn 1982, 75–6). Furthermore, as Rosen's comments about class reveal, the argument for images that are more 'positive' or 'real' always depends on value judgements about what is more 'positive' and 'real'. Their argument also rests on a problematic notion of media effects: Haskell and Rosen assumed that a film's 'message' would be unproblematically transmitted to a passive audience. However, despite these shortcomings, Haskell and Rosen's emphasis on exploring the relationship between film texts and the historical contexts in which they were produced and consumed remains an important one. Furthermore, Haskell, in particular, suggests that, rather than femininity being a monolithic and transhistorical entity, different notions of femininity are negotiated in films, both between, and within, historical periods. This historical understanding of both film and femininity seemed to be forgotten in much of the feminist film criticism that followed.[1]

While there is no straightforward relationship between Haskell and Rosen's work on the one hand, and the film-making which was a product of second-wave feminism on the other, both groups share the concern with putting more 'real' representations on the screen. By 1971, the relationship between feminism and film had been established with the launch of the first feminist film journal, *Women and Film* in the USA, the organisation of feminist film festivals and the production of feminist documentaries (Thornham 1997, 12–13). Feminists in the period were drawn towards documentary film as it seemed to be the film practice which might represent women, and the feminist cause, with the most 'accuracy' and 'honesty'. Much of this work is underpinned by 'autobiographical discourse' in which a woman recounts her story, and, therefore, aimed to operate following similar strategies to those of the consciousness-raising groups (Kuhn 1982, 148).

This documentary practice has been criticised in much the same way as 'images of women' criticism as it assumes that the meanings of feminist films were transparent and had a 'truth' which could be unproblematically communicated to the audience (Kuhn 1982, 149; Citron 1988, 52) Furthermore, this position privileges the director/author as the person with 'the knowledge' and, therefore, reproduces ideas about 'media effects' from mass culture theory (Kaplan 1983, 127). It creates a hierarchy in which the feminist film-maker is positioned as the 'woman who knows' and can reveal the 'truth' to her less aware audience.

Woman as image

If most American feminist film criticism up to the mid-1970s was characterised by the more sociological approach that underpinned 'images of women criticism', in the UK during the same period a very different form of feminist film criticism emerged. Claiming that the operations of the film text produced 'woman as image', these theories would have a far more significant impact on the future of feminist film criticism. In order to understand these theories, it is first necessary to understand that they are not only a product of second-wave feminism but also of a specific type of film criticism underpinned by ideas from structuralism, semiotics and psychoanalysis. This film criticism – often dubbed '*Screen* theory' after the journal in which many of the ideas first appeared – would give feminist film criticism far more theoretical rigour and complexity, while at the same time rendering it largely inaccessible to any 'feminist' or 'woman' who lacked a knowledge of current trends in continental philosophy.

This section examines three key theorists – Claire Johnston, Pam Cook and Laura Mulvey – whose work set a new agenda for thinking about women and film. Their ideas are underpinned by the notion that the very form and language of film works not only to reproduce patriarchal ideology, but also to reproduce its spectators as subjects of patriarchal ideology. From such a point of view, changing the 'content' of films, as feminist documentary practice sought to do, could offer no challenge to patriarchy because it utilised the same 'realist' codes and conventions as mainstream cinema. A feminist film practice which sought to challenge the taken-for-granted codes upon which mainstream cinema depended was needed.

In order to situate Johnston, Cook and Mulvey, it is necessary briefly to explain some of the key assumptions of the *Screen* theory which informed their work. Structuralism and semiotics provided a way of understanding how film texts construct and reproduce our idea of what 'reality' is, rather than reflecting a preexisting reality. This drew on the structuralist idea that language is not a neutral system which refers to 'real' objects in the 'real' world, but instead that it is through language that the world is given meaning. Language divides up the world into classes of objects – including 'man' and 'woman' – and ascribes meaning to them. In this way, language is ideological because it makes what is cultural appear to be 'natural', the way things 'really are'. Meaning in language, for structuralists, is generated through a system of differences: words – or signs – gain their meaning through their difference to other words. For this reason 'man' and 'woman', 'masculine' and 'feminine' only mean through their difference from each other. Feminist appropriations of structuralism would use this insight to argue that in patriarchy, where 'man' is defined as the 'norm', 'woman' only gains meaning as different to – and in opposition to – that 'norm'.

Screen theorists drew on structuralism to argue that the

language of cinema worked in a similar way: while 'realist' films gave the 'illusion' of being a window on 'the real world', they in fact worked to produce particular notions of what 'reality' was. However, it was argued, the 'truth' revealed was ideological. Dominant films produced a non-contradictory view of the world in which conflicts could be resolved and in which the spectator is positioned in such a way as to make the meaning of the world appear transparent. In this way, the position from which to watch a film – the spectating position – is a product of the film text.

This led feminist film critics to claim that dominant cinema does not present distorted 'images of women' but works to construct and reproduce our notions of what 'woman' signifies. Dominant cinema works to reproduce patriarchal ideology, in which man signifies the 'norm' and 'woman' signifies that which is 'other' to that norm. If 'man' and 'masculinity' signify activity, then 'woman' and 'femininity' can only signify its absence, passivity. It is in this sense that Cook and Johnston claim that 'woman' is 'an empty sign' (1988, 27). Within the film narrative woman can only be 'defined negatively' (Cook and Johnston 1988, 27–8).

If cinema works to make culturally produced notions of man and woman, masculine and feminine, appear 'natural', then for Cook and Johnston the task of feminist film criticism is to 'de-naturalise' these images and show them for what they are: ideological constructions (1988, 34). However, Johnston (1988) argued that within dominant cinema it was also possible to identify examples of more 'progressive' films which revealed 'cracks' or contradictions in patriarchal ideology. These films, she claimed, may denaturalise taken-for-granted assumptions about men and women. While the contradictions that Johnston identifies are not assumed to be a product of the director's intentions, they none the less force the spectator to 'read against the grain' of patriarchal ideology and produce a feminist reading. In this way, Johnston differs from many later critics for whom a feminist reading could only be the product of the feminist critic. Johnston claims that these 'progressive' texts can teach feminists how to denaturalise patriarchal ideology and form the basis for 'a feminist counter-cinema' which would 'sweep aside the existing forms of discourse in order to found a new form of language' (Johnston 1988, 44). This practice, which Kuhn terms 'deconstruction', aims to make visible the codes upon which mainstream cinema is founded so as to 'unsettle the spectator' (Kuhn 1982, 160).

Johnston argued that a counter-cinema should reclaim desire and pleasure for feminism (Bergstrom 1988, 82) and that it was necessary to make a feminist intervention *within* the mainstream (Thornham 1997, 30), a position which would be rejected by Laura Mulvey.

Mulvey's 'Visual Pleasure and Narrative Cinema', first published in 1975, is possibly the most frequently cited piece of feminist film criticism. Not only did it provide a way of understanding how the image of woman on the screen served the needs of men, but it was also important in making a debate about gender and spectatorship central within feminist film criticism. While earlier critics had theorised the ways in which spectating positions were 'sewn into' the film text, Mulvey drew on the psychoanalytic film theory developed by critics such as Christian Metz to argue that these cinematic texts were organised in such a way as to produce a spectating position that was male. This would stimulate a debate within feminist film criticism about whether there were any possibilities for female spectatorship within a mainstream cinema that was inherently patriarchal and, therefore, organised around the psychic needs of men.

Mulvey builds on the idea of 'woman' as an 'empty sign' who signifies only her 'otherness' to a male norm associated with activity. As she argues, woman 'acts as a signifier for the male other, bound by a symbolic order in which man can live out his fantasies and obsessions through linguistic command by imposing them on the silent image of woman still tied to her place as bearer of meaning, not maker of meaning' (Mulvey 1988a, 58). However, Mulvey is far more concerned with how the image of woman in narrative cinema is also coded as an erotic object, an object of visual pleasure for the male spectator. In order to explain this, she draws on psychoanalysis to argue that the visual and narrative structures of mainstream cinema both intersect with, and reproduce, the processes through which people become aware of themselves as sexed and gendered subjects. Furthermore, she notes how cinema plays on what Freud had called scopophilia – the erotic pleasure in 'looking at another person as an object', and in the cinema, she argues, it is woman who is coded as an erotic object for a male gaze.

While Cook and Johnston's theoretical framework owed more to structuralism than psychoanalysis, they had drawn on insights from psychoanalysis to argue that 'The male protagonist's castration fears, his search for self-knowledge all converge on woman: it is in her that he is finally faced with the recognition of "lack"' (Cook and Johnston 1988, 27). This notion of 'castration' which is central in both psychoanalytic accounts of the acquisition of sexed and gendered identities in childhood, and in Mulvey's theoretical framework for understanding film, is most easily understood as a metaphor which adds complexity to the notion of woman as 'other'. The idea that woman signifies castration basically refers to the way in which her difference from man signifies an inferiority or 'lack' in relation to man. In this way, the image of woman is potentially threatening to men because she signifies what it is to be powerless, to lack the power and presence which defines what it is to be a man. In short, she signifies the threat that they might become like her. Thus, the 'threat of castration' that woman signifies to men is the threat that they might lose the 'positive' attributes associated with masculinity and become more like the feminine 'other'.

For this reason, the image of woman in cinema always has the potential to be threatening to the male spectator. Therefore, dominant cinema uses mechanisms which alleviate this threat through particular forms of looking: fetishism and voyeurism. Fetishism turns woman into an image that is safe, enjoyable and unthreatening by turning some part of her body into a fetish – that is, by focusing on some aspect of her that can be made pleasurable in itself – for example, the legs or the hair. By focusing on the fetish, the spectator's attention is drawn away from the ways in which woman symbolises 'lack' and in the process the spectator knows, yet disavows, the 'threat' of woman. The alternative mechanism, voyeurism, overcomes the threat that the woman represents by seeking to investigate her, understand her mystery and thus render her knowable, controllable and subject to male mastery. By activating these modes of looking in the male spectator, cinematic structures make woman as image a source of male pleasure rather than a threat.

However, Mulvey argues, that cinema also produces a third type of relationship between the spectator and the image on screen – narcissism – which refers to the male spectator's identification with his own likeness. In this mode of looking, the male spectator misrecognises himself in the idealised image of the male protagonist who controls both the narrative and the look within the film. This gives the male spectator a sense of power and 'omnipotence'. However, while he can identify with the male protagonist as the subject of the film narrative (the person who

makes things happen), the male protagonist's status as the object
of the male spectator's look raises the problem of homoeroticism.
As a result, woman must function as the primary erotic object
within the film, 'with their appearance coded for strong visual
and erotic impact so they can be said to connote *to-be-looked-at-
ness*' (Mulvey 1988a, 62). The spectator's gaze at the male
protagonist is deflected, through identification, onto the female
body. To put it another way, the male spectator looks at a male
who controls the look within the film, a look whose legitimate
object is defined as female.

Therefore, for Mulvey, woman as image in mainstream
cinema is produced as a spectacle for the male gaze. She can only
function as the object of the narrative and signify passivity, while
the man is the active subject of the narrative. As a result,
Mulvey's theory implies that the underlying frameworks of all
mainstream cinema are organised around male desire. Cinema
offers the male spectator a range of pleasures but leaves the
female spectator with no place from which to look that does not
involve her own subordination as the passive object of male
desire. To use the most frequently cited phrase from Mulvey, 'In
a world ordered by sexual imbalance, pleasure in looking has
been split between active/male and passive/female' (p. 62).

By appropriating psychoanalysis for feminist film criticism,
Mulvey explains how 'The images and representations which are
the bearers of ideology are also those through which, by processes
of identification, we construct our identities as human subjects'
(Thornham 1998, 37). For Mulvey, patriarchal meanings cannot
be 'removed' from cinema, because the very structures and
conventions which underpin mainstream cinema are patriarchal.
From such a perspective, the outlook for a feminism which hopes
to effect change is incredibly bleak: if the fact of sexual difference
in which woman is constituted as 'other' is the organising principle for the ways in which we understand the world, it is difficult
to imagine a place 'outside' of this where feminist resistance
might be possible.

Mulvey's analysis not only made a significant impact on the
feminist film criticism that followed, it also stimulated a great
deal of criticism and debate. Many feminists, who agreed that
psychoanalysis was the best tool for understanding women's
subordinate position within patriarchy, asked whether there
could be any place for female desire and a female spectator within
popular cinema, a question which frequently lead them to

consider the woman's film, the focus of the next section. A further problem raised by a number of critics was the fact that psychoanalysis tended to assume that sexual difference is *the* primary difference within cinema and, therefore, neglects 'cinema's role in orchestrating other forms of difference – sexuality outside the heterosexual paradigm, or class or race difference' (Mayne 1993, 61). These questions are taken up in the final section.

However, there are also a number of other problematic assumptions in Mulvey's work. It is not entirely clear in her use of psychoanalysis whether sexual difference – around which she claims that culture is organised – refers to the difference between the sexes (male and female) or genders (masculine and feminine). If the former is the case, then the use of psychoanalysis suggests that culture is in some way organised around a fundamental biological difference. If this were true, we are back to a notion that there are essential differences between men and women, a point which feminisms have, on the whole, attempted to contest. If, as most psychoanalytical feminists are keen to point out, the latter is the case, then this offers the potentially more useful idea that our culture is structured around the difference between masculine and feminine. However, within such a framework, masculinity and femininity become 'transhistorical and "universal"' (Hall 1986, 46). This position becomes clear if we look at E. Ann Kaplan's use of psychoanalysis for feminist film theory where she claims that the 'structuring of woman within . . . narrative . . . transcends the historical and individual specificities' (Kaplan 1983, 2). From such a perspective, the range of 'images of women' that Haskell saw as existing within and between historical periods become merely superficial changes 'in accord with current styles and fashions' (*ibid.*). This implies that while the difference between masculine and feminine may be cultural, there are still 'essential' differences within patriarchal culture. This position not only offers little scope for feminism to effect a change to unequal gender relations, it also ignores the ways in which gendered identities and differences, despite continuities, are the site of struggle and negotiation within historical contexts. Therefore, psychoanalytic film theory – in this form – offers no way of understanding changing representations of woman, or of conceptualising femininity as anything other than 'lack'.

Whereas Johnston favoured 'a feminist counter-cinema' which might occur within the mainstream, Mulvey believed that women could only gain from the destruction of the dominant cinematic apparatus. She argues that feminism needed a 'politically and aesthetically avant-garde cinema' which would make a radical break with the formal conventions of mainstream cinema in order to challenge patriarchal ideologies (1988a, 59). Such a position sees few possibilities for feminism within 'the popular' – indeed concepts like the 'dominant cinematic apparatus' suggests that, as a form of 'popular culture', cinema is 'an essentially repetitive and formulaic system which reproduces the dominant ideology' (Jancovich 1995, 145). In other words, Mulvey's conception of cinema would seem to fit quite well with the notion of 'popular culture' as 'mass culture' discussed in Chapter 2. From such a position, the only way to transform popular cinema is through the creation of a feminist context for viewing which will educate the passive female viewer and transform her into an active feminist viewer (Kuhn 1982, 194). Such a position rests on the assumption that the 'ordinary woman' in the audience watches passively and in 'complicity' with the patriarchal ideologies of popular cinema.

Feminist avant-garde cinema was produced, therefore, in opposition to 'the popular'. It aimed to reject the codes and conventions of popular cinema in order to produce alternative film languages which might offer 'non-patriarchal' modes of expression. Furthermore, because feminist psychoanalysis had tended to see the spectating position – the position from which to watch – as 'built-into' the film text, avant-garde cinema attempted to produce 'radically "other" forms of pleasure' and unsettle the very basis of subjectivity or identity (Kuhn 1982, 168). However, this coalition of feminism and the avant-garde, as was suggested in Chapter 2, is problematic for a number of reasons. First, the exhibition of feminist avant-garde cinema primarily took place in 'art cinemas' which took it away from a 'feminist viewing context' (p. 195), and raised the question of who feminist cinema was for: feminists, arty types or 'the ordinary woman' who was unlikely to be in the art-cinema's audience. Second, the question of how accessible these films were did not only relate to *where* they were shown but also to the 'difficulty' of these films for audiences who did not have the competences required to consume avant-garde art (p. 196). Put another way, if avant-garde cinema was premised on a rejection of popular cinema and its audience, how could it then be consumed by the very audience from which it sought to distance itself? For example, with admirable honesty, the film-maker Michelle Citron has admitted that her attraction to the avant-garde was a product of her desire to distance herself from her working-class background: 'The making of ART was the clearest way for me to put a distance between my parents (who embarrassed me) and myself' (Citron 1988, 48). Third, by being premised on a distance from 'the popular', feminist avant-garde cinema could only define feminist film practice as a marginal practice (Pribram 1988, 4). In conclusion, while feminist film criticism has, on the one hand, wanted to 'recruit' the 'ordinary woman' for feminism, on the other hand, the avant-garde presumes that the 'ordinary woman' viewer is the 'other' of the feminist viewer. As Christine Gledhill argues, 'While the political avant-garde audience deconstructs the pleasures and identities offered by the mainstream text, it participates in the comforting identity of critic or *cognoscente*, positioned in the sphere of "the ideologically correct", and the "radical" – a position which is defined by its difference from the ideological mystification attributed to the audiences of the mass media' (1988, 66).

Images for women? The woman's film and the female spectator

Mulvey's rather bleak portrait of a cinema organised around the needs of the male psyche which only offered a masculine spectating position not surprisingly led some feminist critics to ask 'What is there in a film with which a woman viewer identifies?' (Rich cited in Thornham 1998, 45). This type of question motivated many feminist critics to turn to the woman's film, which after all had been produced for a female audience, in an attempt to discover whether it was possible to identify films which offered opportunities for female spectatorship and which, in the process, might offer some form of 'resistance' within what seemed to be an inherently patriarchal mainstream cinema. In other words, was it possible to find in the woman's film something for women *and* something for feminism?

Mulvey herself addressed each of these questions in two separate articles. In her article 'Afterthoughts' (first published in 1981), she returned to the question of whether there was the possibility of a female spectating position within dominant cinema. While the answer to the question remained a fairly emphatic 'no', she raised the possibility that the female viewer could derive pleasure from taking up the position constructed for the male spectator, where she might take pleasure in 'a phantasy of "action" that correct femininity demands should be repressed': that is, she could take pleasure in an active masculinity which must be rejected in becoming 'feminine' but which is never quite fully repressed (1988b, 78). However, Mulvey concentrates on narrative rather than visual pleasure in this article, and therefore ignores some of the implications of this: that is, whether adopting a male spectating position would lead the female viewer to treat woman as image as an erotic object. None the less, Mulvey argues that while the female viewer may take up a 'trans-sex' or 'transvestite' spectating position – the position of the male spectator – there is no female spectating position for her to take up.

In 'Afterthoughts', Mulvey also raises the question of whether a female protagonist might offer something for women. This point is developed in an earlier article, 'Notes on Sirk and Melodrama' (first published in 1977), where she takes the slightly more optimistic view, finding in those melodramas with a female protagonist and which privilege a female point of view, an acknowledgement of the contradictions faced by women under patriarchy, contradictions that the narrative cannot resolve.[2] While on one hand this can act as a 'safety-valve' (Mulvey 1987, 75) for patriarchy that allows women's feelings of frustration to be defused, on the other hand, these films can be thought of as 'progressive' texts which offer women a sense of the contradictions and problems which patriarchy produces for them.[3] In this way, the woman's film could be thought of as something which offered something for women and which might offer something for feminism. However, in the process, Mulvey skirted around the question of whether female spectatorship was possible. In the debate about the woman's film that followed, the questions about female spectatorship and whether the woman's film could offer some form of 'resistance' within patriarchal cinema, were increasingly addressed together.

A much more thorough, although thoroughly gloomy, theory of female spectatorship would be offered by Mary Ann Doane (1987) in *The Desire to Desire*. Doane turns to the woman's films of the 1940s which were produced for a female audience, feature a female protagonist, deal with 'women's issues', and which might offer the possibility of a female point-of-view. These films, she argues, 'anticipate' a female spectator (Doane 1987, 3–4). However, the female spectator it anticipates is not an active, desiring subject because within the terms of psychoanalytic theory, within patriarchy feminine desire can be only passive.

For Doane, while male spectatorship is characterised by a distance between the male subject/spectator and the female object of his desire (as it was for Mulvey), female spectatorship is characterised by a proximity or closeness between the female subject/spectator and the female object on screen. As Mulvey had argued, the desires evoked by the structures of looking in cinema – voyeurism and fetishism – correspond to the needs of the male psyche. Doane argues that because women do not engage in fetishism – the image of woman poses no threat to them – then there is less distance between the female spectator/subject and women as image/object. This means that female spectatorship is characterised by 'narcissism': an over-identification with the idealised feminine image of the female star. However, because this identification is with woman as the object of a male gaze, it is a 'masochistic' identification with a position of victimisation.

The narcissistic identification also has other extremely negative consequences in Doane's work. She relates the ways in which the female spectator is positioned in the cinema to the ways in which women are positioned as consumers by capitalism, a position in which the female subject is invited to consume in order to turn herself into a commodity and an object for men. When the female spectator identifies with the female star on the screen, she is 'invited to witness her own commodification and, furthermore, to buy an image of herself insofar as the female star is proposed as the ideal of feminine beauty' (Doane 1987, 24). Cinema, by acting as a 'shop window' for commodities, also helps to reproduce the female spectator as a consumer (see Chapter 7). The cinematic image, by operating as both a mirror in which the female spectator misrecognises herself and as a shop-window, 'takes on the aspect of a trap whereby her subjectivity becomes synonymous with her objectification' (Doane 1987, 33). If, however, the relationship of the female viewer to the cinema can only be passive – her spectating position is already constructed by the film text – then the female consumer is also conceived of as inherently passive (for a more extensive critique of this notion, see Chapter 6). As Jackie Stacey argues, the problem with Doane's idea that 'women are tied into these mutually reinforcing relations of powerlessness, is that it robs women of any agency in the reproduction of culture and may even contribute to dominant notions of female passivity' (Stacey 1994, 185).

If this conception of female spectatorship leaves women totally subjected, Doane's discussion of the woman's film also leaves little room for optimism. This discussion rests on Doane's distinction between female spectatorship – a feature of the film text and subject to universal psychic structures – and the film's address to socially and historically produced feminine subjects. What Doane is suggesting here is that while the essential feminine psychical subject is predicated on 'otherness' and 'lack', this is overlaid by a feminine subjectivity that is the product of histori-cally-specific discourses. The woman's film, therefore, is subject, on the one hand, to the same psychic laws that govern all main-stream cinema in which femininity is equated with 'otherness', but, on the other hand, also produces, through its women's discourse, 'a seeing and desiring female subject' (Doane 1987, 37). However, while this seeing and desiring protagonist intro-duces some contradictions which are difficult for the film to contain (and, therefore, the possibility for 'resistance'), they are largely met by 'strategies of containment and discipline' (p. 37). For example, Doane identifies a cycle of the woman's film char-acterised by a 'medical discourse', which includes *Caught* (1949) and *The Cat People* (1942). These films contain the contradic-tions raised by the presence of a female protagonist: woman becomes something to be investigated, known and treated through a masculine 'medical gaze' associated with a (male) doctor. In this way, while the woman's film might appear to offer something for women, patriarchal cinema 'contains' women within these films.

Doane's account might seem to suggest that the woman's film offers little to either a female, or a feminist, audience. However, she argues that if the female spectator's over-identifi-cation with the image is problematic, the solution is to denaturalise these images. *If* the 'poses, postures, tropes' of femi-ninity were exaggerated so as to appear 'unnatural', they would lose their credibility, and femininity might be defamiliarised and denaturalised, creating a distance between spectator and image (1987, 181). This position is extended in later work by Doane where she draws on the concept of femininity as 'masquerade', 'as the decorative layer which conceals a non-identity' (1991, 25). If femininity is but a series of masks, she argues, then this would suggest 'the impossibility of a stable feminine position which seems to align it with female spectatorship' (p. 39). This leaves the female spectator in a position in which 'rather than overidentifying . . . she can *play* with the identifications offered by the film, manipulating them for her own pleasure and purposes' (Thornham 1998, 56). However, Doane sees little scope for such a practice within dominant cinema where women in the audience are left with nothing to do but passively accept their enslavement to the image and, hence, their objectification.

For other critics, however, the search for a more empowering notion of female spectatorship in the women's film was more fruitful. For some psychoanalytic film critics this would involve a search for something 'essentially feminine' in the woman's film (see Modleski 1987) and this led critics such as Kaplan to examine whether motherhood could be 'expressed' 'in a symbolic world that represses it' (Kaplan 1983, 203). However, within the women's films of the 1930s onwards, Kaplan finds little evidence of maternal desire. Instead, she argues, in films such as Stella Dallas (1937), one of the most frequently discussed women's films, the mother is forced to sacrifice her own desires in favour of the 'daughter's psychic and social needs' (Kaplan 1987a, 131). Furthermore, she argues, in the post-war period there had been an increasingly 'negative' representation of the mother: motherhood is frequently presented as 'monstrous' and close mother–daughter bonds as pathological. However, it could be argued that the terms of a psychoanalytic framework, in which woman and the feminine are identified with 'otherness' and 'lack', means that Doane or Kaplan find little in the women's film *for* women.

While Linda Williams (1987) draws on a psychoanalytic framework, her discussion of *Stella Dallas* (1937) suggests that the woman's film has something to offer its female viewers. Williams argues that mainstream cinema is capable of producing films characterised by a female gaze and a female subject, which offer the female viewer 'pleasures of recognition', addressing 'the contradictions that women encounter under patriarchy' (Williams 1987, 305). In order to explain this, Williams draws on the work of Nancy Chodorow. For Chodorow, whereas men must break their identification with their mother in order to gain a mature sexual identity, girls do not. Instead a girl 'takes on her identity as a woman in a positive process of becoming like, not different than, her mother' (p. 306). For Chodorow, mothers and daughters maintain a sense of connectedness, which constructs female identity as 'multiple and continuous . . . capable of fluidly shifting between the identity of the mother and daughter' (p. 306). For

Williams, this offers a way of understanding female spectatorship which, instead of being based on over-identification with the image as Doane suggests, is based on multiple identifications (see Modleski on soap opera in Chapter 5).

In *Stella Dallas*, it had been argued, Stella (the mother) is continually subject to negative judgements about her femininity and her mothering from a range of characters within the film, and is forced to sacrifice her bond with her daughter in order to secure a good future for her. Whereas Kaplan argues that the spectator is encouraged to share these judgements, Williams argues that the 'multiple, often conflicting points of view ... prevent such a monolithic view of the female subject' (1987, 314). Because women's development means that they are capable of shifting between different positions, the female viewer identifies with these conflicting points of view. Therefore, while there may be a patriarchal resolution to the film, 'the female spectator is in a constant state of juggling all positions at once', and identifies with the contradictions rather than the resolution (p. 317). This means that the female spectator, faced with the recognition of the contradictions of patriarchy, produces a radical reading of the film.

This argument has a number of implications. First, Williams, unlike Doane, identifies the possibility of 'progressive' texts within mainstream cinema: the contradictions of patriarchy can be represented in mainstream cinema. Second, she breaks down the distinction between the feminist critic and the female viewer: radical readings are open to all women in the audience because of the ways in which they are, psychically and socially, positioned under patriarchy. Third, in the process, she not only produces a potentially more pleasurable, active and empowering model of female spectatorship, but one in which there is room for resistance. As a result, Williams challenges the idea that popular cinema can only reproduce patriarchal ideology, and in *Stella Dallas*, she finds a woman's film which offers women a 'shock of recognition', a powerful recognition of the contradictions of living under patriarchy. In this way, *Stella Dallas* can be seen to not only offer a female spectating position, but also something for *both* women and feminism. However, Williams is still largely caught within the ahistoricism of psychoanalytic theory, a problem compounded by her use of Chodorow whose theory tends towards universalism and runs the risk of essentialising feminine identity (see Chapter 4).

In contrast, the final account of female spectatorship in this section emphasises the importance of the *differences* between femininities in the woman's film. In her article, 'Desperately Seeking Difference', Jackie Stacey (1988) returns to the questions of whether there is a place for female desire and a female gaze within patriarchal cinema. In this essay, she concentrates on two films, *All About Eve* (1950) and *Desperately Seeking Susan* (1985), both of which feature women gazing at women or, as Stacey puts it, 'representations of fascination between women' (1988, 115). For example, in *Desperately Seeking Susan*, we see the figure of Susan (Madonna) through the fascinated and desiring look of Roberta (Rosanna Arquette), who wishes to 'know' Susan so that she might become more like her, a relationship which evokes the relationship between the female spectator and the female star.

A number of significant points follow from this observation. First, Stacey identifies both a female gaze and a female desire, a desire which is not so much erotic as a desire to become more like the other woman. In this way, while psychoanalytic film theory tends to see a 'rigid distinction between *either* desire *or* identification', the films that Stacey discusses construct 'desires which involve a specific interplay of both processes' (1988, 129). De Lauretis has criticised Stacey for confusing desire and identification, arguing that Stacey is describing a narcissistic form of identification (de Lauretis 1994, 116–17). In response, Stacey has argued that 'female identification contains forms of desire which include, though not exclusively, homoerotic pleasure' (Stacey 1994, 29). In this way, while Stacey's article does not concentrate on lesbian spectatorship, it none the less questions the assumptions about the heterosexuality of the female spectator in much psychoanalytic criticism. Second, in the process, Stacey is able to conceive of an active, desiring and pleasurable model of female spectatorship. Third, Stacey discusses a fascination constructed through the *difference between femininities*: desire is not solely a product of sexual differences, as it must be within the psychoanalytical frameworks discussed above, but a product of 'the difference between two women in the film' (Stacey 1988, 128). In this way, Stacey points towards a very different conception of femininity to that assumed by psychoanalytic theory.

If femininities are taken to be cultural, social and historical products, then this offers a different starting point for understanding the women's film as a space in which the female viewer has the cultural competence to actively make distinctions between the different femininities on screen, which itself may be a source of pleasure. Furthermore, it offers a space to consider how mainstream cinema in general, and the woman's film in particular, produces and negotiates different constructions of feminine identity, offering a 'repertoire' of femininities (Brunsdon 1997, 85). Whereas Doane claims that these differences between femininities are merely *superficial* differences, as she must from within the terms of psychoanalysis, the debates that follow in the next section suggest, in different ways, that the differences between femininities are *significant* differences.

From the female spectator to the female audience

If the debates about female spectatorship provided some answers to the question of how the female viewer watches film, they still tended to regard 'the female spectator' as a position produced by the film text. This section examines some examples of feminist criticism which shift the debates from the film text and female spectatorship to questions about films in context and the female audience (Kuhn 1984). The shift to thinking about the relationship between film texts and women in the audience has a series of implications. First, it involves thinking about how meanings are produced in an encounter between the text and different audiences rather than how they are simply organised within the text (as the work of Dave Morley discussed in the previous chapter suggests). Second, in looking at the women's films of the past, it is also necessary to consider 'the historical and cultural *conditions of meaning-making*' (Partington 1991, 55). This raises questions about the 'intertexts' within which films become meaningful. For example, Maria LaPlace (1987), in her analysis of *Now Voyager* (1942), has examined how the meanings the film generated for female audiences in the period can only be understood in relation to wider discourses of consumerism, the female star and women's fiction, discourses which are utilised by both the film and audience members. Third, if audiences are actively involved in meaning-making activities, this not only questions the assumed passivity of the audience in much psychoanalytic theory but also suggests that, just because a film's preferred meaning may be patriarchal, these meanings are not necessarily accepted by the audience. However, this said, it is also necessary to remember that equally 'women may be active viewers in the sense of actively

investing in oppressive ideologies' (Stacey 1994, 47). There is no
reason to suppose that an active viewer is necessarily a radical
one. Finally, the shift from spectator to audience, and from text
to context, allows us to think not only about the meanings of
cinema texts, but the wider range of meanings that cinema-going
may have for female audiences. As Maria LaPlace suggests, this
also means that it is necessary to situate films within the wider
'feminine' cultures of a period, of which they are a part.

Angela Partington has examined how Hollywood melodramas of the 1950s – such as *Written on the Wind* (1956) and *All
That Heaven Allows* (1955) – may have been used to produce
particular kinds of meanings by working-class women in the UK
during the period. She starts from the premise that psychoanalysis has 'a tendency to take reading positions "produced" in the
texts . . . as a substitute for a view of the audience in its historical
context' (Partington 1991, 53). In order to understand the meanings and pleasures that these melodramas offered working-class
women in the period, Partington argues, we need to not only
consider how they drew on what Brunsdon calls 'traditionally
feminine competences' but also how feminine competences are
both 'classed' and the product of specific historical contexts
(p. 53).

Partington, like Doane, is interested in the ways in which
cinema may operate as a shop-window for consumer goods.
However, whereas Doane portrays women as passive in relation
to the dual forces of cinema and consumerism, Partington
demonstrates why women in the 1950s may well have made
active use of the images of consumer goods presented in the
lavish melodramas of the period. First, she argues, these goods in
themselves may have been a source of visual pleasure. Second, by
reading the ways in which consumer goods are used in these
films, working-class women had the opportunity to use the feminine consumer competences which they were being taught to
acquire during the period (see Chapter 6 for a detailed discussion
of this). Indeed, as Partington suggests, by understanding the
significance of the differences between consumer goods such as
furniture and fashion in these films, women may not only be able
to predict the fate of different characters within these films, but
also produce meanings that exceed those of the narrative. Finally,
by reading the ways in which different femininities were
produced through consumer goods in film, working-class women
were able to read the ways in which different feminine identities

are put together. Indeed, they are distanced from the image, instead of over-identified as Doane had suggested. This suggests that female audiences are not only capable of making distinctions between femininities, but that they understand that femininity is a 'masquerade' produced through the use of clothes, interiors, and so on. Furthermore, this knowledge that feminine identities could be made and remade, it is argued, allowed working-class women in the period to negotiate and resist 'the "housewife" identity . . . they were supposed to adopt' by identifying it as only one among a 'repertoire of femininities' (Partington 1991, 67). This enabled them to use consumer goods to create alternative definitions of femininity to the one they were encouraged to inhabit.

Jackie Stacey's *Star Gazing* also raises questions about the relationship between female audiences and the range of feminine images in the Hollywood films of the 1940s and 1950s. Whereas Partington is forced to speculate about how women made meaning from 1950s melodramas, Stacey's research is based on questionnaires and letters she received from British women who were asked to recount their memories of the female stars of the period. In this way, Stacey aims to reinstate the female audience who had been forgotten in psychoanalytic theories of spectatorship. In the process, she not only pays attention to the meanings produced in the encounter between audience and film text, but also raises questions about the meanings that cinema-going as a practice had for female audiences in the period. While cinema-going did represent an 'escape', she argues that the forms of 'escape' offered by the cinema were more complex than is commonly assumed. For example, cinema was seen not only as an 'escape' from the harsh realities of working-class life in war-time Britain and into an 'other world' in the luxurious comforts of the picture 'palace', it also offered an 'escape' from the constraints of British life into the 'other world' of America which signified 'abundance and glamour' (Stacey 1994, 105). Furthermore, the cinema offered a collective sense of 'escape', creating a 'shared intimacy' between women which was reproduced in their talk about the films and their stars (see also Taylor 1989a). In this way, she demonstrates that the practice of cinema-going is itself meaningful.

However, the main focus of Stacey's work is the relationship between female audiences in the UK and Hollywood's female stars of the period. In the process, she develops the ideas she had

raised in her earlier article discussed above. While female audiences did identify with female stars, she argues, 'identification'
encompasses a far more complex range of processes, practices
and meanings for audiences than had been suggested by psychoanalytic theories. For example, Stacey distinguishes between
what she calls 'cinematic' and 'extra-cinematic' identificatory
practices. 'Cinematic' identifications are usually based on a
recognition of the differences between the star and the female
viewer. Pleasure may be generated through being 'inspired' by
your favourite star – for example, by her glamour or confidence –
or might involve what Stacey calls 'transcendence', 'the imagined
transformation of self which produces the cinematic pleasure'
(Stacey 1994, 145). This refers to the pleasure of believing, for
the time that you are in the cinema, that you are the actress on
screen. 'Extra-cinematic' identificatory practices extend beyond
the encounter between viewer and star in the cinema and into the
viewer's everyday practices. In these practices, women tended to
try to reduce the difference between themselves and the star – for
example, by copying hairstyles, dressing like her or taking on
some of her personality traits. For example, in the cultural practice that Stacey terms 'copying', the difference 'between the star
and the spectator is transformable into similarity through the
typical work of femininity: the production of oneself as both
subject and object in accordance with cultural ideals of femininity' (p. 168).

The insights from Stacey's research produce a much more
complex and contradictory notion of female spectatorship, identification and desire than those often associated with
psychoanalysis. First, as Stacey had noted in her earlier article,
desire may not only be a product of sexual difference, but also of
the difference between femininities. Second, she notes that the
relationship between star and spectator is not just at the level of
the 'imagination' but can also become incorporated into the spectator's cultural practices outside the cinema (p. 171). Third, like
Partington, and in opposition to Doane, she notes how consumption is not simply a site of female subordination but, instead, may
be a source of resistance and empowerment. Like Partington,
Stacey argues that by drawing on the modes of feminine identity
enacted by Hollywood stars, British women, through their
consumption practices, may have resisted feminine ideals of the
period which portrayed women as primarily wives and mothers.
As she notes, 'American feminine ideals are clearly remembered

as transgressing restrictive British femininity and thus employed as strategies of resistance' (p. 204). Women were not simply invited to choose between different notions of feminine beauty, but also 'the production of a feminine self in relation to Americanness signified "autonomy", "individuality" and "independence"' (p. 238). In this way, Stacey appears to move towards an understanding of the importance of recognising competing definitions of femininity and how popular film may be a site where, in specific historical contexts, the meanings of femininity are reworked and negotiated. However, Stacey cannot quite escape from the theoretical agenda set by psychoanalysis and, in places, falls back on a more singular understanding of femininity where it is equated primarily with the visual image of feminine beauty.

None the less, the debates examined in this section suggest a way of understanding female pleasures, looks, identifications, desires and practices which were difficult to produce within feminist psychoanalysis. They begin to break down the distinction between the critical, distanced feminist critic and the passive, over-identified female spectator. Furthermore, these critics move beyond an understanding of popular culture as an undifferentiated mass culture and, drawing on frameworks from cultural studies, point to popular culture as a site of struggle over the meaning of femininity. This does not mean that popular cinema is necessarily characterised by 'resistance' to patriarchy, nor that audiences necessarily produce 'resistant' readings and activities from their uses of cinema. However, it does provide a framework in which struggle and resistance, where they exist, can be acknowledged and explored.

Cinema, femininity and difference

While the 'images of women' criticism of Haskell and Rosen had a tendency to conflate 'positive images' of women with an image of the (white) educated, middle-class, professional, heterosexual woman, the underlying framework of the discussion of 'woman as image' also tended to assume that both this image, and the female spectator, were white and heterosexual. However, some of the work discussed in the previous section explored how the differences between femininities on screen, and the differences between women in the audience are also significant for feminism. If Stacey's work raises the possibility of the 'homoerotic pleasure' of cinema for women, and Partington's work raises questions about how white working-class women in the UK might produce distinctive readings of films, then this section goes on to examine work which has taken issue with the assumptions about whiteness and heterosexuality in feminist film theory.

Critics who wished to develop analyses of lesbians as image, and about lesbian spectatorship, aimed to 'challenge the concept of women as inevitable objects of exchange between men, or as fixed in an eternal trap of "sexual difference" based on heterosexuality' (Becker *et al.* 1995, 43; see also Stacey 1994 and Traub 1995). Furthermore, it was argued, these assumptions create a position in which lesbian desire 'cannot be sexual desire' and can only be thought of in terms of a 'masculine' desire (de Lauretis 1994, 111). As Wilton argues, if feminist psychoanalytic film critics had conceived of a heterosexual, feminine subjectivity as 'impossible', it had difficulty beginning to think about the implications of this for a lesbian subjectivity (Wilton 1995, 10). Debates about lesbian as image have had to start from the fact that lesbians in cinema have been 'virtually invisible' (Weiss 1992, 1). As Hammer succinctly puts it, 'there could be no semiotics if there was no sign' (cited in Wilton 1995, 10). For this reason, lesbian film criticism has often revolved around the small number of film narratives which feature lesbian protagonists such as *Lianna* (1982), *Desert Hearts* (1985) and *Personal Best* (1982). For some critics, there is no possibility of a lesbian image within a mainstream cinema characterised by 'a heterosexist authority system' (Hammer cited in Wilton 1995, 4) which means that a 'lesbian cinema' can only exist in opposition to the mainstream. An alternative view is put forward by Cindy Patton in her discussion of *Internal Affairs* (1990) in which, through the point-of-view of the lesbian detective, we see the hypermasculinity of the male protagonists as pathological, and their heterosexual partners as implicated in this. In this way, Patton argues, the film 'situates *a* lesbian *character* as the film's reference point for the normal psyche' (1995, 22): she acts as a 'signifier of a space untouched by heteromasculine pathology' (p. 32).

Thinking about the lesbian viewer also problematises debates about female spectatorship. While critics such as de Lauretis (1994) have tried to address this from within psychoanalytic theory, others have tried to analyse the role of lesbian spectatorship within a wider lesbian subculture (Mayne 1993, 166). For example, Andrea Weiss (1994) argues that cinema – and, in particular, gossip about cinema and its female stars – played a part in the formation of a lesbian subculture in the US in the 1930s. The lack of images of lesbians in the Hollywood of the period forced lesbian spectators to track down 'traces' of a lesbian subject within the film text. Weiss argues that not only did lesbian spectators negotiate the meanings of texts to produce 'a more satisfying homoerotic interpretation' (1994, 332), they also 'appropriated elements of star images [from stars such as Marlene Dietrich] in forming the characteristics of a lesbian subculture' (p. 334). For Weiss, 'the subtext of films also provided the opportunity to see in certain gestures and movements an affirmation of lesbian experience – something that, however fleeting, was elsewhere rarely to be found, and certainly not in such a popular medium' (p. 334). In this way, as in Stacey's work, Weiss shows how cinema can be drawn on as a resource in wider cultural practices.

If a psychoanalytic model predicated on the centrality of sexual difference had difficulties accounting for lesbians as image and lesbian spectatorship, then it also worked to erase the significance of racial difference. As Lola Young argues, cinema does not just reproduce patriarchal ideologies but 'is complicit in the structuring and naturalising of power relations between black and white people' (1996, 33). As bell hooks has noted, the category 'woman' in psychoanalytic theory is always white. As a result, critics who have highlighted the importance of 'racial' difference in structuring cinematic codes and conventions have highlighted the ways in which the gaze in cinema – the right to 'look' – may not only be male, but the prerogative of the white male. For example, Jane Gaines explains how in *Mahogany* (1975) the body of Diana Ross is only available to the audience via the gaze of the white photographer because 'the black male protagonist's look is either repudiated or frustrated' (Gaines 1994, 182). Gaines argues that this demands a historical, rather than a psychoanalytic, explanation: while white men have historically had the right to 'look' at both black and white women, the idea that a black man has the right to look at the white female has been constructed as a 'threat'. In this way, Gaines argues, 'race could be a factor in the construction of cinematic languages' (pp. 184–5). Furthermore, Lola Young has shown how the emphasis on sexual difference within psychoanalytic theory has blinded critics to the ways in which the differences between femininities are also significant: 'black and white femininity may be linked by their common sexual unknowability, but white femininity is both foregrounded and privileged in relation to black women' (Young 1996, 53). In this way, she argues, the production of black women as images can only be understood in relation to the production of white femininity as an ideal.

Some critics have also argued that 'race' problematises ideas about an undifferentiated 'female spectator'. This raises the question of whether black women 'see' differently (hooks 1992, 128). While cautious of assuming that all black women share a similar perspective, Roach and Felix (1988) suggest that there is a distinctive black female gaze. However, hooks suggests that this ignores the extent to which many black women's perceptions are 'profoundly colonised ... by dominant ways of knowing' (hooks 1992, 128). While hooks usefully notes the problems in 'essentialising' a black female gaze and a mode of black female spectatorship, she makes an equally problematic distinction between the 'critical' black female spectator and 'duped', 'victimised' and 'unaware' black female spectator (p. 127). The 'critical' black female spectator, she argues, develops an 'oppositional gaze': aware of racism, she places herself 'outside the pleasure in looking' and refuses to 'identify with white womanhood' (p. 122). The unaware black female spectator is 'complicit' with cinematic racism: she misrecognises herself as white and adopts a 'masochistic look of victimisation' (p. 121). In this way, hooks overcomes the problems of assuming all black women spectators 'look' in the same way but, in the process, creates a problematic dichotomy between the 'enlightened' and the 'duped', between a black feminist viewer and her unaware, passive 'other'.

Whereas hooks' account of an oppositional black gaze is speculative and rests largely on anecdotal evidence, Jacqueline Bobo studied the ways in which black women made particular readings of the film of *The Colour Purple* (1985). Based on the use of interviews, Bobo's work is a rare attempt, within film studies, to collect data on the actual responses audiences make to films rather than simply generalising about readings from an analysis of the operations of the film text. Whereas there had been widespread criticism of the film version of *The Colour Purple* – especially from black men – Bobo drew on Hall's encoding/decoding model (discussed in Chapter 2) to argue that black women tended to find something more positive in the film because they 'have a different history and consequently a different perspective from other viewers of the film' (Bobo 1988, 101). Not only did the film offer a rare opportunity to see the lives of black women depicted on screen, but also, Bobo argues, their responses to the film created a sense of unity among black women. However, in the process, Bobo also tends to reproduce the notion that black women share a common experience, identity and consciousness (Thornham 1998, 145).

If Bobo, like Stacey, drew on empirical data to analyse how 'real' women in the audience make meanings from popular cinema, this has remained a marginal strategy within film studies, although, it would be a key method in research into soap operas. As this chapter has made clear, feminist film studies has tended to privilege a textual analysis which sees the spectator as an 'effect' of the text. Within this mode of criticism, there is a tendency to see any potential for resistance to patriarchy to be located either in the text itself or in the activity of feminist critique. For this reason, there has been a tendency within feminist psychoanalysis to see popular cinema as a site of domination rather than struggle. As a result, the meaning-making activities of 'real women' have been marginalised to such an extent that many critics could only assume that the viewing practices of 'ordinary women' in the audience were 'complicit' with patriarchy. This neglects the ways in which audiences may produce diverse meanings and uses from both film texts and cinema-going, meanings and uses which may not always be 'complicit' with patriarchy. Furthermore, for those feminist critics who saw popular cinema as inherently patriarchal, a feminist 'alternative' could only be produced 'outside', and 'against', 'the popular', a place which was doomed to remain 'marginal'.

Although there are exceptions in the work discussed above, the majority of feminist film criticism – especially psychoanalytic criticism – conforms to what Brunsdon calls a 'hegemonic' relationship between 'the feminist' and 'the ordinary woman'. In such work, 'the feminist' is set in opposition to 'the ordinary woman': although both are 'women', the 'feminist film critic' is often identified by her ability to distance herself from the seductive 'feminine' pleasures of 'popular cinema' to produce her own 'feminist' reading of it. A further distance, from both the film text and the 'ordinary woman' is produced by the heavyweight theories the feminist film critic wields. While such a position, Brunsdon argues, tends to be 'recruitist', in the case of feminist film criticism of the mid-1970s onwards, there is not a clear sense of what the 'ordinary woman' is being recruited to join, whether it is a 'feminist cause' or a degree in film studies (Brunsdon 1991; 1993).

Notes

1 However, see Walsh (1984) for criticism on the women's film which while reproducing some problematic notions about 'reflection', produced work on the women's film which was indebted to the historical and sociological emphasis in Haskell and Rosen, while also overcoming many of their limitations. For work which seeks to evaluate the significance of this earlier criticism for contemporary feminist film criticism, see Byars (1991).

2 The debate about whether some film melodramas – often those directed by Douglas Sirk and Vincent Minelli – were 'progressive' was already on-going before Mulvey's article. It was claimed by critics such as Elsaesser (1987) that because these privileged contradiction, they therefore disrupted the workings of 'realist' cinema and, in the process, resisted ideological closure. However, these earlier debates had not considered melodrama as a women's genre and, therefore, paid little attention of the implications of this for feminism. For an overview of these debates, see Gledhill (1987) and Klinger (1994).

3 In this article, Mulvey appears to move away from the idea that spectating positions are a product of the film text and towards the idea of a social audience of women who draw on feminine codes and competences to produce readings of the film text. However, this is left rather undefined.

Further reading

Gledhill, C., ed., *Home is Where the Heart is: Studies in Melodrama and the Woman's Film* (London, British Film Institute, 1987)

Kuhn, A. *Women's Pictures: Feminism and Cinema* (London, Routledge, 1982)

Penley, C., ed., *Feminism and Film Theory* (New York, Routledge, 1988)

Pribram, D., ed., *Female Spectators: Looking at Film and Television* (London, Verso, 1988)

Stacey, J. *Star Gazing: Hollywood Cinema and Female Spectatorship* (London, Routledge, 1994)

Thornham, S. *Passionate Detachments: An Introduction to Feminist Film Theory* (London, Arnold, 1997)

Wilton, T., ed., *Immortal, Invisible: Lesbians and the Moving Image* (London, Routledge, 1995)

4

Reading romantic fiction

Romantic fiction is the genre that tends to be most commonly associated with women. Not only are most of its readers women, so are most of its authors.[1] For this reason, romantic fiction has been seen by its critics as a ghetto which imprisons women and by its sympathisers as an 'imaginary community' of women sharing 'utopian' dreams. Indeed, it was romantic fiction's association with women which, for many years, acted as 'proof' of its lack of value. Many literary critics regarded romantic fiction as the ultimate example of the trivial and dangerous fantasies which characterised a mass culture produced for mindless, passive consumers. In fact, as this chapter shows, many feminists have come to similar conclusions. For such feminists, romantic fiction was politically dangerous, a mechanism through which patriarchal culture was reproduced: women were fed fantasies of true love, fantasies which most women were seen to unquestioningly accept. These critiques need to be understood as part of a wider critique of romantic love within second-wave feminism (see below). It is only in recent years that new approaches generated in literary and cultural studies have allowed feminists to produce a more complex analysis of the significance of romantic fiction. Not only have women working in these fields inspected romantic fiction more closely to uncover the complex and contradictory meanings it contains, they have also carried out research with women readers to discover what romance reading means to them. In this way, recent work goes beyond noting that romantic fiction is read by large numbers of women and begins to explain *why* women read it.

The emergent field of cultural studies played an important role in allowing female critics to take romantic fiction seriously. Following the lead of writers such as Raymond Williams (1993), cultural studies broke with the idea that culture could be simply equated with 'great works of art' and instead asserted that 'culture was ordinary'. First, this created a space in which popular texts could be analysed to understand their cultural significance. Tania Modleski's *Loving with a Vengeance* can be seen as both an example of such work and as an attempt to counteract a rather masculine bias in the interests of cultural critics. Second, in Williams' work, culture was no longer simply equated with texts but with the complex relationships between cultural industries, cultural forms and cultural practices. Although her work initially came out of a different tradition, Janice Radway's *Reading the Romance* demonstrates that in order to understand the meaning and significance of romance, it is necessary to analyse the complex relations between publishing industries, romance texts and romance readers. In particular, she goes beyond textual analysis to explore the activity of romance reading as an important cultural practice.

It is in this way that approaches to romantic fiction have developed differently to approaches to the woman's film within film studies. As the last chapter demonstrated, film studies tends to privilege textual analysis, often claiming that the way in which the spectator views a text is inscribed within the film's form. However, members of an audience are not a 'blank canvas', nor is the audience a homogeneous group. Film studies has often ignored the idea that 'texts are selected, purchased, constructed and used by real people with previously existing needs, desires, intentions and interpretive strategies' (Radway 1987, 221). As a result, while the formal organisation of a film or novel may privilege a particular reading or set of meanings, it does not necessarily determine how different audiences interpret them. As Dave Morley's work suggests, different readers inhabit different social and cultural structures which will shape their interpretations, as will their knowledge of other texts. The impact of cultural studies on the study of romance has been to shift analysis away from a hypothetical reader towards specific readers. However, there is still a tendency to treat women romance readers as an undifferentiated group. As Helen Taylor puts it, 'it is certain that the readers of this large, varied group of writings are a mixed and contradictory group about whom far too many easy generalisations are always being made' (1989b, 59).

Taylor's observation raises a further problem – the wide variety of texts which might be classified as romantic fiction. In recent years, most critics have felt the need for some definition in order to specify the features of romantic fiction and so better analyse it. Furthermore, as Jean Radford argues, it is only by specifying the codes and conventions used in romantic fiction

that it is possible to understand how they undergo transformations in different historical contexts. In attempting to specify the
contemporary romance, Radford, like many other critics, draws
on John Cawelti's definition of the features of romance. These
central features are: a) the central narrative concerns a love relationship; b) the central relationship is between a hero and
heroine; c) most romances have a female protagonist; and d)
there is a close identification between reader and protagonist
(Radford 1986, 8). Radford argues that not only is such a definition useful for thinking about romance writing, it is also useful in
'thinking through the romance element in the mainstream novel'
(p. 8). This is an important point but also raises a number of
problems. First, while the scope of this definition is quite wide on
one hand, it rules out a number of possibilities. For example, by
this definition, the idea of a lesbian romance becomes problematic: indeed, it is necessary to recognise 'the heterosexism of
"classic romance"' (Stacey and Pearce 1995, 20). Second, can
clear distinctions be drawn between romantic fiction and 'mainstream' and 'literary' fiction? Indeed, is it desirable to make such
distinctions? Third, 'romantic contents' may be as much a
product of how the text is read as it is of the text itself. For
readers with a knowledge of romance conventions, it is possible
to transform novels with minimal 'romantic contents' into
romances. These points highlight the fact that romance is a
highly complex genre and contains many sub-genres (Taylor
1989b, 59). In the rest of the chapter, a range of ideas about the
characteristics of romantic fiction and romance readers will be
discussed. In particular, the chapter will explore why romantic
fiction has a particular appeal for women, while also considering
the particular pleasures of the romance and the often uneasy relationship between feminism, romances and their readers.

Devaluing romance

It has become part of contemporary 'common-sense' that romantic fiction is a 'formulaic' 'trivial' and 'escapist' form read by
'addicted' women. Indeed, as will become clear, some of these
ideas still permeate contemporary feminism. Many of these
assumptions have their roots in the mass culture criticism which
emerged in the nineteenth century. Mass culture criticism
claimed that when modes of industrial production were applied
to culture, the result was a standardised and formulaic mass

culture. Because mass culture was produced for profit, they claimed, it had to appeal to the 'lowest common denominator'. For this reason, the products of mass culture could be consumed without effort, offering easy pleasures to passive consumers who had difficulty distinguishing between 'reality' and the fantasies they read.

These claims about 'mass culture' and its consumers are not only the same ones that are still commonly made about romances and their readers, they are also claims which are commonly made about women generally. Indeed, as Andreas Huyssen argues, in critiques of mass culture, there is a 'persistent gendering of mass culture as feminine and inferior' (1986, 196) and an association of modernist high art with a heroic masculinity. Put simply, in debates about mass culture, feminine qualities – emotion, sentiment, passivity – are used to signify the worthlessness of mass culture. Therefore, as Huyssen points out, left cultural critics such as Adorno and Horkheimer in the 1930s could claim that mass culture 'cannot renounce the threat of castration' (quoted in Huyssen 1986, 192). These threats about the emasculating effects of mass culture often resurface. In Britain in the 1950s, Richard Hoggart (1958) bemoaned the decline of an 'authentic' working-class culture and the rise of an 'inauthentic' mass culture. Because Hoggart believed that mass culture transformed an active working class into a passive mass, he believed mass culture had an emasculating effect (Webster 1988, 187). The threat of mass culture was to 'feminise' men – no one, at the time, felt the need to contest the idea that 'feminine' qualities were inferior qualities.

What is striking about mass culture criticism is that writers from radically different political positions came to such similar conclusions. Claims about the masses' addiction to easy pleasures, their passivity and their conformity were repeated so often they gained the status of 'truths'. These critics draw distinctions between 'us' – an educated, cultured minority – and 'them', the masses who must be taught to see the error of their ways. As Ien Ang points out, many feminist critics who have been hostile to romantic fiction and other 'feminine' forms have been inspired by 'the paternalism of the ideology of mass culture' (1985, 118). These feminists share the same reforming zeal as mass culture critics – they imply (explicitly or implicitly) that if 'housewives' can be weaned off their addictions to romances and soaps and read feminist books, they may overcome their 'false conscious-

ness' and join with their feminist sisters in the struggle to overthrow patriarchy. For these feminists, romantic fiction was
represented 'as "dope for dupes" – a means of brainwashing
women into subservience' (Jackson 1995, 50). Some writers went
as far as implying that romantic fiction was part of a conspiracy
against feminism. For example, Ann Douglas argues that as the
feminist movement grew so did the readership of Harlequin
fictions in which 'woman's independence is made horribly unattractive   and   unrewarding,   her   dependence   presented   as
synonymous with excitement' (1980, 28).

The most common responses by feminist critics to 'feminine
narratives'   and   their   readers   have   been   'dismissiveness',
'mockery' and 'hostility' (Modleski 1984, 14). For example,
Germaine Greer describes romance novels as the 'escapist literature of love and marriage voraciously consumed by housewives'
(1970, 214). The 'housewife' becomes a key figure in writing on
romance and soaps. A stereotypical figure, she is characterised by
her passivity, dependence, childishness and addiction to romantic fantasies. In this way, the 'housewife' becomes the negative
opposite of the heroic feminist.

The critique of romantic fiction was part of a wider critique
of romance for many feminists. As Stevi Jackson notes, 'love was
seen as an ideology which legitimated women's oppression and
which trapped them into exploitative heterosexual relationships'
(Jackson 1993, 204–5). Indeed, this is made clear in the feminist
slogan, 'It starts when you sink into his arms and ends with your
arms in his sink' (p. 204). Romance was not only seen as a mechanism to secure women's domestic exploitation in the patriarchal
family, but also legitimated the emotional and sexual exploitation
of women. For example, Kate Millett claimed that romantic love
legitimated 'emotional manipulation' and 'obscures the realities
of female status and the burden of economic dependency'
(Millett 1977, 37). Furthermore, romantic love was blamed for
the ways in which feminine identity was predicated on a loss of
self through the idealisation of, and dependence on, men. In
these ways, romantic love was centrally implicated in reproducing 'compulsory heterosexuality'.

One of the most forceful critiques of romance can be found
in what is often seen as one of the key texts to come out of
second-wave feminism. In *The Dialectic of Sex*, Shulamith
Firestone claimed that 'romanticism is a cultural tool of male
power to keep women from knowing their conditions' (Firestone

1979, 139). Romantic love is pathological, she argued: it is love corrupted by the unequal relationship between the sexes and is used to reproduce patriarchy. This is achieved in various ways. First, love becomes a woman's vocation, diverting her energies from other pursuits. Second, a woman's sense of identity and self-esteem depends on a man's valuation of her as worthy of being loved. Third, because romantic love makes women economically dependent on men, it is not about mutual vulnerability but female vulnerability, leaving women open to abuse. Finally, because romantic love helps to maintain the family, it is centrally implicated in the reproduction of women's oppression as a class. For these reasons, Firestone argued, love under patriarchy is doomed – a 'holocaust' – because 'real love' can only occur between equals and not in an 'unequal *power* context' (Firestone 1979, 127). However, more recent feminist critics have argued that such a 'love uncontaminated by cultural and social structures is inconceivable' (Jackson 1993, 206). Furthermore, Firestone's argument 'effectively precluded the possibility of confronting the potency of this emotion and seeking an explanation for it' (p. 206).

There are a number of more general problems with the critiques of romance and romantic fiction which come out of second-wave feminism. First, romance is treated as a monolithic and unchanging ideology. This ignores the ways in which, despite continuities, there are a range of romantic narratives both within and between historical periods. Second, it was assumed that readers not only unquestioningly accepted this ideology – a 'hypodermic syringe' model of media effects – but also that readers could not distinguish between fantasy and reality. For example, Greer argues that 'Although romance is essentially vicarious, the potency of the fantasy distorts actual behaviour' (1970, 180). This relates to a third problem, what Jean Radford calls 'Mistaking the thing on the page for the experience itself' (1986, 14): the ways in which women read romance texts cannot be deduced from the text alone, nor can the meaning of the activity. Furthermore, this meant that critics failed to understand the importance and pleasures of romance as fantasy. It may be that fiction as fantasy allows 'the explorations and productions of desires which may be in excess of the socially possible or acceptable' (Light 1984, 7; see also, Ang 1996 and Kaplan 1986).

A further problem with the feminist position outlined above is that traditionally 'feminine' attributes were treated as negative attributes. In demonstrating their distance from trivial romantic fantasies, they accepted a 'critical double standard' based on masculine contempt for the feminine (Modleski 1984, 14). One of the ways in which this double standard operated was in the opposition between romance, which was equated with femininity, and sexuality, which was equated with masculinity. For example, Greer claimed that romance was 'compulsorily sexless' (1970, 172) and that it transformed 'sex into fairy-tales' (p. 184). The same opposition can be found in Angela McRobbie's early work on the ideology of romance in the girl's magazine *Jackie* (see Chapter 8). One of the main problems that she identifies with the ideology of romance is that it displaces all 'traces of adolescent sexuality . . . replacing it with concepts of love, passion and eternity' (1991, 107).[2] Like Greer, McRobbie assumes that sexuality is a positive and 'natural' force which the negative 'cultural' force of romance distorts.

Rather than seeing sexuality as something which can be 'expressed' or 'repressed', many critics have turned to Michel Foucault's argument that sexuality is 'produced' through discourse. For Foucault, discourses are meaning-producing systems which are both instruments and effects of power (Foucault 1981, 101). From such a position, discourses of sexuality are not a power which 'represses' a 'natural' sexuality but instead produce effects of power which organise and produce what sexuality is in specific historical and geographical contexts. This questions the idea that romantic love is an 'ideological appearance' which distorts a 'natural sexuality'. Furthermore, such a position also suggests that romantic love may also be produced through discourse. This challenges notions of romance as a monolithic and unchanging entity and allows a historically and geographically informed analysis of romance which acknowledges the ways in which discourses of romantic love are 'constantly in the process of being remade and reconstituted' (Stacey and Pearce 1995, 28).

The contradictions of romantic fiction

Tania Modleski's *Loving with a Vengeance* (1984) was one of the key texts which, inspired by developments in cultural studies, took the romance and its appeal to women seriously. This was part of a wider critical process in which feminist critics both tried to resist the 'critical double standard' which deemed cultural forms and practices associated with women 'the lowest of the low' and tried to deal with 'a fear of rejecting women who enjoyed such forms, indeed a fear that feminists were rejecting their own past pleasures in an attempt to be equal to male cultural standards' (Tasker 1991, 85–6). Modleski's book concentrates on three 'feminine' forms – Harlequin romances,[3] Gothic novels and soap operas – and treat them, and the pleasures they offer, as worthy of serious analysis.[4]

Modleski argues that, rather than simply dismissing or deriding these 'feminine' forms, it is necessary to understand their contradictions to show how they deal with real social problems, rather than simply keeping women in their place. In doing so she combines textual analysis with theories from psychology and psychoanalysis to explain the functions that romance fiction performs in relation to women's psychic conflicts and struggles. Therefore, while she is critical of the way in which Harlequin novels invite women to escape into passivity, she also takes seriously the reasons why women might want this form of escape. The escape offered by romance narratives is the possibility of being able to transcend the demands made on women in their everyday lives, by losing oneself in a state of romantic bliss, in which, like the heroine, one can exist in a state of pleasurable dependency where one is taken care of (1984, 37).

Modleski identifies certain features of Harlequin narratives that have a particular appeal to women. For example, the romantic hero often mocks or is angry at the heroine. However, because the reader knows the conventions of romance, she is able to interpret them as signs of his love for the heroine. In the process, Modleski claims, although the reader has an emotional identification with the heroine, she is 'intellectually distanced from her' because the reader knows more than the heroine (p. 41). In this way, Modleski challenges the assumption that the reader passively identifies with the heroine. The function of the hero's initial mockery of the heroine is that it assures women that men's meanness signifies overwhelming love. 'Thus romances to some extent "inoculate" against the major evils of sexist society' (p. 43). As a result, while Modleski doesn't necessarily condone the ways in which romances help women accept patriarchy, she acknowledges that they help women cope with it. For example, the way in which the Harlequin heroine finally brings the contemptuous hero to his knees not only challenges the common assumption that the romantic heroine is passive and childlike, but it also 'conceals a deep-seated desire for vengeance' (p. 45). In this way, romantic fiction does not simply portray feminine passivity, but also contains powerful 'revenge fantasies' and, therefore, a form of protest, even though this anger is eventually neutralised (p. 47). However, she argues, the fact that the novels have to 'go to such extremes to neutralise women's anger and make masculine hostility bearable testifies to the depth of women's discontent' (p. 58).

The romance narrative also deals with a basic conflict that Modleski claims faces all women – women's goal in life is meant to be getting a husband, but they must not let it appear to be a goal which is consciously or calculatedly pursued. The youth and innocence of the Harlequin heroine, however, means that she is spared the conflict that real women experience. Furthermore, the story is told in the third person, and, as a result, it is possible to present the heroine as unaware of the feelings she stirs up in the hero. The heroine escapes the psychic conflicts that real women have but, as a result, they 'inevitably increase the reader's own psychic conflicts, thus creating an even greater dependency on the literature' (p. 57). Modleski returns to the assumptions of mass culture criticism, which stressed the consumer's addiction to the narcotic powers of popular fiction. There may be evidence to suggest that this is indeed how readers perceive themselves, but the extent to which this is the result of readers having inter-nalised the popular and academic stereotype of the romance reader remains unclear.

Although Modleski reaffirms the metaphor of addiction, she challenges the stereotype of the 'passive' reader, claiming that the reader 'is engaged in an intensely active psychological process' (p. 58). Furthermore, instead of blaming Harlequin novels for women's oppression, she believes it is women's oppression that creates the need for Harlequins. Harlequin novels offer their readers a way of 'adapting' to the constraints and conflicts produced in women by a patriarchal culture. Furthermore, if Modleski finds certain parts of the romance narrative 'regressive', she also identifies elements of protest against male behaviour and a 'utopian' longing for a different world, albeit a world in which heterosexual relations are still granted a centrality.

Modleski's work marks a shift in feminist thought from a superficial condemnation of romances to a greater sense of the complex and contradictory nature of these texts. As a result, although they are seen, in the last instance, to reproduce women's subordination in patriarchal culture, they also seen to expose some of the contradictions of women's oppression and as signalling forms of female discontent. The magical solutions that they offer differ from those provided by feminism but, for the most part, Modleski does treat them seriously on their own terms, even if they ultimately must be labelled as 'regressive' and found lacking in comparison with those offered by feminism.

Modleski's work also marks an attempt to treat the romance reader seriously, and seeks to explain why women read romances. However, 'real' readers may not read the romance in the same way as the implied reader of Modleski's argument. Furthermore, the dependence on abstract psychological theory to explain how and why women read romances, simultaneously annihilates social and cultural differences between women readers. As Helen Taylor puts it, do all readers from 'Taiwan to Tallahassee' share common fantasies? (1989b, 65).

Reading the romance

In *Reading the Romance* (1987), Janice Radway turned her attention to the romance *reader*, analysing not only what romantic fictions mean to their readers, but also what the *practice* of reading meant to them (anticipating the ways in which Stacey had considered the practice of cinema-going). For this reason, Radway combined methods of textual analysis from literary studies with 'ethnographic' methods from the social sciences which attempt to understand the meanings people bring to their cultural practices. In order to discover the meanings that readers bring to their romance reading, Radway used open-ended interviews, individual and group discussions and observation with a self-selected group of avid romance readers. These readers were all women who used the services of Dot, an employee at the local bookstore who advised the readers about which romances to purchase. This 'ethnographic' methodology has become increasingly popular in media and cultural studies as critics have turned away from textual analysis alone to consider the importance of what Taylor calls 'texts in use' (1989b, 66) (see Chapter 5). In this way, Radway addresses the problem of the absent or abstract reader in studies of romantic fiction.

Radway also explores the complex cultural relations and exchanges between the organisation of the publishing industry, the texts produced and reading practices. The spectacular sales of romantic fiction from the 1970s onwards, Radway argues, cannot be seen simply as an expression of women's demand for the product but is also the result of publishing practices. Romance readers are, therefore, to some extent, the product of publishing practices. Publishers such as Harlequin aim to predict demand by controlling 'the interaction between an identifiable audience and a product designed especially for it' (Radway 1987, 29). Harlequin's marketing strategies depended on the ability to identify an audience (women); find a way of reaching them (by putting romances 'where the women are' – drugstores, supermarkets and mall bookstores); forging an association between a generic product and the company name (romantic fiction and Harlequin become synonymous); and offering a pleasure women want to repeat. This final strategy was achieved through in-depth market research into the audience's preferences and motives for reading. Some companies even went as far as pretesting books with readers so they could programme 'publications as completely as possible to serve an already constituted desire and taste' (pp. 43–4).

In producing lines of romantic fiction, publishers aim to produce an undifferentiated product for a mass audience, reproducing some of the assumptions of critiques of romantic fiction as mass culture. However, one of the key insights of Radway's work is to show that, unlike publishers and most academics, readers make important distinctions between what is supposedly indistinguishable. Publishers may address a mass but readers devise ways of serving their own tastes. For example, the readers that Radway studied learned to meet their own needs and tastes by 'learning to decode the iconography of romantic cover art and the jargon of the backcover blurbs and by repeatedly selecting works by authors who have pleased them in the past' (p. 46). They also use the services of Dot in their local bookstore who acts as a mediator between publishers and readers, and creates 'generic distinctions within a category that the publishers are themselves trying to ... standardise', empowering readers 'with a selective ability' (p. 53).

Radway's readers had very strong ideas about what characteristics and conventions make a love story a romance: as Dot puts it, 'Not all love stories are romances' (p. 64). The readers define a romance as a story about a woman, which is told from her point of view: the reader should be able to identify with the heroine and feel her emotions. A romance must be about a developing love and include details about the relationship after the hero and heroine have got together. For a love story to be a romance, it must also have a happy ending. Rather than explicit sexual details, the readers are interested in the 'verbal working out' of the romance which gives them the space to actively 'project themselves into the story' (pp. 66–7). Radway claims that the readers rejected stories which contained sad endings, promiscuity, male violence and rape because these are things that they fear. For Radway's readers, the ideal romance offers the opportunity to escape from a world characterised by the excesses of male power and into a utopian world in which heterosexual relationships can work.

Because Radway's readers bring different value systems, knowledges and discourses to the romance when they read it, they often interpret the text in radically different ways to feminist critics. For example, the readers believe that an intelligent, independent heroine with a sense of humour is a key ingredient in a good romance whereas feminist critics have often perceived the same heroines as passive and helpless. In this way, the readers make distinctions between the feminine heroines whereas feminist critics have often found these same heroines to be homogeneous. The reasons for feminist disapproval of the romance heroine is because their ideal woman is 'the autonomous woman capable of accomplishing productive work in a nondomestic sphere' (p. 78). However, while feminists who believe that men and women have equal abilities might find the romance heroine foolish or pathetic, Radway argues that 'she appears courageous, and even valiant, to another still unsure that such equality is a fact or that she herself might want to assent to it' (p. 78). Radway shows an ambivalence here that is evident throughout *Reading the Romance*: she wishes to sympathetically reconstruct the readers' interpretations based on their world-views but at the same time frames these interpretations in the light of her own world-view which is closer to the feminist critic who disapproves of romance described above. For example, she constantly undercuts the pleasure that the readers gain from their reading by calling it 'vicarious', even though they experience it as 'real'. To give one example, Radway argues that

> the good feelings this woman derives from reading romantic fiction are not experienced in the course of her habitual existence in the world of actual social relations, but in the separate, free realm of the imaginary. The happiness she permits herself is not only second-hand, but temporary as well. By resting satisfied with this form of

vicarious pleasure, the romance reader may do nothing to transform
her actual situation which itself gave rise to the need to seek out
such pleasure in the first place. (p. 117)

Not only is this distinction between real and vicarious pleasure
highly questionable, Radway feels compelled to judge the readers
for their lack of feminist values (Ang 1996). While this is not to
suggest that Radway's role as a cultural critic is to uncritically
describe her readers' opinions, it does point to a continuing
tension between feminism and romance even in the most sympathetic accounts.[5]

Radway's explanation of why women read romance plays
around different meanings of 'escape'. First, the readers want to
'escape' into the heroine's life: they experience what it is to be
loved and nurtured by identifying with a heroine who is loved and
nurtured by the hero. In this way, Radway argues, romances offer
their readers the experience of being passive in a world in which
women are positioned as carers who must meet the demands of
their husbands and children. However, Radway not only considers the social and material contexts which draw her readers to the
romance, but also, like Modleski, she considers the psychological
functions of the romance for women. Like Linda Williams (see
Chapter 3), Radway draws on the work of Nancy Chodorow who
argues that women never totally escape the desire to return to the
close emotional bond of the 'self-in-relation' (thinking of yourself
as an extension of others), that they experienced with their
mother as a child. Although women enter into heterosexual relations as their erotic desires become focused on the father, they
still desire the emotional commitment and nurturance they experienced with their mothers. Although women can again establish
themselves as a 'self-in-relation' by becoming mothers, in the
process, they become the nurturer and therefore are still denied
the emotional nurturance they crave. For this reason, Radway
argues, there is a correlation 'between some romance reading and
the social roles of wife and mother' (1987, 138). She claims that,
because women think of themselves as a self-in-relation, and men
cannot function properly as relational partners, women turn to
romantic fantasies. The romance narrative not only charts female
personality development but also 'represents real female needs
within the story' (p. 138): in the readers' 'ideal' romances, the
heroines are nurtured in an intense emotional union with the
hero. Through identification with the heroine, the reader can
experience this state and satisfy her own needs before returning

to a world in which she must care for others. For this reason, Radway suggests that despite their preoccupation with heterosexual love, romances are really about 'the original, blissful symbiotic union between mother and child' (p. 156).

As a result, Radway's readers choose romances which offer a form of escape that fulfils their psychological needs, needs which are produced by patriarchy but aren't satisfied within patriarchal institutions. Although these romances do explore reservations about men, they hold out the promise that all men can be magically transformed from inconsiderate brutes into tender, caring lovers. For this reason, Radway argues, the romance reader 'insulates herself from the need to demand that such behaviour change' (p. 151). However, in the process Radway presents 'feminism . . . as the superior solution to all women's problems as if feminism automatically possessed the relevant and effective formulas for all women to change their lives and acquire happiness' (Ang 1996, 103).

None the less, romance reading offers another means of 'escape', the escape provided by the act of reading itself. Picking up a book provided Radway's readers with a way of blocking out the surrounding world and the demands of their family, a way of giving themselves a treat and taking care of their own needs. Radway's readers 'use traditionally female forms to resist their situation *as women* by enabling them to cope with the features of the situations that oppress them' (Radway 1987, 11). Although Radway finds that the texts which the women select in order to escape into ultimately confirm patriarchal relations, the practice of reading is a form of *resistance* to their social and material situation in patriarchy. Furthermore, while Radway insists that the romance text helps to reproduce these readers as wives and mothers, the readers also believe that their reading has transformed them, encouraging them to think of themselves as independent and intelligent and causing them to re-evaluate their relationships.

Their image of themselves as intelligent and their reading as worthwhile is crucial to these women in a culture in which, as we have seen, romances are seen as trivial and their readers stupid. Indeed, the women are keen to distinguish themselves from mere 'housewives' who are addicted to soap. It is by stressing the educational value of their reading that they justify this distinction and overcome their guilt at spending valuable time and money on a cultural form which the wider culture denigrates. However, by legitimating their reading for its educational function – they are instructed about history, geography and different cultures – they do so according to an 'ideology of hard work or productive labour' that is prevalent in the wider culture, not to mention feminist criticism. Some of the women also enjoy the details about household objects, maybe a result of the types of knowledge which women deem to be important (as shown by Partington's work discussed in the previous chapter). Indeed, Radway argues, it is this 'craving for knowledge' that draws these women to reading rather than other cultural practices.

Reading the Romance, by focusing on the ways in which women interpret both the romance text and the activity of reading, shows that readers of popular fictions are not merely 'cultural dopes'. Furthermore, Radway demonstrates how readers' active engagement with mass-produced forms can be a form of protest and resistance. Romance reading can be seen as a form of struggle over what it means to live as a woman under patriarchy. However, it is important to remember that Radway's romance readers are not necessarily typical of *all* romance readers: the differences between women might produce different engagements with romantic fiction. Just because most readers are women, they will not necessarily read the romance in the same way (although the use of Chodorow's work largely implies this). Furthermore, women similar to those studied by Radway might find the romance reading irrelevant and turn to other cultural forms and practices (1987, 8). The problem with generalising from Radway's readers to all 'ordinary women' is that they quickly lose their specificity and can easily 'join that generalised other to feminism, "the housewife"' (Brunsdon 1991, 373).

Although *Reading the Romance* was groundbreaking in terms of studying why women read romances, Radway maintains a distinction between the resistance embodied in romance readers' practices and the conservative ideology embedded in romance texts. From her feminist perspective, and despite the fact that her readers 'insist that romantic fiction is fantasy', she is still worried about the effects of romance on her readers. For example, she wonders 'how much of the romance's conservative ideology is inadvertently "learned" during the reading process and generalised as normal, natural, female development in the real world' (1987, 186). The distinction between 'us-feminists' who know better and 'them-readers' who need to learn the error of their ways remains. Indeed, as Ang argues, Radway's work is a 'drama-

tisation of the relationship between "feminism" and "women"'
(1996, 100). Furthermore, 'The distribution of identities is
clearcut: Radway, the researcher, is a feminist and *not* a romance
fan; the Smithton women, the researched, are romance readers
and *not* feminists. From such a perspective, the political aim of
the project becomes envisaged as one of bridging this profound
separation between "us" and "them"' (p. 102).

Social change, feminism and romantic fiction

If Radway believed that, at the time of writing, the conservative
ideology of romance texts was still very much at odds with feminism, she did also identify signs of hope in changes in the
romance field. First, she finds hope not only in new forms of
collective organisation among romance writers with the founda-
tion of the Romance Writers of America, but also that these
writers seemed open to some feminist ideas. Second, she notes
the rise of a new wave of more sexually explicit romances – for
example, Harlequin Temptations and Silhouette Desire. In these
books Radway is heartened by the new sexually desiring heroine
and explicit descriptions of premarital sex because they valorise
an active female sexuality, but is dismayed by the continuing
connection between female sexual desire, love and marriage.

These themes are taken up in more detail by Ann Rosalind
Jones. Her textual analysis of sixteen Mills and Boon romances
published in 1983 and 1984 reveals that all the novels dealt with
feminist issues – for example, issues about women's work, female
independence and sexuality (1986, 197). However, she claims,
'that certain positions put forward by feminism are taken for
granted, along with the economic and ideological benefits it has
brought many women, while the movement itself is perceived as
alien, threatening, excessive' (p. 201). If feminist critics cannot
align their feminism with the romance, then it seems that the
romance cannot completely come to terms with feminism.[6]

Jones looks at how generic conventions in the romance have
changed in response to the social changes associated with feminism. When romantic fiction and feminism meet, she argues, the
results are often incoherent and produce contradictions. For
example, she identifies 'narrative discontinuity' as the heroine
shifts from being an independent and ambitious working woman
to someone whose future is defined in terms of the hero (p. 204).
The heroine's career often serves to establish the heroine's

glamour 'but for the love conflict to occupy centre stage, the job that gives the heroine glamour must always be temporary' (p. 207). However, Jones also identifies positive changes: not all heroines sacrifice their career for love, gender inequality in the workplace is open to criticism and there appears to be a new 'erotic equality' (p. 213). In this way, it could be argued that romantic fiction has negotiated a form of popular feminism and with it new modes of feminine identity in its heroines (see Chapter 9). However, other research points to a 'backlash' in the romantic fiction of the 1980s. For example, Linda Christian-Smith argues that the adolescent romantic fiction of the period presented a 'vision of traditional femininity . . . which can be interpreted as a transformed version of new Right thinking on women' (Christian-Smith 1988, 95). In these novels, she argues, 'femininity consists of administering to the heart and tending the hearth' (p. 97).

Jones' new sexually desiring heroine, along with more explicit sex scenes in some contemporary romance lines, raises questions about the pleasures of romance reading. However, the idea that the pleasures of romance reading might include sexual pleasures has its roots in an older debate about whether romantic fiction is 'pornography for women'. In this debate, if pornography is a source of sexual pleasure for men, then romantic fiction operates in a similar way for women. Originally, this was used as a way of condemning romantic fiction. For mass culture critics, designating romances 'pornography' was a means of signifying their self-evident lack of worth and the cheap pleasures they offered. For feminists like Ann Douglas (1980), pornography was an expression of men's desire to break down female independence and brutalise women into submission. Romantic fiction portrayed the same 'male fantasies' showing the pleasures of male brutality and female dependence.

More recently, feminist critics have demonstrated a sympathetic understanding of romance as pornography for women. Ann Barr Snitow suggests that the atmosphere of Harlequin novels is sexually charged. They offer a 'romanticised sexuality' in which 'waiting, anticipation, anxiety . . . represent the high-point of sexual experience' (1983, 250). This experience of 'sex as anticipation' corresponds to Alison Light's observation that foreplay may be the high-point of sexual experience for many women (Jones 1986, 200). In her textual analysis of Mills and Boon romances, Alison Assiter not only finds a new eroticism but also shows how these books play out many basic sexual fantasies. By arguing that romantic fiction shares many characteristics with pornography, she not only challenges the idea that the pleasures of pornography aren't just for men, but also shows how these books offer women sexual pleasure by making them the subject of sexual fantasies not the just the object of male fantasy (1989, 121). The problem with this analysis is that there is little evidence to suggest that women readers interpret and use romances primarily for the sexual pleasures they offer. Indeed, Radway's readers not only vehemently wished to defend romantic fiction against the claim that is was pornographic, they also disliked graphic sexual descriptions and did not define their pleasure in sexual terms. Alternative evidence is offered from readers who responded to Thurston's questionnaire about the pleasures of the new 'erotic' romances. According to Thurston, these readers 'consciously perceive these novels as erotica and said they use them for sexual information and ideas, to create a receptive-to-sex state of mind, and even to achieve arousal' (1987, 10). These contradictory accounts seem to suggest that the sexual pleasures of the romance are as much a product of the way in which the text is read as a product of the text itself. However, these debates are useful because they begin to break down the opposition between romance and sexuality, even if there is a tendency to redeem the (feminine) romance by labelling it sexual.

Questioning romance

Despite the recent work on romantic fiction, there is much more that needs to be explored. We still know little about distinctions within the genre or about the range of romances on offer, especially those which are published outside the major romance publishers such as Harlequin. Furthermore, there is still little known about historical variations within the genre as too often romance is treated as a monolithic ideology rather than as open to transformation. As Radford argues, 'if generic forms are ... signals in a *social* contract between writers and readers, changes in these conventions will be regulated by transformations at other levels of social relationships' (1986, 9). Further work also needs to be carried out in order to understand what the romance means to different social groups in different national contexts.[7] For example, Moss has analysed romantic fiction written by teenagers in British schools which highlights the problem of how black women readers relate to heroines in the romance who are nearly always white. For example, one student claimed, 'Usually when I'm writing a romance, a story, it's usually just me, but playing a white character, d'you know what I mean?' (1989, 74). Another area ripe for investigation is both the lesbian reader's relationship to heterosexual romances and to the new sub-genre of the lesbian romance (Taylor 1989b, 62–3).[8] In both lesbian and/or inter-racial romance narratives 'obstacles are shown to be *integral* to romance: they are not something to be magically "disappeared" through comsumation/resolution' (Stacey and Pearce 1995, 24).[9]

Bridget Fowler's study from a socialist feminist perspective, *The Alienated Reader* addresses historical changes in the romance, particularly in relation to changing class relations, and the ways in which class influences what, and how, women read. Her study contains some useful and sympathetic vignettes and she demon-strates how class relations not only underpin changes in the form of the romance but also why some women find some romances relevant and not others. However, while Fowler wishes to take the romance seriously, many older assumptions reappear. The only romances which can be validated are those which engage with the public sphere of work rather than the private sphere of relationships, because Fowler's socialist-feminism equates politi-cal struggle with working-class struggle in the workplace.[10] Therefore, while Fowler does attend to differences between women, stressing the importance of class and class struggle, in the process, she largely denies the political struggle over personal life which has been seen as central to feminism. Furthermore, Fowler reiterates many of the assumptions of mass culture criti-cism: profitable fiction is 'conservative' fiction; romance is formulaic and 'pre-cooked' and acts as a drug; and if the people were given improving (socialist feminist) literature, they would see the error of their ways (1991, 30–1).

The problem is that the moralising that underpins much of the work on romance cannot come to terms with the question of plea-sure – indeed, these works are often built on the refusal of pleasure (Bourdieu 1984). There is still a tendency in much academic work on popular culture to make 'things like responsibility, critical distance or aesthetic purity central – moral categories which make pleasure an irrelevant and illegitimate criterion' (Ang 1985, 116). For feminist critics who take this position, pleasure is ultimately ideological and helps to maintain patriarchy and/or capitalism. In recent years, an alternative position has emerged in cultural studies which acknowledges that the pleasures people gain from popular forms are important. However, not only does this position have a tendency to result in an uncritical celebration of anything that gives people pleasure, it also does little to advance our understanding of it (see, for example Fiske 1989). Pleasure is neither an essentially positive nor an essentially negative force and remains one of the centrally under-theorised concepts within cultural and media studies: as Ang argues, Radway fails to get to grips with 'the *pleasurableness* of the pleasure of romance reading' (Ang 1996, 104).[11] Romance reading offers, as critics like Modleski and Radway note, 'utopian' dreams of a better world. As Helen Taylor argues, dreaming is not necessarily a reactionary pleasure, 'dreaming is also about imagining other possibilities, change, difference' (1989b, 72). Indeed, it is this emphasis on pleasure and visions of utopias that feminism could usefully learn from romance fiction. (These debates are returned to in the next chapter.) As Ann Jones asks (and many romance readers might also feel entitled to ask), 'what's wrong with a happy ending?' (1986, 23). Romantic fictions are enjoyed as fantasies that we might have while happy fulfilling loving relationships, fantasies that many feminists (and men) are not immune to in their own personal lives (Jackson, 1993).

Although I have stressed both that romance readers do not passively act out the roles laid down in romantic fiction and that romantic fiction is enjoyed as fantasy, it is worth pointing out that not only are romance narratives important in other cultural forms such as film and popular music, but also that most people construct, adapt and use romance narratives at some point in their lives. As Jackson puts it, 'Narratives are thus not merely a form encountered in novels, plays and films. They are very much part of everyday cultural competences' (1993, 213). Women and men are not passive recipients of an ideology of romance, instead romance narratives are 'a resource they draw upon in making sense of the emotional and social world' (p. 215). An acknowledgement of the importance of romance in everyday life makes it crucial to move beyond condemning romance narratives, to understand their diversity, their uses and how they might be subject to transformation.

Notes

1 Although many studies point to the existence of male authors and readers, unfortunately little is known about them.

2 For more on young women and romantic fiction, see also Christian-Smith
   (1988) and Moss (1989).
3 Harlequin is the publisher name which is seen as synonymous with romantic fiction in the US in the same way as Mills and Boon is seen as
   synonymous with romantic fiction in the UK.
4 She also demonstrates some of the relationships between these forms. For
   example, in charting the historical precedents for Harlequin romances –
   from Samuel Richardson's *Pamela*, through the 'sentimental' novel to works
   like *Pride and Prejudice* and *Jane Eyre* – she points to how the roots of soaps
   and Gothics intertwine. For her discussion of soap operas, see Chapter 5.
5 In her textual analysis of the romance narrative, Radway expresses a contin-
   ual amazement at the fact that readers read romances for the content or story
   and can't understand the formal devices used in the romance. Radway's
   'incomprehension' of how the Smithton women read romances is a product
   of her class and educational position which predispose her to consider form
   over function which the work of Pierre Bourdieu (1984) illustrates. For a
   different but related critique of Radway's problems with her reader, see
   Purdie (1992) and Ang (1996). For an intelligent and critical discussion on
   the relationship between academic researchers and their respondents, see
   Seiter *et al.* (1989).
6 However, this is partly a question of how you define feminism. For example,
   Carol Thurston's *The Romance Revolution* makes a case for the new erotic
   romance as reflecting the changes brought about by 'women's liberation' but
   her argument is severely undermined by a naivity about sexual politics
   as well as a host of theoretical and methodological problems.
7 See Giles (1995) for a useful alternative to Radway's work in which she
   demonstrates why working-class women in the UK in the inter-war years
   chose to refuse romance.
8 See Vice (1995) and Collecott (1995) on lesbian romances.
9 For work on inter-racial love as forbidden love see, for example, Blackman
   (1995), (charles) (1995), Nkweto Simmonds (1995) and Perry (1995).
10 Furthermore, Fowler's work retains a rather old-fashioned Marxist class
   essentialism in which the better romances are those which express 'working-
   class and plebeian experience' (1991, 4).
11 For good exploratory work on the pleasures of the romance, see Kaplan
   1986 and Light 1984.

Further reading

Fowler, B. *The Alienated Reader: Women and Popular Romantic Literature in the
    Twentieth Century* (Hemel Hempstead, Harvester Wheatsheaf, 1991)
Modleski, T. *Loving with a Vengeance: Mass-produced Fantasies for Women*
    (London, Routledge, 1984)
Pearce, L. and Stacey, J., eds, *Romance Revisited* (London, Lawrence and
    Wishart, 1995)
Radford, J., ed., *The Progress of Romance: The Politics of Popular Fiction* (London,
    Routledge & Kegan Paul, 1986)
Radway, J. *Reading the Romance: Women, Patriarchy and Popular Literature*
    (London, Verso, 1987)
Taylor, H. Romantic Readers, in H. Carr, ed., *From My Guy to Sci-Fi: Genre and
    Women's Writing in the Postmodern World* (London, Pandora, 1989)

5

Soap operas
and their audiences

Just as romances and their readers have been treated as objects of derision and contempt, so soap operas and their viewers have had a hostile response from cultural critics. Indeed, even the pioneers of cultural studies, such as Raymond Williams, who wished to treat popular culture as worthy of serious analysis, found it easy to dismiss soap opera (Modleski 1984, 12–13). More recently soap operas and their viewers have been subject to the same process of recuperation by feminist critics that was evident in the analysis of romantic fiction. Indeed, as will become clear, feminist critics working in cultural and media studies have not only found it easier to admit to being soap fans than romance fans, but they also identified a 'progressive' politics in the soap text and 'resistance' to patriarchy among soap fans.

The turn to soap operas by feminist critics can be situated within a wider debate about femininity and 'feminine genres' within feminist television criticism (Brunsdon *et al.* 1997, 2). While feminists have also been concerned with TV programmes which feature feminine/feminist heroines, soaps have proved to hold a particular fascination for feminist critics. As Brunsdon (1995) has argued, many earlier feminist critics were attracted to soaps as a 'woman's genre' in order to expose the negative and limiting images of women in them. However, Brunsdon continues, there have been three further reasons why feminists have been so preoccupied with soaps. First, the importance of the idea that 'the personal is political' within second-wave feminism (see Chapter 1) meant that feminist critics would argue that 'the home and personal life are in themselves significant' (Brunsdon 1995, 59). Studying soaps not only gave the opportunity to analyse representations in which the private sphere and personal relationship were central, but also the turn to the study of television audiences led to a preoccupation with the domestic context of viewing. Second, studying soaps gave feminists the opportunity to challenge an aesthetic hierarchy in which soaps and 'the feminine' were devalued through their association with each other. Third, Brunsdon argues, the preoccupation with soaps is also characterised by a 'feminist ambivalence': 'there was no way in which a political movement which was challenging gender definition could ignore soap opera. But neither could it, finally, repudiate these pleasures and identifications, nor simply celebrate them' (Brunsdon 1995, 61).

This ambivalence has produced a slightly different relationship between the feminist critic and the 'ordinary woman' than was evident in the study of romantic fiction. While, as will become clear, there has still been a tendency to envisage the soap viewer as the feminist's 'other', the 'housewife', increasingly there has been an attempt to close down the gap between the feminist and the 'ordinary woman'. This can be seen in Laura Stempel Mumford's claim that her study of soap is motivated by the question of why *she* liked soaps rather than mere speculation about 'other' women (1995, 3–4).

Although it was initially tempting to apply psychoanalytic film theory to understand how the spectator is positioned by the soap text, many critics stressed the need to understand the specificity of television as a cultural form (Flitterman-Lewis 1992; Kuhn 1984). It was argued that not only were soap operas formally different from film narratives – for example, in soap there is no final narrative closure – but also that psychoanalytic models of the relationship between the cinematic text and its spectator might be difficult to simply apply to the different context of the audience watching television. Therefore, while some work on soap operas has been concerned to demonstrate how soaps address female spectators and construct feminine subject positions through textual analysis, other critics have engaged with the social context of watching soaps by studying the meanings that social audiences bring to their soap viewing (Kuhn, 1984). Therefore, in analysing the appeal of soap operas to women, critics have both drawn on theories of gendered spectatorship from film theory and research into audiences which examines 'texts in use' generated within media and cultural studies. The former position considers how soap operas contain female-centred narratives which anticipate and address a female spectator – for example, the work of Tania Modleski – and the latter position starts from the ways in which actual women interpret and make use of soap operas. Textual analysis has tended to emphasise resistance to patriarchy within the formal features of the soap text, whereas audience studies have tended to emphasise how female soap viewers use their soap viewing as a mode of resistance to patriarchy. As will become clear, both positions have their own problems.

Soap opera as feminine genre

If there are problems in defining the characteristics of romantic fiction, melodrama and the woman's film, then the same problems abound in thinking about soaps. In trying to pin down the characteristics of soap, it should be remembered that different soaps will share these characteristics to a greater or lesser extent, and that many of these features are also present in other forms of television drama. Soaps are usually characterised as continuous, open-ended, episodic serials. As a result, unlike the formal features of film, resolutions in soaps are at best precarious and always open to further disruption. Soap narratives are linear and often unfold in 'real time' (Geraghty 1991). In this way, soaps observe the seasons and rituals such as Christmas and the viewer can imagine that soap characters' lives continue as usual when they are absent from our screens. Soap operas are also characterised by multiple narratives running simultaneously and a large body of characters which give multiple opportunities for identifications. These characters often occupy a shared familiar space – for example, the British prime-time soap *Eastenders* is centred around various locations in Albert Square which provide places for interaction such as the Queen Vic pub, the 'caff' (cafe), the market and the launderette. It is within these spaces that soaps strive to maintain a sense of 'community' which is often modelled on the family, but does not necessarily equate with a 'real' family (Geraghty 1991). Similar patterns can be found in other British prime-time soaps and Australian soaps such as *Neighbours* and *Home and Away*. In American prime-time soaps such as *Dallas* and *Dynasty* the soap 'community' was more likely to be centred around a single family – the Ewings or Carringtons – and the central location is the family home – Southfork or the Carrington mansion. It is these familiar locations and characters that intensify the pleasures of soap watching.

The appeal of soaps to the female viewer is often related to their emphasis on the domestic sphere, personal relationships and emotions. As Charlotte Brunsdon argues, these are realms which have been culturally coded as feminine and in which 'feminine competence is recognised' (1981, 34). Therefore, although the action of soaps takes us into public spaces – for example, the oil business in *Dallas*, the motel in *Crossroads* or the Lassiter's complex in *Neighbours* – these masculine, public spaces are colonised 'from the point of view of the personal' (p. 34). Brunsdon argues that watching soaps not only requires a generic knowledge of soap conventions and serial-specific knowledge, it also requires 'cultural knowledge of the socially acceptable codes and conventions for the conduct of personal life' (p. 36). Because women are more likely to be trained in the skills used in personal life, because they are deemed to be 'feminine' skills, it is argued that soaps draw on women's knowledge and competences.

More recently, Christine Geraghty in *Women and Soap Opera* (1991) builds on Brunsdon's observations to argue that not only do soaps encourage the use of feminine skills, their appeal to women is compounded because they are told from a women's point of view. In this way, work on soaps draws on ideas raised by the study of the woman's film where critics had attempted to discover films which privileged a female point of view within a dominant cinema which was organised around a male protagonist and a male point of view, and which emphasised masculinity as the 'norm'. As Geraghty puts it, 'the soap's basic premise [is] that women are understandable and rational, a premise that flies in the face of much TV drama' (1991, 47). According to Geraghty, not only do soaps validate feminine competences, they also deal in the common emotional situations which women share, allowing a sense of 'female solidarity' to be built. Therefore, unlike romantic fiction, in soaps (as with some women's films), relationships between women are seen to be important. Not only do women in soaps often motivate the action, but also 'The centrality of women in soaps has the effect of making them the norm by which the programmes are understood' (p. 51). Furthermore, Geraghty argues, because soaps offer a space in which emotional relationships are 'tested out' they offer the female viewer the pleasure of 'rehearsing the decision-making process without responsibility for its consequences' (p. 42).[1]

In thinking about these characteristics of soaps, it is important to bear in mind that not all soaps are the same and that the differences between them are as important as the similarities in defining the genre (p. 5). Geraghty offers a couple of useful ways of classifying soaps. First she draws on Laura Mulvey's distinction between the patriarchal and the matriarchal melodrama. She argues that patriarchal soaps such as the US prime-time series,

Dallas and *Dynasty*, concentrate on the positions and problems of powerful men but offer women pleasure because they also demonstrate that male power can be challenged 'on one hand by moral questioning and one the other by women's refusal to be controlled' (p. 74). In matriarchal soaps, such as the UK prime-time serials *Coronation Street* and *Eastenders*, the challenge to male authority has traditionally been bypassed by 'handing emotional and patriarchal control to the mother' (p. 83). Soap matriarchs need not be biological mothers but can act as a mother to the community. This role was perhaps best demonstrated by Bet Gilroy, the pub landlady, in *Coronation Street*, who asserted power in the street's soap community. This again emphasises the importance in these soaps of being on women's side and of showing female characters as strong, capable and, often, as economically independent.

Geraghty also offers a way of distinguishing between soaps by considering the three different elements at play in the soap aesthetic. First, soaps draw on a light entertainment aesthetic which privileges spectacle and conspicuous consumption. This is particularly evident in US prime-time soaps such as *Dynasty* and *The Colbys* where the sets, locations and clothing are often excessive so that lavishness can become an end in itself and a source of pleasure for the viewer. Second, the emotional engagement which soaps offer draws on melodramatic aesthetics. The 'excessive expressiveness of the *mise-en-scène* and performance' in soaps heightens their emotional force in a similar way to 1950s film melodrama (p. 31). In terms of *mise-en-scène* this is most evident in the US prime-time serials mentioned above, but the intense expression of performance is also featured strongly in US day-time soaps. Third, realism provides an important aesthetic in British prime-time soaps. Indeed, the battles for ratings and prestige among UK soaps are usually based on their commitment to a 'realist' aesthetic. For the UK soaps, 'realism' was originally equated with a commitment to representing the working-class and now includes a commitment to discussing social problems such as AIDS and representing ethnic minorities and a variety of sexualities. Indeed, in the mid-1990s claims to realism appeared to be grounded on the inclusion of lesbian characters, with other soaps responding to the success of the character of Beth Jordache in *Brookside*. It is against this 'realist' tradition in Britain that US soaps are usually derided as melodramatic and, hence, inferior. In the US, however, the survival of prime-time serials which draw on soap conventions seems to rest on the rejection of a realist impulse and the intensification of light entertainment and melo- dramatic aesthetics. For example, both *thirtysomething* and *Melrose Place* started out with some claims to realism but these were rejected in favour of increasingly sumptuous clothing and increased emotional intensity.[2] In analysing specific soaps, it is therefore important to be aware of the particular characteristics of that soap. It is not always possible to generalise from the features of one soap to another across and within national contexts.

Geraghty's work is useful because it allows us to consider the similarities and differences between romantic fiction, the women's film and soap and also offers the basis for analysing what other genres may or may not have in common with them. First, she argues, each genre has 'central female protagonist(s) whom the reader is invited to support and whose reasons for action are understood by the audience although not necessarily male characters' (p. 116). Second, in each genre, there is a sepa- ration between the masculine public sphere and the feminine private sphere, the latter being the sphere of the emotions in which women are shown to be skilled and have some control. Third, the narrative is not organised around action but instead around how relationships are built and maintained, in which it is 'the verbal expression of feeling or indeed the withholding of such expression [that] is crucial to the resolution' (p. 117). Finally, Geraghty argues that each genre allows 'readers to imagine an ideal world in which values traditionally associated with women are given space and expressed and in which there is some model of the way in which relationships, particularly those between men and women, could be differently organised on women's terms' (p. 117).

For Geraghty then, romances, women's pictures and soaps all offer glimpses of 'utopias', although the nature of these utopias will differ. Drawing on Richard Dyer, she argues that entertainment, rather than offering a prescription for what utopias would *be like*, offers a glimpse of what they would *feel like* (p. 117). These 'utopian possibilities' fall into five broad cate- gories which are 'related to specific inadequacies in society' (p. 118): abundance, energy, intensity, transparency and commu- nity. Although access to all these utopian possibilities is available in soap as a genre, they will not be represented equally in all soaps. For example, while *Dallas* and *Dynasty* offer the chance to experience what it feels like to enjoy material abundance, this opportunity is not available in the main British prime-time soaps. In the same way, there is a far greater emphasis on building the feeling of belonging to a community within the British soaps than there is in *Dallas* and *Dynasty*. What both these categories of soap share, is the opportunity for forms of intense emotional expression and the possibilities of transparency, the ability to be open and honest in your feelings.

The possibility of intensity and transparency in emotional relationships are offered in all three women's genres discussed so far, particularly because they fit in with the 'emphasis on a female viewpoint and the concentration on the personal and domestic sphere' (p. 128). Whereas romantic fiction offers the most utopian visions, in soaps, Geraghty argues, 'utopian possibilities are expressed in quite practical, down-to-earth ways' (p. 128). Furthermore, whereas the utopias offered by romances are rather rigid, soaps have the possibility to handle change. In this way, in the 1980s, soaps became an arena in which possible solutions to emotional problems were offered which translated the utopian possibilities of intensity and transparency into 'the practical competences of women's experience and offered a means of testing out how they could be lived in the day-to-day world' (p. 130).

Soaps and the female spectator

For Brunsdon and Geraghty, soaps have a particular appeal to women because of their concentration on, and validation of, the spheres and skills which have been traditionally aligned with femininity. Whereas both Brunsdon and Geraghty argued that soaps offered something to a social audience of women because they allowed them to use culturally produced feminine competences, some critics have attempted to discuss soaps in terms of the debate about female spectatorship familiar from film studies. Critics such as Tania Modleski have used textual analysis in an attempt to reveal the connection between soap's formal features and women's lives by analysing 'the particular *textual mechanisms* that are responsible for engendering spectator identifications' (Ang and Hermes 1996, 112). These critics try to pinpoint what is meant when we say that soaps are aimed at a female audience by showing how soap operas have a feminine address (Kuhn 1984). In particular, within this body of feminist work, there is an attempt to show how soaps are indeed radical, and therefore 'progressive', texts because of their formal features are seen to express a 'feminine aesthetic'.

Tania Modleski's analysis of US daytime soap operas, in *Loving with a Vengeance*, was instrumental in developing such an approach, demonstrating that the narrative pleasure of soaps needs to be understood in relation to the social position of women in the home. She notes the similarity between the formal features of these soaps and women's experience of family life. For example, she argues, unlike the classic realist text, soaps privilege constant disorder and lack of resolution which resonates with women's experience of family life. Similarly, soaps acknowledge what women experience – that there can be no final happy endings for all. Furthermore, the soap opera both 'reflects and cultivates the "proper" psychological disposition of the woman in the home' (Modleski 1984, 98). Drawing on Chodorow (see Chapter 4), she claims that just as the classic realist text relates to the goal-orientated nature of men's work, so there is a unique fit between the structures of soap opera and women's work in the home.[3] Soap opera emphasises repetition, lack of progress or end and connections to others, all of which characterise women's work in the home.

Modleski also claims that the soap aesthetic privileges disruption, interruption and fragmentation. Not only does this reflect the characteristics of women's work in the home, soaps also 'habituate' women to this way of life because they 'keep her from desiring a focused existence by involving her in the pleasures of a fragmented life' (p. 101). In this way, despite the compensations that soaps offer their female viewers, they ultimately keep women in their place. The structure of soaps anticipates distracted viewing, making distraction pleasurable and available to women while they work. As a result, Modleski challenges the idea that soap operas distract women from their work by encouraging escapism, and she argues that the housewife needs a 'distractible state of mind' in order to function.

However, there are a number of problems with Modleski's hypothetical model of the distracted housewife. By providing a theoretical model of how all women in the home watch daytime soaps, Modleski fails to acknowledge that 'reality is much more complicated and diversified than our theories can ever acknowledge' (Ang 1989, 111). Not only have audience studies suggested other models of daytime viewing for women (see below),

Modleski also fails in her study to acknowledge how there might be any pleasure for anyone other than 'the housewife'. Furthermore, as Geraghty notes, Modleski ends up reiterating a model of the isolated, distracted and passive housewife that appears in the mass culture criticism she wishes to challenge (1991, 45).

For Modleski, both the subject of the soap opera and the spectator

> is constituted as a sort of ideal mother: a person who possesses greater wisdom than all her children, whose sympathy is large enough to encompass the conflicting claims of her family (she identifies with them all) and who has no demands or claims of her own ... Thus soap operas convince women that their highest goal is to see their families united and happy, while consoling them for their inability to realise this ideal and bring about familial harmony. (1984, 92)

This subject/spectator position is reinforced by the character of the good mother, who like the spectator is powerless to bring the family to order and, therefore, unlike the manipulative bad mother, can only sympathise with, and tolerate, the problems that surround her. This character is not just present in US daytime soaps but has been present in figures such as Helen Daniels in *Neighbours*, Pippa in *Home and Away* and Krystle in *Dynasty*. However, when we turn from the abstract to the specific, the good mother is not necessarily a constant character – for example, Hope in *thirtysomething* was originally constructed a good mother of sorts only to be transformed into a judgmental manipulator. Nor is the 'ideal mother' always equated with a female character – in the early episodes of the twenty-something soap *Melrose Place*, the position of the ideal mother was occupied by a gay man who, lacking any storylines of his own, listened patiently to problems of other residents of *Melrose Place*, a position which was compounded by his occupation in the caring profession of social work.

For Modleski, the negative side of the ideal mother is the villainess, who unlike her powerless opposite tries to exert control. Modleski believes that the housewife viewer is fascinated by the villainess because she acts out 'the spectator's fantasies of power' (p. 97). However, the spectator does not identify with the villainess – indeed, she wants the villainess to be punished. In this way, while soaps constitute the spectator as the ideal mother, they 'provide in the person of the villainess an outlet for feminine anger' (p. 97), the fury that 'the housewife' has learned to repress.

Underlying Modleski's conceptualisation of the ideal mother is the assumption that all women will take up this spectating position inscribed in the text. Furthermore, as Robert C. Allen points out, Modleski often comes close to conflating the ideal mother as 'textually inscribed position' with the actual position of the viewer (in Seiter *et al.* 1989). As Ang and Hermes argue, 'textual generalisations about "the female spectator" turn out to foreclose prematurely the possibility of empirical variation and heterogeneity within actual women's responses' (1996, 113). Modleski ignores the fact that some viewers may not take up a position based on 'a middle-class and white feminine ideal' and, indeed, may instead consciously resist this position (Seiter *et al.* 1989, 237). Seiter *et al.*'s audience research suggests that working-class women not only rejected the position of the ideal mother, but also that they saw the 'ideal mother' as a 'whiner' because she was so passive and dependent on men (p. 238). As they put it, the problem with the spectator position of the 'ideal mother' is it 'implies a specific social identity – that of a middle-class woman, most likely with a husband who earns a family wage. The textual position is not easily accessible to working-class women, who often formulate criticism of the soap opera on these grounds' (p. 241). Geraghty argues that contrary to Modleski's suggestions, the soap viewer does not take the position of the passive and bemused ideal mother. 'The viewer understands that these are not her children and is therefore free to speculate and gossip about the characters knowing they are not her responsibility' (1991, 23). Furthermore, for many of the women interviewed by Seiter *et al.*, it was the villainess who was loved and admired for her transgressions and independence (1989, 239). This is backed in studies of prime-time US soaps which have illustrated the attractions of characters like Alexis in *Dynasty* to female viewers (Gray 1992; Budge 1988) and to gay men (Finch 1986). Many of the problems of Modleski's work stem from the level of abstraction at which she operates, eradicating the differences between both daytime soaps and their viewers by isolating a single viewing position which all women (as 'housewives') are assumed to share. As Seiter *et al.*, among others, suggest, the differences between women may shape their readings of soaps. Furthermore, part of the pleasure of soaps may well be the ability to take up a range of subject positions and identifications.

Despite Modleski's rather unflattering depiction of the distracted, passive 'housewife' and her acknowledgement that soaps contribute to this state, she also is keen to demonstrate the seeds of a feminist aesthetic in soap conventions. She formulates this argument drawing on post-structuralist distinctions between the conservative closed text and the radical open text. According to this theory, the classic realist text reaffirms men's sense of self, privileges action and resolves contradictions by progressing towards a closure in which order is achieved. The radical text privileges the pleasures of language rather than action, breaking down the illusion of order and unity by showing a lack of progress and disorder. Thus, Modleski suggests, within the very structure of soap opera are the seeds of resistance to patriarchal ways of being. The problem with this argument is that, despite Modleski's rejection of mass culture criticism which opposes a radical avant-garde to a conservative popular culture, she still accepts the terms of the debate by trying to prove that soap operas are in some ways like avant garde art. Furthermore, in the process, she creates a distance between herself, 'the feminist', who can recognise this radical potential and the distracted 'housewife', who lacks her cultural capital, and views with a duster in one hand and a child in the other. Rather than understanding soap as a popular form, Modleski legitimates it by showing that soaps are open to feminist interventions which can have the political impact of avant-garde art.[4]

Indeed, for many feminist critics, it is the lack of resolution in soaps which marks them out as a potentially radical feminine form. Despite the fact that such critics find the themes of soap such as the family and marriage extremely conservative, they continually point to the open-ended narratives as a sign of hope. For example, Nochimson extends Modleski's argument about the way in which open-ended narratives are feminine narratives. Nochimson draws on psychoanalytic feminist theory to argue that while Hollywood produces patriarchal fantasies which privilege closure and a male subject, soap operas reverse this structure by creating a place for the female subject. Whereas the supposedly linear narratives of Hollywood cinema work to suppress women, she claims that soaps, without their demands for linear narratives, create 'an opening through which the female subject, ordinarily repressed from the patriarchal narrative, can emerge' (Nochimson 1992, 35). Such a position suggests that the very structures of Hollywood film on one hand, and daytime US soaps on the other, express masculine or feminine views of the world. It rests on the assumption that Hollywood narrative is 'essentially' masculine and daytime soaps are 'essentially' feminine.

The pleasure of soaps

In *Watching Dallas* (1985), Ien Ang combined an analysis of the soap text with research into audiences' responses to soaps. She based her argument on letters which she received in response to an advertisement in a Dutch women's magazine in which viewers explained why they did – or didn't – like *Dallas*. Underpinning Ang's argument is an attempt to theorise the *pleasures* women gain from watching soaps in order to challenge the 'monstrous alliance' between feminism and mass culture which is based on a distrust of pleasure (1985, 119).

However, Ang's research also challenges those accounts which see room for feminist optimism in the 'openness' of the soap opera's form. This position, implicit in the work of critics like Modleski, is made explicit in Deming's claim that despite the fact that soaps are 'intensely conservative', 'resistance to narrative closure provides an opening for speculation . . . as to how the case itself may be reopened' (1990, 56). Ang argues that the optimism in this position rests on the hope that 'viewers will make use of the freedom offered to them, so that the latent narrative potential contained in this narrative form will actually be translated into the manifest production of subversive, feminist meanings' (1985, 120). However, research into viewers responses to *Dallas* revealed that this 'feminist potential' is not necessarily realised in the positions that female viewers take up in relation to *Dallas*. Her research demonstrated that the dominant way in which women who like *Dallas* gained their pleasure from it was through a 'tragic structure of feeling' rather than feminist subversion.

Ang explains the ideas behind her argument by noting that respondents who liked *Dallas* perceived it as 'realistic'. This may seem strange in a British context in which 'realism' is judged by how accurately soaps are seen to 'represent' the 'real world': by this 'empiricist' conception of 'realism', which many respondents who disliked *Dallas* employed, the programme is doomed to be seen as 'unrealistic'. However, such a conception of 'realism', as was suggested in Chapter 3, ignores the fact that texts – even 'factual' texts such as documentaries – are *produced* and, therefore, cannot simply express and reflect the 'real' world. Ang argues that those viewers who found *Dallas* pleasurable because they found it realistic, employed a different notion of realism. For these viewers, although they are aware that the world of *Dallas* is fictional, the programme had an 'emotional realism'. Their pleasure was aroused by a 'recognisable' experience of the world in the soap, a recognition of 'general living experiences: rows, intrigues, problems, happiness and misery' (1985, 42). For these viewers, the 'psychological reality' of *Dallas* is pleasurable because it deals with a subjective experience of the world as being made up of emotional peaks and troughs, what Ang calls the 'tragic structure of feeling'.

The tragic structure of feeling in *Dallas* is invoked through a range of melodramatic conventions which deal with exaggerated emotions and emphasise life's torments. Through exaggeration, events become 'bearers of a melodramatic effect' which intensifies the emotional force, and hence the pleasure, of *Dallas* (p. 64). While for many people, exaggerated events such as kidnappings and obscure illnesses might seem clichéd and ridiculous, within melodrama they are 'meaningful in so far as they solicit a highly charged emotional impact' (Ang 1990, 80). As Ang continues, 'Their role is metaphorical, and their appeal stems from the enlarged emotional impact they evoke: it is the feelings that are being mobilised here that matter' (p. 80). For example, one of the metaphors used in *Dallas* is alcoholism. Sue Ellen's alcoholism made 'visible areas of internal psychological disturbance' (1985, 68) so that it was recognisable to viewers and functioned 'as a metaphor for her enduring state of crisis' (1990, 80). The repetition of these metaphors, both within and between TV programmes, is important if viewers are to recognise and comprehend them. The crisis that both Dylan in *Beverly Hills 90210* and Sipowitz in *NYPD Blue* feel about the failure of their family situation and their general lack of direction is signified through alcoholism. Alison's inability to deal with an attempted rape in *Melrose Place* is made visible through a period of alcohol abuse. Even the seemingly mundane can be made a bearer of the melodramatic effect: for example, when Jenna in *Dallas* was distressed, her sleek straight hair was frequently transformed in a mass of frizzy curls.

Ang argues that the melodramatic imagination is also revealed in *Dallas*'s concentration on the problems of the family and the lack of progress, which is a condition of the open-ended narrative structure, and strengthens a sense of 'aimlessness and directionlessness' (1985, 75). If conflicts are structured into the narrative then the tragic structure of feeling is compounded by characters' lack of awareness of their hopeless situation. It is 'this *gradual* facing of one's own impotence [which] makes it all the more tragic: illusions and ideals are steadily undermined' (p. 73). The pleasure that *Dallas* offers viewers, Ang argues, is that it 'makes the melodramatic imagination present and palpable' (p. 82). However, this pleasure is only accessible to viewers who have access to a tragic structure of feeling, viewers 'for whom a tragic look into daily life is in principle logical and meaningful' (p. 61). *Dallas* will be pleasurable to those viewers who can connect with this subjective experience, who experience it as a 'dimension' of reality (p. 83). Given the traditional association between the private sphere of the emotions, caring and women, it is not surprising that some women are likely to find pleasure in the melodramatic imagination.

Ang claims that, for feminism, this tragic structure of feeling is often seen as a problem because it not only contains little hint of feminist resistance to patriarchy, but also appears to be 'a rather passive, fatalistic and individualistic reaction to a vague feeling of powerlessness and unease' (p. 82). She argues that soaps such as *Dallas* explore the contradictions of patriarchy but not solutions to them. The pleasures offered by the tragic structure of feeling are 'fantasies of powerlessness', fantasies which seem at odds with 'the fantasies of protest and liberation inscribed in the feminist imagination' (p. 132). However, Ang's treatment of pleasure of such 'politically incorrect' fantasies offers a corrective to the problems encountered in much feminist writing on romantic fiction. She argues that engaging in fantasies of passivity is not the same as being politically passive. Fantasy offers a space in which we can 'try out' positions without having to live with the consequences (p. 134). Women who find pleasure in the tragic structure of feeling do so because it allows them to be temporarily sentimental or fatalistic, feelings there may be no space for in the battles that they face in their everyday lives. Just because feminism is about a struggle for a better future, doesn't mean that women (feminists included) do not need some consolation for the problems of living in the present.

To identify with different heroines through a range of genres then is, for Ang, a little like 'dressing up'. It allows viewers the opportunity to engage in fantasy with different modes of femininity that they often cannot, or would not want to, take up in real life. As Lesley Stern puts it, 'gratification is to be achieved not through acting out the fantasies but through the activity of fantasising itself' (in Ang 1990, 84). For some women, the sense of giving oneself up to the forces of fate, as Sue Ellen does, might be experienced as a sense of release (Ang 1990, 86). For others, the fantasy of controlling – even enslaving – men and plotting your own destiny offered by Alexis in *Dynasty* might offer gratifications. Indeed, for many of us, pleasures may be produced by a whole range of fantasies and identifications which we can take up at different times. Some of these fantasies may be more 'politically correct' than others but, in different ways, they all offer ways of living in the present.

Ang's analysis is useful on a number of levels. It provides us with the important ways of thinking not only about the specific pleasures of the melodramatic imagination found in *Dallas* but also of thinking about the relationship between pleasure, fantasy and the identifications different audiences make in their engagement with a range of cultural forms and genres. By drawing on Williams' concept of a 'structure of feeling', Ang is able to bring together texts and audiences to show the complex relationships between cultural forms and practices. Furthermore, rather than disdaining the sentimentality and emotion that is a major source of pleasure in a range of cultural forms, she tries to show that it is both understandable and rational (1990, 87). She moves beyond a model of the female viewer as distracted 'housewife' to argue that the pleasures of the melodramatic imagination, while more appealing to women, are not merely a function of women's role in the home. This is not to underestimate the importance of power relations in a domestic context but to show that female subjectivity is not just a function of the domestic environment and power relations in the family.

Soaps and the female audience

Like Ang, other critics who have carried out research into the soap audience also explore their appeal to a social audience of women. Textual analysis, while often recognising the specificity of television as a cultural form, relied heavily on modes of analysis developed within literary and film studies. The development of audience research within media studies, in contrast, was driven by a sociological impetus. This can be seen in the use of ethnographic research methods, developed in anthropology and sociology. Although associated with in-depth, long-term participant observation studies in sociology, ethnography in media studies has usually been associated with face-to-face unstructured interviews which allow the researcher to start from viewers' own perceptions of television texts and how these texts are used. Rather than reading the meaning of soaps off from the text, these studies tried to reveal the ways in which 'real' women decoded and used soaps. In this way, ethnographic audience research was in a much better position to deal with the different ways in which different women read soaps rather than treating women as a homogeneous category and was also able to reveal the ways in which soap viewing was woven into a range of cultural practices. Audience research therefore aimed to restore a sense of what Raymond Williams calls the 'normal television experience' by concentrating on the practice of soap watching (Gray 1992, 16), and by revealing the range of uses female viewers made of soap. In this way, audience researchers were not only interested in soap opera as a cultural form, but also emphasised the ways in which soaps were woven into a range of cultural practices.

Like the work of Modleski, some studies of soap-watching considered the relationship between 'the housewife's' working day and soaps. Many studies suggest that women who work in the home have difficulty perceiving the home as a site of leisure: because 'a woman's work is never done', they feel guilty about watching television (for example, Morley 1986). However, as Ann Gray's ethnographic research reveals, just because housework may be based on the principles of interruption and distraction and the formal features of daytime television may work on similar principles, this does not mean that women are forced to watch in this way. As Gray puts it, 'Modleski's model of the rhythms of reception tends to leave no space for the active female subject who may want to resist both flows. The women in the present study switched the television on and stopped working to watch it' (1992, 78). In a similar way, the data produced by Seiter *et al.*'s audience research also indicates that women in similar situations watch soap operas in different ways. For women, who organise their housework along the same lines of efficiency and rationality that underpins men's work in the public sphere, uninterrupted soap viewing can be scheduled into their timetable as a reward. It is only those women who do not adhere to the norms of rational organisation and planning who watch in a more 'distracted' way (Seiter *et al.* 1989, 229–31). This suggests that generalisations about 'housewives'/'ordinary women' and their mode of viewing might mask important differences *between* women viewers.

As was demonstrated above, Modleski's conception of how women read soaps from the position of the 'ideal mother' is also complicated when we can consider the meanings that 'real' women, rather than the hypothetical female spectator, get from soap viewing. As I have already suggested, audience studies have shown that the pleasures of soap are not the same for all women – some may take up the position of the 'ideal mother', others identify with the villainess while some women may enjoy the opportunities in soap for multiple identifications (Seiter *et al.* 1989). The differences between the ways in which women read soaps, and the pleasure they gain from soaps have been shown to be related to class differences. For example, Seiter *et al.* (1989) argue that their middle-class respondents were more likely to take up the position of the ideal mother than working-class women who, because of material differences, were more likely to see the ideal mother as a 'whiner'. Andrea Press (1990), in her study of women's responses to *Dynasty*, found that not only did middle-class and working-class women interpret *Dynasty* in different ways, but also that working-class women's pleasure in the glamorous lifestyle presented on *Dynasty* was more a product of their class position than their gender. Class-specific competences which are related to educational achievement and cultural capital also cut across women's viewing preferences in Ann Gray's ethnographic study. Therefore, audience research suggests that women's relationships to soaps cannot simply be understood in terms of gendered skills and competences: they are also a product of classed cultural competences. However, while this research suggests that cultural identities are not totally reducible to gender, there is still the danger of 'essentializing' classed and gendered responses and to assume, for example, that all working-class women will share a similar relationship to soap operas (Ang and Hermes 1996).

Audience research has also added a further dimension to our understanding of women's use of soaps by going beyond both how meaning is organised in soap operas and how meanings are produced in the act of viewing. These studies consider what Mary Ellen Brown calls the 'spoken text' – 'the text people create when they talk about soap opera' (1994, 67). In a similar vein, Dorothy Hobson argues that talking about soaps represents a further stage

in the communication process which moves 'television into a
further dimension from that which ends with the viewing
moment' (1989, 167). Like other audience studies, work on
women's use of soap aims to show how women make active use
of soap operas rather than passively absorbing them. For
example, Hobson's study of soap talk in the workplace shows
how women use television as part of discussions about everyday
life, to 'share experiences and opinions' and create 'their own
culture in the workplace' (1990, 71). Not only do viewers actively
speculate about future developments – which is part of the pleasure of soap watching (see for example Seiter *et al.* 1989; Brown
1994) – they also put themselves in the characters' shoes. This
not only challenges Modleski's picture of the isolated soap
viewer, it also backs up Geraghty's suggestions about the importance of soaps for women as a space for 'testing out'
relationships.

The collective consumption of soap operas in the gossip and
fan networks that surround soaps forms the basis for Mary Ellen
Brown's analysis which stresses the resistance to patriarchy
embodied in this oral culture. Brown's study is illuminated by
joyful accounts of the use of soaps in female fan networks. For
example, she tells how 'one group in a remote section of Western
Australia meets for a wedding breakfast every time there is a
wedding on *Days of Our Lives*' (1994, 81). She also demonstrates
how soaps use the structures of women's talk or gossip. Far from
seeking to devalue gossip, she claims that this female oral culture
is a mechanism through which women resist patriarchal ways of
speaking. She uses the work of Deborah Jones to conceive of
gossip as 'a way of talking between women in their roles as
women, intimate in style, personal and domestic in topic and
setting, a female cultural event which springs from and perpetu-
ates the restrictions of the female role, but also gives the comfort
of validation' (Jones in Brown 1994, 30). This form of talk is not
only used by women talking about soaps but informs the structure of soaps. While it is questionable whether this form of speech
is 'essentially' female, as Brown sometimes seems to suggest, the
skills and competences employed in gossip are those associated
with traditional definitions of femininity, competences on which
soaps draw. However, Brown's suggestion that women talking
about soaps might constitute a form of resistance to patriarchy is
overstated to the point where the very act of watching soaps
becomes an act of resistance. She claims, 'Soap opera networks

are a popular form of resistance partly because of the way women use them and partly because the form of soap opera itself defies hierarchies of cultural dominance' (p. 113). It is one thing to challenge dominant assumptions about cultural value which claim soap to be worthless. It is quite another thing to argue that because soaps are seen to be worthless, they embody a resistance to dominant definitions of value. Furthermore, while watching soaps or reading romantic fiction, rather than viewing avant-garde art, may involve a rejection of the validity of the cultural distinctions which say fine art is 'better', this does little to displace the power relations underpinning these distinctions. Brown also fails to consider that cultural hierarchies are not only the result of the unequal distribution of cultural power between men and women, but also of the unequal distribution of cultural power between classes. It is Brown's own class position as an academic that enables her to interpret her female interviewees' responses as a form of resistance to patriarchy, a position which is simply not open to most women soap viewers.[5]

Audience studies of soaps have managed to displace the hypothetical spectator who is deduced by bringing psychoanalytic frameworks to bear on the soap text. In some of the better work, these studies have revealed that the differences between women's engagements with soaps might be as important as the codes and competences that women share. Furthermore, audience research has added a whole new dimension to our understanding of soaps by considering them as texts in use. However, this form of research is not without its problems. For example, Hobson's (1989) discovery that women actively talk about soaps is based on a couple of hours spent chatting with a few women. On the one hand, this tells us something that most soap viewers might have already known and therefore sounds rather banal, but on the other hand, this chat becomes the basis for a whole series of generalisations about how women talk about soaps. Furthermore, in the case of critics like Hobson, the transcripts from the chat are reproduced with little attempt at explanation of *why*, and little analysis of *how*, women talk about soaps.

This audience research is often motivated by a desire to relinquish some form of feminist control: instead of the feminist critic speaking *for* 'other' women, it is 'characterised by an awareness of the necessity to let "other" women speak' (Ang and Hermes 1996, 114). As a result, as Ang and Hermes argue, this has lead to an emphasis on recognising the struggles and resistance that characterise not only the lives of feminists but of 'ordinary women'. However, this can result in a celebration of any signs of 'resistance' – a strategy which can end up sounding somewhat condescending. Furthermore, this resistance is sometimes claimed *for* feminism *by* the feminist critic. While this aims to break down the distinction between the feminist critic and 'the ordinary woman', the ordinary woman is none the less celebrated because she shares some similarities with the feminist critic.

In general, then, studies of women's genres have tended towards analysis of femininity in relation to 'the politics of representation' rather than cultural practices. However, the study of soaps in particular has not only analysed how texts with 'feminine' characteristics might offer something to women within a patriarchal society, but also the ways in which female audiences make use of these texts in order to cope with the experience of living under patriarchy. None the less, there remains the problem that some female audiences have been more visible than others in audience research. In particular, as Bobo and Seiter (1997) argue, black female audiences have been largely marginalised.[6]

Furthermore, the study of gender in soaps has been dominated in the main by feminist television studies, and, as a result, little attention has been paid to the male audience: gender is assumed to be significant to the activity of viewing from the outset and little comparative research has been done on the similarities and differences between masculine and feminine viewing practices. As Ang and Hermes argue, 'the a priori assumption that there is a continuous field of experience shared by all women and only by women tends to naturalise sexual difference and to universalise culturally constructed and historically specific definitions of femininity and masculinity' (1996, 118). Indeed, this comment would seem to apply even more to most studies of the woman's film and romantic fiction than it does to soaps. While studies of soaps have paid attention to the significance of differences between women, they still 'do not go as far as problematizing the category of "woman" itself' (Ang and Hermes 1996, 117).

Notes

1 The structures of soap are also used to make sense of the lives of the rich and famous. For example, Coward (1984) and Lury (1995b) have shown how the story of Princess Diana and her relationship with Prince Charles has been written about in the press using soap conventions. Furthermore, once

established, their relationship has been used in the same 'testing out' process played by soap characters. For example, the UK daytime show, *This Morning* featured a phone-in debate on the morality of Prince Charles' affair with Camilla Parker-Bowles, aided by contributions from experts. However, while what Coward calls the saga of 'the royals' continues, Diana's death could have been argued to have brought about some form of narrative resolution.

2 For more on *thirtysomething* and its viewers, see Heide (1995).

3 Although this begs the question of what kind of men's work she is discussing and which kind of men perform this kind of work.

4 For an extended critique of Modleski on these points, see Gripsrud (1995, 169–74).

5 For a much more thorough critique of this kind of position, see Morris (1988b).

6 Bobo and Seiter argue, 'women of colour will probably be less likely to welcome white researchers into their homes than will white women ... Thus, while theoretically sound, the increased emphasis of late on the crucial role of the domestic sphere in shaping media consumption must be scrutinised in terms of the limitations it may set on the kinds of participants available for studies involving the home as both site and object of research' (1997, 171).

Further reading

Ang, I. *Watching Dallas: Soap Opera and the Melodramatic Imagination* (London, Methuen, 1985)

Brown, M. E. *Soap Opera and Women's Talk: The Pleasure of Resistance* (London, Sage, 1994)

Brunsdon, C. *Screen Tastes: Soap Opera to Satellite Dishes* (London, Routledge, 1997)

Brunsdon, C., D'Acci, J. and Spigel, L., eds, *Feminist Television Criticism: A Reader* (Oxford, Oxford University Press, 1997)

Geraghty, C. *Women and Soap Opera: A Study of Prime Time Soap Operas* (Cambridge, Polity, 1991)

Seiter, E., Borchers, H., Kreutzner, E. and Warth, M., eds, *Remote Control: Television, Audiences and Cultural Power* (London, Routledge, 1989)

Part III

CONSUMPTION PRACTICES and CULTURAL IDENTITIES

6

Consumption
and material culture

Part II of this book raised questions about consumption by challenging the view that there is a single meaning of a text that is inscribed in it through the production process. It demonstrated a shift in thinking about film, literature and media forms which not only raised questions about how texts are capable of producing a range of meanings, but also highlighted the importance of thinking about how the same text can be interpreted and used in different ways. This, it was argued, is not to claim that the consumer is all-powerful and that consumers are free to make whatever meanings they want. Instead, focusing on consumption challenges the view that audiences passively absorb meanings, arguing instead that they are actively involved in practices of meaning-making (see Morley 1995, for an overview of these debates).

There is obviously a lot more to thinking about the consumption of goods and services than thinking about media texts. This chapter introduces debates about consumer cultures, shopping, domestic consumption and consumption and lifestyle. Similar themes are replayed in the following chapters which deal with consumption practices in relation to fashion and the body in Chapter 7 and youth culture and popular music in Chapter 8. However, just as work in media and cultural studies has challenged the lingering influence of mass culture theory which claimed that consumers of the media passively absorbed meanings inscribed in the production process, so work on consumption in a range of disciplines such as sociology, design history, cultural studies and anthropology has questioned the idea that the meanings of commodities are inscribed in the production process and are simply reproduced, and passively absorbed, by consumers. In particular, I explore work which considers how consumption is not simply a process in which commodities are bought but also how they are 'given meaning through their active incorporation in people's lives' (Jackson 1993, 209). Furthermore, the ways in which these consumer goods are used are practices through which cultural identities are formed and reformed.

Thinking about consumption

In this section, I want briefly to explore two main issues: first, how contemporary debates about consumption and material culture are a response to an earlier orthodoxy, in which production was not only seen as more important than consumption but as determining consumption; and second, the ways in which the terms of these debates are gendered. This involves examining how production is valued positively as a masculine activity and consumption is seen as negative and is identified with women and/or as 'feminine'. Indeed, these assumptions are built into Betty Friedan's *The Feminine Mystique* where the female consumer was portrayed as passive, dependent and gullible and the world of work was seen as the key to fulfilment.

The way in which production is privileged over consumption is evident in a range of critics of different theoretical persuasions, but the work of Marx serves as an excellent example. Marx shared in common with many other Victorian theorists the idea that labour is 'the site of self-creation' (Miller 1994, 46). By stressing the 'utilitarian value of work', Marx argued that 'we create our identity through socially useful labour' (p. 47). Therefore, productive labour is not only valued as the fundamental human activity but it also produces our sense of identity. From such a perspective, consumption is not only *not* work (which might come as a surprise to anyone who has spent a Friday evening in Safeway or is responsible for transforming that shopping into a family meal each night), but it is also not a source of our 'real' identity. For Marx, our sense of who we are is a product of our relationship to production and, therefore, in a capitalist society – in which our relationship to production is structured by unequal power relations between social classes – the identities produced through productive labour are class identities. It is for this reason that many later critics would claim that the development of consumer culture led to a weakening of class identity because people increasingly saw themselves in relation to what they consumed rather than in relation to production. Furthermore, identities formed through consumption were seen as forms of 'false consciousness'; as 'inauthentic' or not 'real' identities. This alleged dilution of (male) working-class identity was often seen as a process of 'emasculation'. The sphere of production – which is seen as the site of human identity and useful labour – is, therefore, identified as masculine and privileged over the sphere of consumption which came to stand for 'destructiveness, waste, extravagance, triviality, and insatiability – in fact all the things that men traditionally hate or fear about women' (Pringle, cited in Jackson 1993, 217).

The idea that production determines consumption leads to one further key issue – that the meaning of goods is inscribed in the production process and, therefore, consumption is seen as simply the passive consumption of these meanings. However, the meanings and values of an object are not simply inscribed in the design and production processes and neither are they fixed by advertising, as is sometimes argued. This is not to argue that objects reach the consumer as a blank page on which they can inscribe meanings and values. Instead, it means considering the total trajectory of an object as it moves from production through exchange, distribution and mediation to consumption (Hebdige 1988). This includes a consideration of how the meanings of objects change as they are recontextualised (Miller 1994). Furthermore, as Appadurai (1986) argues, things have 'social lives' and their value changes over the course of their life as they move between different 'regimes of value'. Debates about youth subcultural styles have often illustrated these points. For example, the meaning of army combat gear changes from its original functional and display purposes in the military as combat trousers and flying jackets have become recontextualised in youth subcultures and used to express alternative meanings. In this process, they re-enter the commodity state in different regimes of value from those for which they were originally produced, regimes such as the second-hand market which deals in subcultural styles where these clothes are valued for their 'authenticity' (McRobbie 1994).

The way in which production is privileged over consumption has resulted in a 'negative consensus' (Hebdige 1988) about consumption which Daniel Miller argues is embodied in a range of myths about consumption. Miller acknowledges that, in debates about consumption, the 'housewife' has been portrayed as an 'intensely competitive, status-seeking, emulator, as superficial as she is inauthentic' (1995, 38). However, he does not develop an analysis of how these myths which see consumption as the negative 'other' of production have been persistently gendered. As Mica Nava argues, 'The activity of the consumer is likely to be constructed as impulsive and trivial, as lacking agency, whereas the work of the producer ... tends to be "hard", "real", dignified, a source of solidarity and a focus around which to organise politically' (1992, 190). In this way, consumption can be derided by aligning it with 'feminine' qualities and femininity can be derided by aligning it with consumption. Furthermore, the female consumer enslaved by her desire for goods has been seen as politically dangerous not only in those neo-Marxist and feminist academic analyses which portray her as being in a state of 'false consciousness' but also in more popular accounts. For example, Terri Lovell argues that the British social realist cycle of films of the late 1950s and early 1960s 'persistently portrays the status-conscious woman as the vulnerable point of entry for seductions which might betray a class and its culture' (1990, 367). Similar claims have been made about the ways in which women are portrayed in the work of black Hollywood directors and in rap music. Finally, if a distinction has been made between good, masculine production and bad, feminine consumption then gendered characteristics are also used to discriminate between good and bad consumers. The 'rational' masculine consumer, 'calculating, efficient and aware of his aims and wants' is opposed to the 'romantic', feminine consumer who is passive, impulsive and irrational (Bowlby 1993, 99).

As I suggested earlier, myths about the female consumer which draw on a class analysis in thinking about production also marginalise questions about consumption as a form of labour rather than leisure. Within a traditional Marxist model, domestic labour is not recognised as socially valuable labour. As Celia Lury argues, 'Shopping may be seen as an instance of consumption in relation to the cycle of commodity production (that is, production of goods for exchange on the market), but also as a moment of production in relation to household or domestic production' (Lury 1996, 123). Indeed, as Judy Attfield's (1995) study of women in Harlow in the 1950s (discussed below) demonstrates, women's consumption practices in the home can sometimes be guided by an attempt to make their labour visible.

In the rest of this chapter, I isolate three debates about gender and consumption in three different historical formations of consumer culture: late-nineteenth-century modernity, mid-twentieth-century Fordism and late-twentieth-century post-Fordism. This section explores debates about the department store as a 'feminine space' within the masculine 'public' sphere in the nineteenth century. The following section considers how women consumed housing and used consumer goods to create a sense of 'home' and to articulate classed and gendered identities in the post-war period in the UK. The final section examines debates about gender, identity and contemporary consumer cultures, and explores how the heroes of contemporary consumption have been portrayed as both masculine and middle-class. In the process, consumption is not simply identified with shopping but also the ways in which 'commodities are taken "home", adapted and reinterpreted in establishing relationships and social positions' (Clarke 1997, 154).

The department store, modernity and consumer culture

The department store has gained a central place in debates about both the formation of a modern consumer culture and the modern female consumer. Debates about the significance of the department store tend to focus on the period 1860–1920 and, although there are crucial differences between patterns of development in department stores in different national and regional contexts (Glennie 1995, 189), there are recurrent themes in debates about their significance in the US, UK and France. Department stores of the period, such as Harrods and Selfridges in the UK, are usually portrayed as enormous, luxurious and sumptuous shopping emporia, bringing together the world of consumer goods under one roof. These stores are often portrayed as the vanguard of a new, distinctively modern, consumer culture and as signifying an 'epochal change in cultural meaning' (Lears cited in Glennie 1995, 185). As a result, debates about the significance of other retail outlets during the period, and the ways in which people developed consumer knowledges, skills and competences prior to this period, have been marginalised (p. 188). Department stores have come to be seen as the main site in which an emergent middle class learned to use commodities as symbolic goods, which was crucial in the formation of a distinctive middle-class culture. With women being given the responsibility for consumption, the skills in consuming they developed have been seen as not only distinctively feminine skills but also as crucial in forming a distinctively feminine form of taste (Sparke 1995).

In order to understand the ways in which the department

store has become so central in debates about the production of classed and gendered identities in the late nineteenth century, it is necessary to explore the way in which an 'ideology of separate spheres' is claimed to be increasingly important from the mid-nineteenth century onwards. This ideology rests on the assumption that the domestic, private sphere is the responsibility of, and proper place for, women and the public world of work, the world of men. 'The attempt to confine women to the domestic sphere was both a specifically spatial control and, through that, a social control on identity' (Massey 1994, 179). The 'cult of domesticity' produced an idealised notion of middle-class femininity in which women were seen as the centre of a moral community and equated with 'goodness' and 'beauty'. Women's work in the home was central in displaying new middle-class identities. As a result, women became associated with the exercise of taste through consumption as they were marginalised from the public sphere and the world of production (Sparke 1995, 16–31).

This is significant for a number of reasons. First, middle-class women were increasingly responsible for the symbolic dimensions of consumption – middle-class femininities, it has been claimed, were produced and displayed through the 'correct' use of commodities. In this way, the use of commodities becomes a mechanism through which classed and gendered identities are made visible, a way in which people are classified, and their morality judged, according to their tastes and preferences. Second, the idea of separate spheres highlights the ways in which the spaces of modernity are gendered: the home was seen as the sphere of feminine influence and the masculine public sphere as a dangerous and inappropriate place for women. However, as Vickery argues 'the stress on the proper female sphere in Victorian discourse signalled the concern that more women were active outside the home rather than proof that women were so easily confined' (cited in Nava 1996, 42). Furthermore, it is important to recognise the uneasy position of working-class and lower-middle-class women whose employment brought them into public, masculine spaces and who were, therefore, threatened with being labelled 'unrespectable' (Ryan 1994). Third, Penny Sparke has argued that the cult of domesticity led to the production of distinctive masculine and feminine cultures and the creation of 'two distinct ideological systems' (1995, 23). For Sparke, this division is the historical basis for a distinctively feminine aesthetic which has since been reproduced by women so it appears that it is 'simply "in their bloodstream"' (p. 145). This distinctively feminine taste, Sparke argues, is based on notions of comfort, fashion and display. However, this notion of an epochal, 'essential' feminine taste is highly problematic as it generalises from a model of middle-class Victorian femininity to all women and is seen as only slightly modified within different historical contexts, a problem to which I return below.

The department store has been seen as significant in ideas about the gendered spaces of modernity because it offered a 'feminine space' in public life (Wilson 1985, 150). The stores and the activity of shopping were 'one of the main contexts in which women developed a new consciousness of the possibilities and entitlements that modern life had to offer' (Nava 1996, 53). Rudi Laermans (1993) claims that department stores operated as 'female leisure centres' which would variously offer reading rooms, meeting places, nurseries, sick-bays, exhibitions and – in one instance – even a bicycle academy (Nava 1996; Dowling 1993; Chaney 1983). Indeed, they have even been seen as enabling feminism. For example, the owner of Selfridges claimed that he had 'helped to emancipate women' (Chaney 1983, 24). Owners of some department stores in the UK produced goods in the 'symbolic colours' of the suffragette struggle and store owners saw no conflict between their own interests and women's demands for independence (Nava 1996, 55). If the stores offered freedoms to their middle-class female shoppers, then it has been argued that they also offered, albeit more limited, freedoms to their working-class and lower-middle-class female employees by offering them an alternative to domestic employment, a space in the public sphere, and some 'financial and cultural autonomy' (Chaney 1983, 29).

Critics have also frequently stressed the pleasures that department stores offered middle-class women. The luxurious and glamorous interiors and the service offered by sales staff created an 'aristocratic ambience' in which the middle-class shopper could feel like she was 'a lady for the day' (Laermans 1993, 93). Nava argues that the stores legitimated 'the desire of women to look as well as being looked at' (1996, 53). Bowlby claims that middle-class women were given the opportunity to explore their own desires outside the domestic sphere in which they became involved in the new 'image-worlds' of modernity (Lury 1996, 144). However, these public opportunities for feminine pleasure were not without their critics and if the female shopper was the heroine of the store-owner, she was frequently labelled as 'pathological' and 'irrational' by her critics (Wilson 1985, 150; Lury 1996, 128; Dowling 1993, 302). The freedom shopping presented led some to condemn the activity as a vice among women (Laermans 1993, 87). Shoplifting, medicalised as kleptomania, caused a series of 'moral panics' (Chaney 1983, 29). Women were seen to be all too easily seduced by the world of goods 'as women who had "fallen" spoke of the irresistible touch of silk and satin, the visual seduction of the displays, and their thirst for possessions' (Wilson 1985, 150). However, alongside these ideas of the seduced innocent woman, Nava identifies another set of fears that the world of goods might release 'an unbridled sexuality, an ominous transgressiveness' (1996, 59) which echoes fears about demands for female emancipation more generally. The anxieties about the woman out of control, with an insatiable thirst for goods, also shaped the way in which women were treated in department stores. For example, Robyn Dowling has noted how Woodward's store in Vancouver employed male floorwalkers until the 1920s to guide women around the store and help them control their urges to purchase (1993, 302). In this way, the response to department stores demonstrates clearly the ways in which femininity and consumption became articulated and also identified as a 'problem'.

However, the stores didn't simply see their customers as irrational but also addressed them as rational homemakers and mothers. Indeed, they attempted to redefine femininity 'in terms of the optimum consumption of certain products' (Laermans 1993, 95). In the department store, the shopper no longer haggled over prices but got her 'bargain' by moving between stores and comparing prices (Chaney 1983, 23). However, it has often been claimed that retailers also sought to educate women in particular consumer skills and knowledges through demonstrations and the advice of sales staff so they could control consumption more effectively (Glennie 1995, 185). If the new consumer goods were used symbolically to mark out classed and gendered identities, it was women who were at the forefront in developing these skills. 'As those most literate in the complex signifiers of social hierarchy – a literacy acquired largely from magazines and stores themselves – it was women who decoded and encoded the changing images of class' (Nava 1996, 48). As Nava's comment suggests, it is important that the stores are not seen as solely responsible for the development of consumer skills: 'shops were just one of several everyday social spaces in which people learned about commodities, styles and their uses and meanings and where people deployed their understanding' (Glennie 1995, 188). Furthermore, critics writing on the twentieth century have emphasised how women have drawn on a wide range of media forms in honing their consumer knowledges and competences (Nava 1996; Partington 1991; Stacey 1994).

In conclusion, the literature on department stores suggests that department stores were not only crucial in producing modern consumer culture but also an 'urban sense of self' in which one displayed 'one's social identity before the eyes of strangers' (Laermans 1993, 100). This 'mastery of a language of possessions' was seen to be a feminine competence (Chaney 1983, 29). As well as being displayed through clothing, women were often judged by their ability to 'express' their femininity in the interiors of their homes (Lury 1996, 127). However, it is important to remember that these consumer knowledges and competences are not just gendered but also cross-cut by other forms of difference. For example, as I suggested earlier, critics such as Sparke have seen the department store as a site where feminine taste and culture was validated (1995, 95). However, by privileging the existence of separate spheres, Sparke sees a world only divided by gender, universalising middle-class experiences and obscuring 'class specificities in the gendering of consumption' (Glennie 1995, 189). Furthermore, as Judy Attfield argues, 'There is no such things as a complete and identifiable set of totally feminine or masculine attributes which make up the "essential" man or woman' (1989, 218).

Sparke aims to identify a distinctively feminine form of taste arising from the social position of women in the home and to show the internal logic of feminine culture. She writes in response to the constant devaluing of these tastes by the design establishment and aims to show that women's taste for display and comfort are inherently meaningful because of women's position in the domestic sphere. While she seeks to validate feminine tastes, her argument is undermined by her lack of attention to the ways in which tastes and preferences are not epochal but are defined and redefined historically. As Celia Lury argues, it is important to consider how changes in gender relations shape 'changes in cycles of production and consumption and vice versa' and that these are cross-cut by class, race, age and sexuality

(1996, 119–20). These themes are developed in the next section which explores a case-study of working-class women's domestic consumption practices in the UK in the postwar period to show how their tastes and preferences cannot simply be understood as gender-specific.

However, before leaving the department store, it is important to recognise that they have not simply disappeared from high streets, but instead their role has changed in more recent formations of consumer culture. While it has been argued that in contemporary consumer culture, department stores have been superseded by the increase in specialist or niche retail outlets, they are still used by shoppers in mapping their ways around the city and are still built into their shopping plans (Taylor *et al.* 1996, 136). The relative lack of attention paid to the department store in the twentieth century has meant a lack of attention to the ways these shops have changed. For example, Robyn Dowling's study of Woodwards store in the postwar period highlights how low- to middle-income shoppers were addressed by the store (1993, 305). As well as creating a place-image of the store as a 'family' place, Woodwards also negotiated discourses of rationalisation in producing a 1950s version of modernity. The Woodwards of the period became a 'new, up-to-date, and a scientific and rationally controlled environment' (p. 306) embodied in the design of the store, the dress of employees and the position of the sales staff as experts with scientific knowledge. The 'bewildered housewife' was treated as irrational and in need of expert knowledge to help her select the right product for herself and her family (p. 310). For example, in the food hall there were promotions, demonstrations and displays in which the shopper received an education in how to use new, modern foods (p. 314). In the display of new 'ready-made' foodstuffs, Dowling identifies a reconstruction of domestic labour and femininity: 'A mixture of familial and rational femininity was being constructed. Caring for the family remained a primary component of domestic labour, but this was to be achieved in a scientific manner, requiring the use of ready-made commodities' (p. 313). This rationalisation of domestic labour and femininity as 'the housewife' was made over as a 'home manager' or 'domestic scientist' is a major theme of the next section.

A house is not a home: women and domestic consumption in the post-war UK

As Angela Partington has argued, feminists have traditionally seen the 1950s as 'an all-time low in terms of feminist history' (1995a, 212). It is often claimed that women gained some measure of emancipation during wartime by taking over men's roles in paid employment but that in the post-war period, they were turned into passive consumers and reimprisoned in the domestic sphere. The superficial, status-seeking housewife-consumer lusting after consumer goods to satisfy the 'false needs' constructed by advertising has become a dominant image of femininity in the post-war period in left and feminist criticism. More recently, feminists have set out to challenge the portrait of the American 'zombie-housewife' in Betty Friedan's *The Feminine Mystique* (see, for example, Clarke 1997; Meyerowitz 1994; Spigel 1997). This section concentrates on work in the UK. It explores how consumption in the 1950s was not only a site of struggle between different tastes, but also how, through consumption practices, women were active in producing gendered and classed identities in the ways they made their houses into homes. In particular, the British context not only highlights women's relationship to the new commodities produced during the period, but also their relationship to attempts by the design establishment to educate them into principles of 'proper' consumption and 'good taste'. Furthermore, this allows an exploration of how ideas about the design of houses and goods are also bound up with ideas about family life and women's role in it. Material culture comes with particular ideas about gender 'built-in' (Attfield 1989, 203) but this does not necessarily determine how they are consumed. Finally, if the previous section considered struggles over the gendering of public and private space, this section emphasises struggles over the meaning of domestic space.

In order to understand how struggles over the meaning of femininity take place in particular historical contexts, it is necessary, albeit sketchily, to attempt to partly reconstruct that historical context. In the UK, the post-war period is usually understood as a period of political stability and consensus: concessions on welfare issues in the formation of the Welfare State and full (male) employment 'secured just the measure of popular legitimacy the revival of capitalism required' (Hall *et al.*

1978, 229). This stage of capitalism transformed methods of production requiring new modes of consumption which differentiated it from nineteenth-century capitalist modernity and is usually termed Fordism. Although Fordism had its roots earlier in the twentieth century, the post-war period is usually seen as the time in which Fordism enjoyed its greatest successes. The mass production methods of Fordism depended on a large workforce of semi-skilled labour performing routine, rationalised activities. Full employment meant that workers could bargain for *relatively* better wages, and that they were *relatively* more 'affluent'. However, this 'affluence', it has been argued, was necessary to sustain production because it enabled mass consumption of the new consumer goods which were being mass-produced (*Manifesto for New Times* 1989, 25–6). This 'affluence', it was claimed, 'dismantled old class barriers' as the working class adopted more 'consensual' middle-class values which, in turn, produced increased political stability (Hill 1986, 7). During the 1950s, while the Conservative government claimed the end of class divisions (as Macmillan put is, 'the class war is over and we have won'), left-wing critics mourned the '*emasculation* of the revolutionary powers of labour' (Lee 1993, 82; my italics). This idea that working-class men were becoming more like women rests on the idea that women are inherently conservative and materialistic, a view that not only echoes earlier ideas about consumption in mass culture criticism but portraits of femininity in the 1950s more generally.

This post-war reconstruction also involved the transformation of femininity around notions of domesticity, motherhood and consumption. While it is commonly claimed that women were forced back into the home and out of their war-time jobs to make room for their returning husbands, and while there was a severe reduction in opportunities for women to work in better-paid masculine occupations, this tends to oversimplify the case. First, it underestimates the extent to which women might have been happy to return to the home, rather than being forced or persuaded, and second, it underestimates the number of married women who actually continued to work during the post-war period, albeit often in part-time and low-paid jobs, because full employment required the participation of women in the workforce. Indeed, the expansion of consumer culture was, to some extent, dependent on a female wage (Partington 1995b, 249; Hill 1986, 17). None the less, women's role in the post-war economy has been primarily seen in terms of their role as consumers rather than producers. In Fordist culture, the family became the site in which the 'spirit of modernity' entered everyday life and in which the self-sufficient family unit had to be transformed into a 'modern consumption unit' (Lee 1993, 90–1).

The post-war period saw attempts to alter the housewife's job description. With the rationalisation of labour in Fordist production came corresponding ideas about rationalising the housewife's labour. The principles of Taylorism which had sought to rationalise factory production along scientific lines to maximise efficiency were applied to kitchens in the hope that the domestic 'machine' could operate more efficiently. Time-and-motion studies were applied to the kitchen in order to eliminate wasted movements so the housewife in her workplace could operate more efficiently. The production of the scientific and rational home can be seen clearly in the following recommendations in Joan E. Walley's *The Kitchen* which advises '1. Eliminate all unnecessary work. 2. Combine operations and elements. 3. Change the sequence of operations. 4. Simplify necessary operations.' (1960, 172). If, on one hand, the rationalisation of housework made it sound increasingly mechanised, there was also a corresponding attempt to 'professionalise' the housewife's role so that household management could be seen as a vocation.

The design of housing in the post-war period also contributed ideas about family life and women's role in it. Feminist work on architecture and design has highlighted the ways in which 'the physical form of housing mediates and structures gender relations' (Madigan and Munro 1990, 25). In particular, types of public-sector housing are legitimated by 'their perceived appropriateness to a particular image of working-class and/or family life' (Boys 1995, 50–1). The design establishment of the post-war period was heavily influenced by the principles of Modernist design developed earlier in the century. For Modernists, the built environment was a way of producing order by injecting 'rationality and purpose into everyday life' (Sparke 1995, 98) and this was embodied in claims such as 'a house is a machine for living in' (Lee 1993, 96). Modernists believed that good design was underpinned by universal, utilitarian and functional values and the *form* of housing and household equipment should determine its use: 'The architect's task was to supervise the equipping of the house in such a way that no further subsequent "arranging" was necessary on the part of inhabitants' (Sparke 1995, 109). The principles of modernist design have been seen to embody a 'masculinist rationality' (Boys 1996, 245) and to be the product of a position of upper-class privilege from which objects can be valued for their form rather than their function. Modernism is based on a refusal of 'the passions, emotions and feelings which "ordinary" people invest in their "ordinary" lives' (Bourdieu 1984, 4). As a result, modernist design, as a classed and gendered practice, is based on the idea that it is the *form* (or structure) of housing where 'true' values can be revealed while decoration is seen as 'trivial, superficial, false, feminine' (Boys 1996, 234–5).

Judy Attfield's study of Harlow 'New Town' in the 1950s provides an excellent example of the ways in which the planners' and architects' values, and their ideas about domestic life, were integrated into the built environment. Indeed, ideas about gender were built into the design of the town, not just the houses themselves: Harlow's planners separated the public sphere of work from the feminine private sphere of the home. Indeed, the lack of a female public sphere isolated women in the home and helped to create the phenomenon known as 'New Town Blues' (Attfield 1995, 215). Furthermore, in the early 1950s, Harlow Development Corporation's belief that married women with young children, the majority of Harlow's female residents, should not work outside the home led them to refuse applications from firms who needed to employ high numbers of workers in this category (a decision they were forced to revise in the face of high demand from Harlow's women) (p. 228).

The architects attempted to transform the traditional gendered spaces of the working-class home and change the meanings of domestic space. First, they tried to change the traditional idea that the front of the house was for 'the public display of status' by putting the kitchen at the front of the house. This was so that the woman in her workplace could feel involved in the life of her neighbourhood. However, they failed to recognise how this might exacerbate women's feelings of isolation by making them feel 'marooned' in their kitchens, cut off from the outside world (pp. 217–18). Second, many Harlow homes replaced the front parlour room, 'traditionally kept for best', and the more private back room, with an open-plan living room in order to 'dissolve divisions that separate life into compartments' (pp. 218–19). This notion of a single public room reflected ideas about family 'togetherness' in the period, irrespective of whether families wanted to spend all their time together or not.

However, the ideas about domestic life, and women's position in it, which were built into the design of Harlow were not necessarily reproduced in women's consumption of domestic space. This is made clear in the following comment from a member of Harlow's architects department:

> Every architect thought that after his house had been built . . . it should be furnished as he thought it should be . . . Of course, that didn't happen. At one time we used to be very conscious of the interior decoration . . . fairly early on we came to the realisation that we were utterly wasting our time because no matter what we put on the walls . . . no sooner had people gone in . . . they'd paper them direct with some of the most awful wallpapers. And you'd throw your hands up in horror . . . Right from the beginning people did things themselves . . . They wouldn't be allowed to change fireplaces and things like that but a lot of them did it surreptitiously. (p. 222)

Because the architects produced houses which were totally at odds with residents' understanding of what a 'home' was, the residents appropriated the built environment in such a way as to make it meaningful to them. People used consumption strategies in order to 'own' and take 'possession' of their homes, even though the majority were rented, and invested them with their own meanings (Miller 1990). The window on the world which the front kitchen was meant to offer was quickly obscured when Harlow women put up net curtains (Attfield 1995, 219). 'Through the appropriation of privacy by the concealment of the interior from the uninvited gaze, people took control of their own domestic space and at the same time made a public declaration of their variance from the architects' design' (p. 228). These women also used furniture and room dividers to break-up and compartmentalise the open-plan living space, in order to make the space more meaningful to them by recreating the traditional parlour area for 'display'. However, in doing so, they had to resist the design establishment's attempts to train them into the 'proper' consumption of consumer goods, and to reform their 'feminine' taste for decoration and display.

If many architects working for the public sector tried to build Modernist principles into public housing, then the Council of Industrial Design, established in 1946, drew on Modernist ideas in an attempt to promote good design in consumer goods (Morley 1990). While producers and retailers tried to 'libidinise' consumption by flooding the market with a whole range of 'sexy' new products, the design establishment attempted to regulate it

(Partington 1995b). The wartime Utility scheme, introduced during rationing in 1943, was an attempt to legitimate an aesthetic based on the principles that the functions of an object 'determines the choice and handling of materials, that the object should be easy to manufacture and that decorative visual features should be eliminated' (Partington 1995a, 208). When the Utility scheme was finally scrapped in 1952, the 'Good Design' movement encouraged people to voluntarily accept their principles (Attfield 1990, 85). The 'contemporary' style, launched at the 1951 Festival of Britain, softened some of the harsher features of Modernism and gained both the approval of the 'Good Design' movement and some of the public. However, these design professionals primarily approved of objects which emphasised their 'functional' qualities through their 'form': for example, electric fires which *looked like* electric fires rather than those disguised as something else. 'Their images of the electric fire articulate the post-war ideal of the machine-like home, smooth-running, scientifically operated, everything in its proper place, efficient and tasteful' (Partington 1995a, 209). In this way, both dominant economic and aesthetic models worked to produce the model of the home as machine with the rational and scientific housewife at its centre.

However, the universal meanings that the 'good design' movement believed resided in these objects were often either rejected or negotiated and redefined in use. The attempts by design professionals to educate the female consumer into principles of good taste met with resistance as many working-class women refused models of 'proper' consumption. First, Modernist-inspired styles were rejected at times because they were too machine-like: in particular, women working in paid employment had no wish to return home to another machine environment (Partington 1995b, 259; Forty 1986, 217). Second, the idea of a harmonious designed interior met with problems as people, on economic grounds, mixed and matched old and new styles and maintained the wartime emphasis on 'make do and mend' (Attfield 1995, 223; Partington 1995a, 211). Third, women resisted attempts to educate them into principles of 'good taste' and produced and asserted their own class- and gender-specific tastes and preferences, refusing to 'isolate the practical functions of objects from the social contingencies and circumstances of everyday life' (Partington 1995a, 212). For example, the idea that a fire has a single function – heating – ignores the ways in which the fireplace in the context of the home assumes different meanings such as family gathering place or decorative focus for display (p. 209).

This emphasis on display can be seen clearly in the way in which the traditional parlour, which had been designed *out* of Harlow interiors, was brought back *in* through the creation of 'parlour-substitutes'. The ways in which cocktail cabinets were used in some working-class homes epitomises the struggles between the tastes of the 'Good Design' movement and those of working-class women. These cocktail cabinets stood for everything the design establishment hated: ornamental, glittery and glossy, they were given names such as the 'Ultra', 'Curzon' and 'Plaza' summoning up the luxury, glamour and other-worldliness of the cinema (Attfield 1990, 86). As Attfield comments, 'What better vehicle for display than a piece of furniture which was rarely, if ever, used?' (p. 87). The emphasis on display, decoration and ornament in making a house into a home, as I have shown, has been a central theme in thinking about feminine taste. These feminine tastes have been rejected by design professionals as 'in bad taste' and as based on irrational principles: clutter collected dust and interfered with the efficient running of the household. However, Attfield argues that the way in which Harlow women discussed their interiors was not simply about creating meanings through display but also about creating meanings through the emphasis they put on 'pride and polish' which signified their labour. 'There is no product in housework: it only "shows" when it is *not* done. The signs which announce its efficient completion are more to do with excessiveness – high gloss and shine, brilliant whiteness, non-functional furnishing and collections of ornaments' (Attfield 1995, 234). In this way, we can see that the practices by which these working-class women consumed the home and consumer goods (and used them to articulate different meanings from those which were designed in) were class- and gender-specific practices. The emphasis on 'pride and polish' 'was completely different from the practice of leisured or middle-class housewives, in that it denied the home a status of "haven" from the world of work' (Partington 1995b, 260). In this way, we can see that the type of Marxist model which sees active labour as a source of 'real' identity and passive consumption as involved in the construction of 'false' identities is ill-equipped to deal with women's labour in the home where consumption and production cannot be thought of as separate entities.

In conclusion, this section has explored how the design of material culture in the 1950s tried to produce a particular form of femininity epitomised by the figure of the rational, scientific housewife. However, the images of people built into material culture are not necessarily reproduced when objects are consumed. 'In certain circumstances, segments of the population are able to appropriate industrial objects and utilise them in the creation of their own image' (Miller 1994, 175). Struggles over the meanings of material culture are, in this way, struggles over the meaning of femininity in a particular historical context. While the notions of rationality built into ideas of 'good design' have been identified as masculine, this was not simply a struggle between 'essential' masculine or feminine tastes because this neglects the way in which masculinities and femininities are transformed in different historical contexts and are cross-cut by other forms of difference. Furthermore, studies of women's consumption practices challenge ideas in earlier feminist criticism about the passive 'housewife-consumer' who unquestioningly accepted dominant notions of femininity during the period. They also challenge those critics during the 1950s and early 1960s who saw the new, 'affluent' working-class housewife's thirst for goods as part of a process in which class distinctions were eroded bringing about a 'mass culture'. As Angela Partington argues, 'Working-classness was to be increasingly articulated through the exercise of choices in relation to goods and services, practices which were located in the private domestic sphere and for which women were better equipped than men . . . consumerism provided new opportunities for the expression and celebration of class and gender differences, and of oppositional beliefs and values' (1995b, 248).

Contemporary consumer cultures

Studies of consumption have increasingly challenged the opposition between active production and passive consumption. However, as theorists have increasingly seen consumption as an active practice through which people construct meanings and create a sense of identity, it is no longer necessarily seen as a feminine activity. Indeed, changes in theories of consumption, which have been produced alongside changes in consumer culture, have increasingly been concerned with consumption as a 'heroic' activity which opens up new frontiers. The consumption practices of the 'happy housewife heroine' have not been validated in the process, but have been largely ignored, alongside the marginalisation of women's contemporary consumption practices more generally. The hero of the new consumer culture is usually both masculine and middle class. (The exception tends to be in studies of fashion and youth culture discussed in the following chapters, although there has also been a masculisation of style in each of these areas.) This section briefly explores some of the debates about changes in consumer culture which highlight the increasing opportunities to 'play' with identities that consumer culture now offers. It then questions whether 'consumer culture is a playground for everyone' (Dittmar, cited in Lury 1996, 241) and explores how gender, class and race might limit access to this playground.[1] This is followed by a consideration of more 'mundane' consumption practices before exploring a contemporary case study about femininity, class and consumption (Skeggs 1997).

Contemporary theories of consumption which stress its heroic dimensions need to be understood as a response to previous portraits of consumption as conformist, conservative and as reproducing the status quo. Some critics (most notably Fiske 1989) have tried to reverse the terms of this debate demonstrating the power of consumers to create meanings; the permanent potential for resistance in people's use of goods; and by emphasising the idea of consumption as 'fun' and 'leisure' rather than domestic labour. The argument that consumers are free to make whatever meanings they wish from goods reverses the terms of previous debates: the meanings of goods inscribed in production are no longer seen as all-determining, and are increasingly seen as infinitely plastic and ineffectual. This ignores, the way that struggles over the meanings of goods take place in power relations, as was shown in the previous section, in which neither production, mediation, distribution nor consumption is determining (Appadurai 1986; Hebdige 1988). This sense of struggle is also marginalised when consumers' power to use goods to 'resist' dominant meanings is seen as infinite. Furthermore, Ien Ang has questioned whether just because consumers are active, they are also necessarily powerful (Lee 1993, 54) and Danny Miller has suggested that the consumption practices of subordinate groups might be more 'concerned with gaining access to resources than in using acts of consumption as some kind of "resistance"' (1995, 29). While both shopping as 'fun' and 'leisure' is certainly not the privilege of a class or gender, this idea has been put forward most forcefully when critics have concentrated on the consumption practices of young, relatively affluent men (see, for example, Mort 1989). The study of routine and subsistence shopping produces a more complex picture (Taylor *et al.* 1996).

However, the new consumer heroes are often studied in tandem with changes in consumer culture. Contemporary post-modern and/or post-Fordist consumer culture is said to be radically different from previous formations of consumer culture. There has been wide debate about whether these changes are, in the last instance, driven by changes in the economy with a shift to post-Fordist production (or late capitalism) and/or whether they are the product of a wider cultural shift from modernism to post-modernism. There is not the space here to explore these debates. Instead I want to highlight a couple of key arguments about how these economic and cultural changes have produced a new type of consumer culture.

The shift from Fordist to post-Fordist production methods, it is argued, marks a shift from mass production for a largely national mass market based on 'economies of scale' to international production for 'niche' markets in a global marketplace based on 'economies of scope'. The consequences for consumer culture are that goods are no longer produced for an undifferentiated mass but instead produced for particular niche market segments associated with particular types of people, types of people who do not just exist at a national level but may also exist at a global level. For example, in the British high street Miss Selfridge, The Gap and Laura Ashley can be identified as different niche clothing stores, targeted at different market segments. This relates to another key feature of post-Fordist consumer culture, 'the leading role given to market research, packaging and presentation' (Hebdige 1989, 89). Furthermore, it has been claimed, post-Fordist consumer culture is marked by 'aesthetic obsolescence' where an increasing number of commodities are distinguished only by aesthetic differences (Lee 1993, 136): the sportswear market provides a clear example of this. With more emphasis on the appearance and style of consumer goods, it has been argued that now everyone is engaged in making choices (Lury 1996, 34–6). 'The cultural as well as economic splintering of what in the 1960s and 1970s were solid market blocs – the working class, youth, the housewife, etc. – calls for a rethink ... *Campaign* makes the point that: "Lifestyle advertising is about differentiating oneself from the Jones", not as in previous decades, keeping up with them' (Mort 1988, 208–9).

For many critics, contemporary consumer culture has lead to a situation in which people use consumer goods to mark out distinctive and plural lifestyles. Furthermore, if our sense of who we are increasingly comes from what and how we consume, then this, it has been claimed, makes people aware that our identities are not fixed but something we can *play* with, construct and reconstruct through our use of commodities. One major change arising from this, it has been claimed, is the breakdown of a singular masculine identity, if such a thing ever existed in the first place. 'Young men are being sold images which rupture traditional icons of masculinity', Frank Mort claims: 'They are getting pleasures previously branded 'taboo or feminine' (Mort 1988, 194). These arguments, often linked to the rise of magazines such as *The Face* and *Arena* (Nixon 1993; Mort 1996), frequently suggest that 'constructions of masculinity and femininity are less fixed; shopping and self-adornment have become less gendered ... activities' (Nava 1987, 208). However, this not only maintains a tradition in which young men's use of style is seen to rupture taken-for-granted meanings (see Chapter 8), but also neglects the fact that while shopping for leisure and pleasure might have become a less gendered activity, this does not necessarily mean that shopping as labour has become a male activity. Furthermore, 'feminine' practices are not only validated in this framework when they are performed by men, but also they are divorced from any 'political, cultural or sexual identity' (Lury 1996, 150).

The claim that contemporary consumer culture displaces fixed social identities and encourages us all to 'play' with identity and produce new styles of life has lead commentators to a notion of 'hybrid consumption': for example, for John Sculley, today's 'consumers are not middle class or upper class: they are hybrids. These days someone might buy a cheap digital watch, yet drive a BMW. Or drive to a fast-food restaurant in a Mercedes' (cited in Lee 1993, 137). Tastes and lifestyles in such a picture are so divorced from the economics of class, that the woman who goes to Aldi or Netto supermarkets on the bus has been removed from the picture.[2] Other critics have been more cautious in their theories of lifestyle and consumption, arguing that an investment in the art of lifestyle is part of a process in which the new middle classes engage in a struggle for distinction, a struggle 'to impose their particular tastes as *the* legitimate tastes' (Featherstone 1991, 86). For Featherstone, 'the new heroes of consumer culture make lifestyle a life project ... the modern individual within consumer culture is made conscious that he speaks not only with his clothes, but with his home, furnishings, decoration, car and other activities' (p. 86). On one hand, this is hardly a new phenomenon: the women in Attfield's Harlow study used their 'home, furnishings and decoration' to articulate and construct class- and gender-specific tastes and preferences. On the other hand, the 'new heroes' in Featherstone's account not only appear to be male (Lury 1996, 148), but the relative power of these heroes in shaping contemporary consumer culture is theorised with scant attention to their effects on the relatively powerless. According to Dittmar, 'the argument that all are much freer to acquire the lifestyle – and thus identity – of their choice runs the risk of slipping into an imaginary world of equal opportunities, and thus of becoming a rhetoric that all are equal, even if some remain more equal than others' (cited in Lury 1996, 239).

Questions about difference and inequality add complexity to many accounts of post-Fordist consumer culture: indeed, emphasis on the freedom to play with lifestyles often neglects very basic questions about access to opportunities to consume. Doreen Massey has continued to point out that 'It is the mobility and control of some groups that can actively weaken other people' (1993, 62). For example, out-of-town shopping complexes are often not only inaccessible for those dependent on public transport, they also 'contribute to the rising prices, even hasten the demise, of the corner shop' (*ibid.*, 63). Taylor *et al.*'s study of shopping practices in Manchester and Sheffield not only demonstrates that shopping as 'play' and 'leisure' was only one out of a diverse range of shopping practices, but also that such ideas suppress the ways that 'poverty structures the practice of shopping for a large (and perhaps an increasing) proportion of the urban population' (1996, 115). However, access is not just a matter of economics. American lawyer, Patricia J. Williams has written about how the use of buzzers to regulate entry into New York stores has enabled shops to use 'race' as the grounds for inclusion or exclusion. Indeed, she recounts her experience of being refused entry to a Benetton franchise (Benetton, of course, being famed for their 'united colours' and, in academic debates, for being the epitome of post-Fordist production) on the grounds that they were 'closed'. As she recalls, 'It was two Saturdays before Christmas, at one o'clock in the afternoon; there were several white people in the store who appeared to be shopping for things' (cited in Lury 1996, 168). Skeggs clearly demonstrates that the opportunities for 'play' and 'leisure' in a modern department store are also based on salestaff's and other shoppers' judgements about the 'class' of shoppers. As one of the women in her study commented, 'this woman she just looked at us. If looks could kill ... We weren't doing anything wrong. We weren't scruffy or anything. She just looked. It was like it was her place and we didn't belong there. And you know what we just all walked away' (1997, 92).

As Miller *et al.* argue, 'once the sexual division of labour and the gendered nature of shopping are recognised, the notion of shopping as leisure is much harder to sustain' (1998, 94). Recent studies of shopping suggest that women are still primarily responsible for sustaining the family through consumption (Miller 1998). It is in studies of food that ideas about consumption as a form of domestic labour, and women's role in 'feeding the family', have been most apparent (DeVault 1991).[3] 'The contribution of domestic production to consumption, through the provision of services like cooking and cleaning within the household, frequently goes unrecognised' (Warde 1997, 126).

Skeggs' ethnographic study of white working-class women in Britain also further challenges Featherstone's portrait of contemporary consumer culture. The women in the study know that they speak with their clothes and their homes, but they are embarrassed about what they are saying. As Skeggs argues, 'The pleasure they get from their homes and the time they spend on them is always disrupted by their knowledge of a judgemental external other' (1997, 89). The group of women in her study constantly apologise for why their homes are not up to middle-class standards. 'It's like the drawers upstairs, they're horrible, did you notice them? They shouldn't have house room really but I had nowhere to put things' (Jane). 'I was ashamed to have people round with everyone else's castouts, but we're replacing it bit by bit. It looks odd though, don't you think?' (Sharon). (Skeggs 1997, 89). Consumption practices here are as much a source of pain as pleasure and are experienced as a failure to produce the desired effect rather than a source of a sense of distinction. 'They continually doubt their own judgements. This is the emotional politics of class. They can never have the certainty that they are doing it right which is one of the main signifiers of middle class dispositions' (p. 90). The women in Skeggs' study use consumption practices to disidentify themselves from the working class and to 'pass' as middle class. However, at the same time, they refuse the legitimacy of some middle-class practices by seeing them as pretentious and, therefore, do not simply wish to emulate them. Skeggs' study demonstrates that what it means to be a white, working-class woman cannot simply be shrugged off by using commodities to 'play' with identity. However, consumption practices do not simply 'express', but also involve a 'reworking', of cultural identities (Miller *et al.* 1998, 185).

Just as Skeggs has argued that working-class competences and tastes are denied the legitimacy which might allow the women in her study to experience a sense of distinction, the feeling of 'being what it is right to be' (Bourdieu 1984, 228), Lury suggests that women's cultural competences and consumer practices more generally fail to produce this sense of distinction. Studies such as these problematise accounts of contemporary consumer culture which celebrate consumer pleasures and the free 'play' of identities as empowering and liberating. In the next chapter, I consider the work of feminist critics who have focussed on women's use of fashion and style to 'resist' 'traditional femininity' to produce new forms of feminine identity. However, outside the debates about fashion and the body, there has been a relative lack of feminist work on women's relationship to contemporary consumer culture and a relative lack of attention to more 'mundane' consumption practices (although, see, for example, the work on food consumption cited above). This is doubly surprising given that it is women who tend to be responsible for shopping and 'do the "work" of consumption' (Lury 1996, 121).

Notes

1 The lack of discussion in this chapter of lesbians and consumption reflects the structure of the field (Clark 1995). Those studies of lesbians and consumption that exist tend to focus on fashion and, for this reason, are discussed in the next chapter.

2 Indeed, these accounts rarely discuss 'particular consumers engaged in specific acts of purchase ... particularity and specifics, heterogeneity and difference, are obscured in what need to be seen as over-generalising and over-homogenising theoretical representations of consumption' (Gregson and Crewe 1997, 242).

3 See also Charles (1995); Charles and Kerr (1988); Lupton (1996); Murcott (1995); Warde (1997); and Warde and Hetherington (1994).

Further reading

Attfield, J. and Kirkham, P., eds, *A View from the Interior: Women and Design* (1995 edition), (London, Women's Press, 1995)

Clarke, A. J. Tupperware: Suburbia, Sociality and Mass Consumption, in R. Silverstone, ed., *Visions of Suburbia* (London, Routledge, 1997)

Dowling, C. Femininity, Place and Commodities: A Retail Case Study, *Antipode*, 25(4), 1993

Jackson, S. and Moores, S., eds, *The Politics of Domestic Consumption: Critical Readings* (Hemel Hempstead, Prentice Hall/Harvester Wheatsheaf, 1995)

Lury, C. *Consumer Culture* (Cambridge, Polity, 1996)

Nava, M. Modernity's Disavowal: Women, the City and the Department Store, in M. Nava and A. O'Shea, eds, *Modern Times: Reflections on a Century of English Modernity* (London, Routledge, 1996)

Sparke, P. *As Long as it's Pink: The Sexual Politics of Taste* (London, Pandora, 1995)

7

Fashion and beauty
practices

Although feminist critics have disagreed over the significance of fashion and beauty practices, they all tend to share an interest in the ways in which fashion and beauty practices produce gendered identities. As Elizabeth Wilson has argued, modern 'fashion is obsessed with gender' (1985, 117), defining and redefining femininity and masculinity and playing with the boundaries between them. Although we are used to thinking of the body as a 'natural' entity – and for this reason, the differences between male and female bodies as biological – fashion and beauty practices are a key mechanism through which 'the human body [is made] culturally visible' (Silverman 1986, 145). Indeed, there becomes no way of thinking about bodies 'outside' of culture. While fashion and beauty practices are 'part of the process by which attitudes to and images of men and women are created and reproduced' (Rouse, cited in Barnard 1996, 111), they do not only create gendered identities but also classed, 'racial', age and ethnic identities. In our everyday lives we are often very skilled at reading cultural identities from clothes: for example, Stansted Airport in the UK produced an advertising campaign to create an 'up-market' image in the mid-1990s that proclaimed it was a 'shell-suit'-free zone, a period in which 'shell suits' signified working-classness. However, the significance of fashion and beauty practices is not just about *what* we wear but also *how* we wear things, an issue explored in more detail later in the chapter.

This chapter also explores the ways in which fashion and beauty practices should be understood as part of debates about consumption and consumer cultures. The way in which men have been associated with the 'rational' world of production and women the 'irrational' world of consumption which was discussed in the last chapter, also structures many negative accounts of fashion. Many theorists who are anti-fashion draw on these critiques of mass consumption and mass culture (Wilson 1985, 53). Within these critiques women's investment in what is seen as the shallow, trivial and irrational world of fashion is used

to associate femininity with shallowness, triviality and irrational-
ity (and vice versa).

However, the study of fashion has also been dominated by
the discipline of art history which privileges production over
consumption in a different way. These approaches tend to share
the idea that fashion is produced by men and consumed by
women, denying the high proportion of women involved in the
production of fashion (Leopold 1993, 102). Indeed, the fashion
industry is best thought of as a highly femininised industry
(McRobbie 1997b). However, fashion within an art history tradition has been equated with largely *haute couture:* art historians
have analysed the ways in which great designers as artists have
stamped their clothes with the mark of genius. In such accounts
the meaning of clothes is associated with the intentions of the
designer, which ignores the ways in which meanings are created
through the ways in which clothes are worn and used: as
Elizabeth Wilson argues, clothes without bodies do not really
exist (1993, 15). Furthermore, the emphasis on *haute couture* also
ignores the majority of people's relationships to clothing,
'viewing the history of fashion from the top down rather than the
bottom up' (Leopold 1993, 102).

More recently, critics have drawn on ideas generated within
cultural studies to challenge the idea that women are passive
fashion victims of consumer capitalism and to open out the study
of fashion beyond the realm of *haute couture*. These critics draw
on many of the themes introduced in the previous chapter,
exploring the ways in which the activities of consumers produce
meanings which may not be anticipated in design and production
processes and in the ways fashions are mediated, for example,
through women's magazines and film. Furthermore, as was
discussed in the last chapter, it is necessary to think about how
the meanings of clothes as commodities change as they move
through different 'regimes of value'. However, in the process, as
Angela McRobbie (1997b) has argued, the relationship between
women as consumers of fashion and those women involved in
'the production of consumption' has been largely ignored.

This chapter offers an overview of feminist approaches to the
relationship between fashion and beauty practices and femininity.
In order to have the opportunity to explore the ways in which
different feminine identities are produced in specific historical
contexts later in the chapter, it has been necessary to limit the
scope of the discussion to the post-war period and to a British,

and to a lesser extent US, context. The first section explores feminist approaches which could be classified as anti-fashion, which tend to come out of second-wave feminism, and the forms of cultural politics and practices these critiques produced. The second section explores feminist work which has tended to see fashion more positively by focusing on the aesthetics of fashion, and demonstrates how these approaches are informed by a different notion of cultural politics. The third section acts as a case study of fashion in a specific historical context – post-war Britain – to explore struggles over the meaning of fashion, highlighting the ways in which fashion practices do not just produce gendered identities, but identities which are both classed and gendered. The fourth section picks up on some themes developed in Chapter 3 to explore the role of cultural forms such as cinema in educating female consumers in the codes and competences which are demanded for the production of different feminine selves. The final section examines the idea that fashion and beauty practices are techniques for the production of feminine selves.

It is crucial to recognise from the outset that most debates about women, fashion and beauty have been about *white* women, fashion and beauty. If second-wave feminism was often characterised by a critique of the ways in which fashion and beauty practices work to turn women into objects for men, this neglected the ways in which 'Black and White women are objectified differently' (Weekes 1997, 114). There was little recognition within second-wave feminism of how feminine ideals of beauty were both implicitly and explicitly white. As Lola Young has argued, 'Images of white European women as the standard of beauty are pervasive: those images are the polar opposite of and yet dependent on images of black women's femininity and sexuality' (1996, 44).

Feminism and anti-fashion

Fashion and beauty practices have been a major target for feminist critique. Many feminists have seen these practices as oppressive and exploitative and emphasised the damage they do to women. While many second-wave feminists saw fashion as a form of 'bondage' – for example, the girdle and stiletto heel are frequently cited examples – the fashion and beauty industries continue to receive a great deal of criticism. In recent years, for example, the media has given considerable publicity to feminist critiques of the 'waif' look, and the extra-thin models associated with it have been said to encourage anorexia and bulimia in young women: girls, it is claimed, damage their bodies in pursuit of impossible beauty ideals, damage which can result in death. This section explores the assumptions underpinning these forms of critique. However, while the feminist criticism discussed below emphasises how fashion and beauty practices oppress the female consumer, locking them into 'false' feminine identities, it is important to remember that women are also exploited in the production of fashion. Socialist feminists have reminded us that the fashion industry relies on low-paid female, and often child, labour, not only on a national but also a global level. The emphasis on the female consumer in writing in cultural studies has often been at the expense of an analysis of the exploitative conditions under which women work in the fashion industry (McRobbie 1997b; Wilson 1985).

While there was little attempt to theorise fashion, the rejection of fashion and beauty practices was at the heart of second-wave feminism. The feminist critique of fashion was part of the wider critique of femininity discussed in Chapter 1. Feminist practices highlighted this critique: for example, the protests against beauty pageants encouraged women to literally throw away the paraphernalia of femininity, condemning items such as bras, girdles and curlers as 'woman-garbage' (Morgan 1970, 585). Beauty practices, it was claimed, objectified and, in the process, dehumanised, women: for example, Alice Embree argued that women were seen only as bodies, not people (1970, 206). If women's liberation was to take place, it was argued, women must no longer be 'enslaved by ludicrous "beauty" standards' (Morgan 1970, 586). For this reason, as Elizabeth Wilson has noted, fashion was seen as a form of 'false consciousness' (1985, 57).

These critiques of fashion generated two different types of feminist anti-fashion and anti-beauty practices. Some feminists argued that it was necessary to reject feminine fashion by adopting masculine dress while others argued that it was necessary to step outside of fashion altogether to reclaim a 'natural' female self (Barnard 1996, 135). While both these positions are based on a rejection of femininity, they differ in their assumptions. The first strategy which opts for masculine dress, such as trousers and short hair, is based on a rejection of both the feminine values and the practical constraints of feminine dress. For example, Susan

Brownmiller has argued that, 'Trousers are practical. They cover the lower half of the body without nonsense and permit the freest of natural movements. And therein lies their unfeminine danger [to patriarchy]' (1984, 83).[1] However, in the process, this strategy reproduces the idea that masculinity is the norm by privileging masculine values over feminine ones (Wilson 1985; Barnard 1996). Furthermore, by asserting the 'practical' merits of masculine over feminine dress, this approach distinguishes between feminist and non-feminist clothing on the grounds of how functional they are. For example, trousers were often championed as a more practical and functional form of clothing than skirts and, therefore, were seen as more 'rational'. However, as Elizabeth Wilson has argued, this ignores the ways in which 'dress is never primarily functional, and that it is certainly not rational' (1985, 244).

The second feminist anti-fashion strategy also maintains an emphasis on practicality and comfort, but rejects both 'masculine' and 'feminine' forms of fashion in an attempt to 'escape' fashion altogether. Here fashion is equated with a 'false' feminine mask which – when taken off – will reveal a 'natural' female self. However if there is no dress outside of fashion systems in modern societies (Wilson 1985, 3), this would seem to be an impossible task (Barnard 1996, 135). Instead, Wilson argues, 'feminist' dress should be seen as 'a sub-theme of the general fashion discourse': indeed, feminist dress often shares many similarities with the educated middle-class fashions of a particular period (1985, 242). She notes that while feminists have often asserted a (mythical) notion of 'free choice' to 'do your own thing', not only is there a remarkable similarity between the ways in which feminists 'do their own thing', but the styles they adopt often impact on, or resemble, wider fashion trends of the period. For example, in the late 1970s and early 1980s, one strand of 'feminist style' shared many similarities with punk. Therefore, it is important to understand how feminist identities were constructed through fashion.

Just as it is impossible to think about clothing as 'outside' of fashion in modern societies, so it is also highly problematic to think of a 'natural' and 'authentic' female self 'outside' of culture. This notion of feminist cultural politics can be seen as an example of the 'folk feminism' discussed in Chapter 2. This feminist approach to fashion sets up 'the "natural" as superior to the "artificial" (as if the concept of human culture were not artificial)

... [and has] confused the natural with simplicity, and so the uncorrupt' (Wilson 1985, 235). The feminist endorsement of the 'natural' was not only an attack on 'artificial' modes of femininity, but also 'because fashion and femininity had been identified as so much labour, there was a problem with being seen to have "done" anything' (Evans and Thornton, 1989, 7). However, this 'natural' look cannot be understood as something that lies beneath the 'false' appearance of fashion and femininity: instead, feminist fashion and beauty practices have constructed a different mode of feminine identity. As Evans and Thornton argue, the 'natural' look 'took as much labour as all the other "looks"; its "naturalness" was a function of the denial and concealment of that labour' (p. 13). Therefore, like the 'images of women' criticism discussed in Chapter 2, feminist critiques of fashion in the 1970s often claimed that fashion as a form of representation *mis*represented women and 'used the notion of a real (unconstructed) woman to criticise consumer culture's offerings' (Gaines 1990a, 4). Feminist dress is not outside of fashion, nor does it represent what women are 'really' like. If, as Evans and Thornton argue, fashion 'endlessly defines and redefines femininity' (1989, 13), then feminist styles also negotiate notions of femininity through fashion.

However, notions of 'feminist' style – whether they privilege the 'masculine' or the 'female' – are problematised by both 'race' and sexuality. Black feminists sought to challenge the ways in which fashion and beauty practices presumed that feminine beauty equated with white feminine beauty. For many black women, the turn towards an appearance that was more 'natural' may have been motivated by gender politics, but it was crucially influenced by the black power movement's insistence on redefining 'Blackness' and celebrating 'Afro-centricity'. From this perspective, a pro-black woman's stance demanded a rejection of the hair-straightening techniques and skin-bleaching creams which affirmed white femininity as the desired identity. For example, 'the Afro and the dreadlocks were constructed as a return to nature, and rejected the European notions of "cultivating" and taming Black hair into straightness' (Weekes 1997, 116). However, such a strategy not only rests on the problematic notion of revealing a 'natural' self, but also reaffirmed the equation of 'blackness' with 'nature' and 'whiteness' with 'culture'. Furthermore, as Debbie Weekes argues, 'the ways that such strategic essentialising occurs creates rifts between Black women which means that essentialising on the basis of skin shade and hair texture has limited political possibilities' (1997, 124).

More recently, feminist critics have highlighted the ways in which fashion plays with gender. As Elizabeth Wilson has argued, 'Modern fashion *plays* endlessly with the distinction between masculinity and femininity. With it we express our shifting ideas about what masculinity and femininity are. Fashion allows us to flirt with transvestitism, precisely to divest it of all its danger and power' (1985, 122). Fred Davis picks up on this theme to argue that 'cross-gender clothing' rarely challenges ideas about gendered identities because it is usually 'accompanied by some symbolic qualification, contradiction, jibe, irony, exaggeration, etc.', which suggests that it should not be taken 'at face value' (1992, 42). For example, wearing an over-sized man's shirt can often have the effect of making a woman look under-sized or petite, therefore, emphasising a fragility and smallness which have frequently been identified as 'feminine'. However, while many cross-dressing practices do serve to reaffirm gender differences, Marjorie Garber has argued transvestitism can provide a radical challenge to ideas about sex and gender. For Garber, the cross-dresser challenges 'the categories of "female" and "male"' by forging identities that resist classification (1992, 10). If the cross-dresser is thought of as neither male nor female but as 'something else', then this calls into question the binary opposition between male and female which structures our culture.

The rest of this chapter explores feminist cultural criticism which moves beyond the anti-fashion position of second-wave feminism and engages with the contradictions and possibilities of fashion and beauty practices. As Evans and Thornton put it, 'Fashion can be an experiment with appearances, an experiment that challenges cultural meaning ... The feminist rejection of fashion was an experiment and it is now possible to imagine ways to direct the experiment back into fashion' (1989, 15). However, the condemnation of these practices by feminists has not disappeared and there have been very public denunciations of the damage fashion and beauty practices do to women (see, for example, Wolf 1990).

Fashion, aesthetics and resistance

Whereas second-wave feminism tried to produce oppositional fashions by attempting to get 'outside' of fashion, more recently some feminist critics have highlighted the potential for resistance within the field of fashion. This section examines feminist approaches which highlight the ways in which fashion practices can be used to disrupt taken-for-granted ideas about gender differences. In particular, these approaches have an interest in the ways in which some fashion practices might share the same characteristics as modernist avant-garde art. While in the 1970s there was still widespread feminist condemnation of fashion, critics such as Dick Hebdige (1979) had begun to explore how masculine subcultures used style as a form of resistance (see also Chapter 8). Everyday clothing, Hebdige argued, uses codes which appear as 'natural' when they are in fact cultural. Subcultures such as punk, he argued, disrupt and abuse the codes of 'normal' style and therefore appear 'unnatural'. Therefore, in breaking the codes that are reproduced in 'normal style', subcultural style, it is claimed, exposes the ways in which there is nothing 'natural' about fashion systems: the ability to break the codes of fashion highlights the ways in which fashion is governed by codes in the first place. For example, punks created their subcultural style by taking everyday items such as safety-pins, chains and bin-liners and using them out of their 'normal' context. For this reason, Hebdige sees subcultural style as a form of 'signifying practice' which shares some characteristics with avant-garde art forms that disrupt the form of everyday languages to 'make strange' that which appears to be 'normal'. As Hebdige argues, 'artistic expression and aesthetic pleasure are intimately bound up with the destruction of existing codes and the formulation of new ones' (Hebdige 1979, 129).

Elizabeth Wilson's work on fashion also emphasises the oppositional element of punk. Throughout *Adorned in Dreams* (1985), she is eager to draw out connections between modernist aesthetics and fashion practices. Although more democratic than modernist art, Wilson argues, fashion often shares modernism's 'oppositionalism and iconoclasm, its questioning of reality and perception, its attempt to come to grips with the nature of human experience in a mechanised "unnatural" world' (1985, 63). These fashions acknowledge and play with 'the social construction of the gendered self' (p. 231), demonstrating that there is nothing 'natural' about gender by highlighting its artificiality. For example, Wilson argues that 'punk was the opposite of mainstream fashion which always attempts to naturalise the strange rather than the other way around ... it radically questions its own terms of reference, questions what fashion *is*, what style *is*, making mincemeat of received notions of beauty and trashing the very idea of "charm" or "taste"' (p. 196). Therefore, Wilson maintains the distinction between fashion as a modernist practice and 'mainstream fashion', a distinction which underpins subcultural theory. In the process, she also distinguishes between people engaged in oppositional fashion practices and 'the conformist majority' (p. 184). The forms of fashion and beauty practices claimed for feminism are those which operate as avant-garde art. In this way, while some second-wave feminists saw the cultural politics of fashion in terms of 'folk feminism', Wilson tends towards the cultural politics of 'avant-garde feminism' also discussed in Chapter 2. In the process, however, everyday fashion practices are marginalised.

Evans and Thornton's (1989; 1991) analysis of fashion and femininity also rests on the opposition between a radical 'avant-garde' approach to fashion and 'ordinary' fashion practices. Indeed, they ignore anything that they deem to be 'conformist' and concentrate on the 'radical, demanding and critical' (1989, xiv), spectacular subcultural styles (punk, again), and a handful of female high-fashion designers. While, like Hebdige and Wilson, Evans and Thornton celebrate the 'anti-naturalism' of punk, they give more attention to how punk style disrupts 'conventional' notions of femininity. For example, they argue that punk girls 'jettisoned conventional prettiness and sought instead to look tough, menacing and threatening. In doing so they pinpointed the masquerade of femininity, the unholy alliance of femininity, naturalness, good taste and good behaviour' (1989, 18). Furthermore, when female punks used 'the bad girl *look*, the separation of the look from its signified, sexual availability, constituted a form of deviance' (p. 19). The fashion practices of female punks, they argue, do not represent an attempt to 'escape' femininity, but a challenge to the ways in which femininity is naturalised through 'conformist' fashion and beauty practices. In this way, for Evans and Thornton, punk styles question what it means to be feminine.

If spectacular subcultural styles can operate as one form of avant-garde practice by playing with a field of representation through which femininity is constructed, then Evans and Thornton also find radicalism and critique in the work of female high-fashion designers such as Vivienne Westwood and Rei Kawakubo of *Comme de Garçons*. Both designers, they argue, avoid the 'conventional' trappings of feminine clothing (which the authors dismiss as 'uninteresting fashion') and 'elements of clothing that are *symbolically* masculine' (1991, 57). Westwood, they claim, produces a 'more radical and challenging "version"' of 'femininity' in her clothes because she 'fails' 'to refer to patriarchy' (p. 58). For example, they argue, Westwood's clothes use 'a feminine sexuality ... outside the constraints of male definition and which is, crucially, linked to our experience of our bodies' (p. 61). This argument, like the French feminism upon which it draws, ends up running the risk of essentialism: the 'feminine' sexuality which Westwood expresses through her clothes, which is 'outside' of patriarchal logic, is hard to distinguish from a notion of an 'essential' femaleness (Moi 1985). Indeed, it is important to question whether women share a common 'experience of our bodies'.

While Wilson is right in reminding us that the aesthetic dimensions of fashion should not be ignored, Evans and Thornton over-emphasise the importance of fashion as aesthetic practice. For this reason, they are less interested in fashion as popular culture than fashion as modernist art practice. While punk is a 'popular' style, they read punk as if it were 'oppositional' art (although they admit that their reading is only *one* reading). Vivienne Westwood is treated as a 'philosopher' and 'artist' playing with the codes of representation. In this way, Evans and Thornton's notion of cultural politics is underpinned by an 'avant-garde feminism' in which 'mainstream', 'boring' popular forms are seen as the degraded 'other' of oppositional avant-garde art. However, designers such as Vivienne Westwood are not only the ones valued by the bourgeois culture they are supposed to oppose, they are also a reaction to 'mainstream fashion' and therefore dependent on the very practice they seek to undermine. To read Westwood's designs as a radical play with the codes of fashion depends on class-specific codes, competences and tastes far more than a recognition of gendered experience. It is for this reason, perhaps, that designers such as Westwood are treated as 'incomprehensible', 'ridiculous' and 'impractical' from within a 'popular aesthetic'. For example, these designs are routinely ridiculed in daytime TV magazine shows as 'daft' and 'not exactly the kind of thing you could go to Tesco's in'. In Evans and Thornton's work, oppositional styles are meaningful because of their difference to 'mainstream', 'conventional' fashion. In the process, they assume that mainstream fashions are homogeneous and 'conformist', and produce homogeneous and conforming modes of feminine identity.

Debates about the politics of subcultural style have taken a slightly different direction in discussions of lesbian identity. For many lesbian critics, dressing to make a lesbian identity visible is a political act because it is a refusal to 'pass' as heterosexual. In the 1970s, lesbian style tended to be highly politicised and, like wider feminist styles of the period, was built on a refusal of a 'feminine' identity constructed for men in favour of more 'rational' dress and a more 'natural' look. None the less, this anti-fashion 'expressed allegiances and social attitudes' (Wilson 1990, 72). Style, as Danae Clark has argued, has been crucial for lesbians because the 'resistance to or reformulation of fashion codes ... distinguished lesbians from straight women at the same time that it challenged patriarchal structures' (1995, 487).

The 1980s and 1990s, it has been argued, have been characterised by the decline of a politicised lesbian-feminist identity and the rise of 'lifestyle lesbianism' (Stein 1995). Some lesbians reacted against the 'political correctness' of lesbian-feminism and challenged the idea that a lesbian identity had to be 'aesthetically dull and sexually unattractive' (Blackman and Perry 1990, 69). These lesbians rejected the equation of a specific lesbian style with a politicised lesbian identity and embraced 'a self-conscious aesthetic that plays with style' (Stein 1995, 479), aiming to subvert the codes of femininity while 'using the feminine to attract women' (Blackman and Perry 1990, 69). As a result, lesbian fashion in the 1990s has been increasingly characterised by a range of styles rather than a single identifiable 'look'. However, this move is not without its critics who, while recognising the problems with 'overly politicised or prescriptive notions of lesbianism', argue that lifestyle lesbianism 'comes perilously close to depoliticising lesbian identity' (Stein 1995, 482). Furthermore, as Blackman and Perry argue, while playing with a range of looks 'may be subversive ... it can never become a substitute for direct political campaigning' (1990, 78).

The debate about lifestyle lesbianism and the resulting proliferation of lesbian looks can also be seen in the context of the shift to post-modernism and/or post-Fordism, discussed in the last chapter. This refers to the way that fashions today are no longer produced for an undifferentiated mass but heterogeneous niche market segments. Today, it is sometimes argued that there is no fashion, only *fashions* which are used to mark out a range of lifestyles and identities. On the one hand, this suggests that there can be no clear-cut sense of 'oppositional' dress as there is no longer a monolithic mainstream to oppose. On the other hand, it has been argued, now everyone is encouraged to 'play' with their identity through clothes and assert their 'difference' breaking down any fixed relation between fashion and gendered (among other) identities. However, this tends to neglect the ways in which women have used 'everyday' fashion to negotiate identities and assert difference in different historical contexts, practices which question whether an undifferentiated mainstream ever existed. This is the subject of the next section.

Femininity and difference in post-war British fashion

Post-war fashion cannot be understood outside of the wider context of the consumer culture of the period and, therefore, many of the themes raised in this section are connected to the discussion of women's consumption practices in the post-war period discussed in the last chapter. By looking in some depth at the fashions of a specific historical period, it is possible to challenge both the idea that mainstream fashion practices are homogeneous and the idea that the fashions of a period produce a single, dominant mode of feminine identity.

As earlier chapters have suggested, the late 1940s and the 1950s have often been seen as a deeply anti-feminist period where women were stripped of the 'independence' they had gained during the Second World War and 'forced' back into the home. Many feminist interpretations of the fashions of the period have exhibited this logic, seeing post-war women's fashion as part and parcel of 'the feminine mystique'. After the more 'masculine' women's fashions of the war years, it is often claimed, post-war fashions saw the resurrection of a exaggerated and highly romanticised femininity in women's fashions. The style that epitomised this change was Christian Dior's 'New Look', launched to the sound of both adoration and outrage in 1947. The New Look silhouette consisted of rounded shoulders, a close-fitting bodice emphasising the breasts, a tiny nipped-in waist and long full skirts (often achieved through petticoats and crinoline-like constructions), a total contrast to the 'manish angularity' of the wartime clothing that preceded it (Schreier 1984, 6). The stiletto heel was also introduced as an 'intrinsic element' of the New Look, and worked to emphasise the bottom and breasts (Wright 1995, 8).

Supporters of the New Look in the period claimed it was a return to a 'true' femininity which had been masked by the masculine war-time fashions: as British *Vogue* put it, it is 'manifestly inspired by woman's true form in a renewed avowal of femininity' (in McNeil 1993, 293). The fact that a whole lot of boning and corsetry was necessary to reveal 'the woman within' was conveniently disavowed in the process. Indeed, Maynard has argued that the New Look demanded new kinds of 'body management': the long skirts required a new kind of walk and the small waist demanded 're-educative regimes of exercise and massage' (1995, 46). The New Look demanded the production of 'recognisably feminine bodies through the structures of diet, body comportment and make-up' (p. 46).

It is the nostalgia and romanticism of the New Look, combined with the way in which it is said to allocate women a passive and decorative role that has lead many feminists, past and present, to condemn the New Look as part of a 'feminine mystique' which aimed to remove women from the workforce, and relegate them to their 'traditional' roles as wife and mother, locked in the private sphere. As Valerie Steele puts it, 'Critics have interpreted Dior's New Look as a sartorial expression of the Feminine Mystique, "elegance as bondage"' (1997, 235). Some contemporary critics, while distancing themselves from the 'conspiratorial' edge of earlier critiques, have still presented women as 'victims' of the New Look, its body management techniques, and the consumer culture it helped sustain, arguing that the New Look allocated women 'a quite restrictive role as sexually attractive, ever charming family managers within the expanding capitalist market' (Maynard 1995, 56–7). However, these critiques of the New Look tend to share the view that 'Fashion is purpose-built to secure certain effects' (Craik 1994, 16), ignoring the ways that the meaning and appearance of clothing, like other commodities, can be transformed through use.

The popularity of the New Look in post-war Britain was, in part, due to its symbolic break with wartime austerity and the opportunities it offered to indulge in the pleasures of femininity. The New Look was certainly influential, and was popularised not only through Hollywood's love affair with the style (Turim 1990) but also through changes in fashion production and retailing. The New Look was not restricted to the rarefied world of *haute couture* but made accessible to far more women through both the rise of ready-to-wear fashion and the expansion of mass-market high street fashion chains such as Marks and Spencer (Partington 1993; Dorner 1995). However, the New Look also faced heavy criticism: not only was it seen as a symbolic threat to women's independence, but it was also interpreted as a threat to both the post-war economy (because of its extravagant use of material), and to standards of 'good taste' (Wilson 1985).

During the war, and until the end of clothes rationing in 1949, most clothing in the UK was produced under the Government's Utility Scheme where top British designers were brought in to design 'quality' clothing for mass-production. The Utility scheme was officially governed by the economic principle of making the best use of scarce resources. Although economics partly influenced the idea that simplicity was good and extravagance bad, the virtues of simplicity in design also coincided with the ideals of modernism and some designers also saw the scheme as an opportunity to reform the nation's dress-sense (McNeil 1993, 284). Although clothes rationing ended in 1949, in the 1950s the design profession through bodies such as the Council of Industrial Design, hoped to continue to exert an influence on the nation's clothes by educating the consumer to make proper choices from the new consumer goods available. Just as the design establishment attempted to educate the working-class consumer into the values of simplicity and functionalism over decoration and clutter in their household choices, so they also attempted to educate working-class women's dress-sense into their notions of 'good taste' (Partington 1993). (See Chapter 6 for an extended discussion of these issues.) For these reasons, Utility styles continued to exert a significant influence on notions of fashionable femininity. For example, the 1940s shirt-waister dress became so popular in the post-war period that 'it became almost symbolic of the housewife' (Partington 1993, 154). Furthermore, the design professionals believed that the Utility suit provided an ideal 'image of "modern" femininity, that is, the sensible and restrained attributes of the housewife' (p. 155). Such clothes, it was believed, would enable the housewife to function most effectively within her workplace, the home.

Therefore, in the post-war period, there were two competing definitions of fashionable femininity: the glamorous and romantic New Look and the 'sensible' housewife look. Writing about the US in the period, Schreier identifies the way in which women were invited to shift between these two feminine identities, 'the dutiful homemaker and tempting siren ... Fashion encouraged women to become chameleon-like characters, shifting effortlessly from wholesome homemaker to wanton lover with a change of clothes' (1984, 13). In the UK, as Angela Partington argues, women were being educated to develop a 'taste' for 'restraint' and 'practicality' in their roles as home-makers but 'feminine glamour was being promoted as a feature of high fashion' (1993, 155). The design establishment believed that both styles could co-exist as long as each style was matched to the 'appropriate' situation. For Partington 'this attempt to construct clear distinctions between the utilitarian/practical and the decorative/glamorous and to impose codes of dress as a consequence, inadvertently encouraged consumers to acquire knowledges and competences which enabled them to be "chameleon-like" in the production of different femininities' (p. 155). However, the consumer skills that women acquired would also allow them to break the rules of 'proper' consumption and develop 'improper' uses of fashion by mixing and sampling the two styles together.

Partington identifies these 'hybrid' fashions as characteristic of postwar 'popular' fashion. Working-class women drew on their class-specific consumer skills to mix the decorative and the practical and produced fashions which broke with designers' conception of two separate looks. For example, women incorporated some of the decorative or glamorous elements of the New Look into their working wardrobe (p. 158). To illustrate this, Partington discusses a photograph of her mother in the early 1950s wearing a dress that combined the bodice of the shirtwaister with the skirt of the New Look to produce a style that 'was "free" and comfortable rather than restrictive and ornamental, allowing it to be worn in an "everyday" way rather than for evenings or special occasions' (p. 159). By mixing the practical and the glamorous, working-class women not only challenged 'the dichotomy separating "housewife" (functional woman) and "sex object" (decorative woman)' but also totally redefined the meaning of the clothes: they used 'clothes in meaning-making practices which are dependent on class-specific skills' (pp. 159–60).

Partington's analysis challenges many assumptions about femininity and fashion that have been encountered so far in this chapter. First, she challenges the idea that fashion systems prescribe meanings that are simply reproduced in consumption practices: women use fashion to negotiate feminine identities, not to simply reproduce them. Furthermore, as her study shows, women used clothes to negotiate class-specific forms of femininity. This suggests that clothing is not only used to produce and reproduce feminine identities, but also classed, 'racial', generational, sexual or ethnic identities. Second, Partington challenges the idea that the political meanings of different fashions can be simply read-off from the clothes themselves without looking at them in use. Feminist criticism which simply equates an object such as the stiletto with women's oppression misses how the stiletto in use was capable of generating a far greater range of meanings: for example, it might signify female power and an assertive female sexuality (Wright 1995). Third, Partington challenges the cultural hierarchies which see working-class women's fashion practices (and, indeed, most women's fashion practices) as 'uninteresting'. Working-class female fashions have often been seen as merely diluted and less adventurous versions of high fashion. Partington questions the idea that working-class fashion seeks to emulate higher class fashions, by demonstrating how working-class women used the language of clothes to assert their class difference. Furthermore, she challenges the theoretical frameworks, discussed in the last section, which have dismissed working-class women's fashion practices as merely 'conformist' and 'uninteresting'.

Fashion knowledges and feminine selves

Whereas many early feminist critiques of fashion argued that clothes masked a 'real' female self, more recently a number of feminist critics have explored how everyday fashion and beauty practices work to construct, produce or 'perform' a feminine self. While from the critical distance of modernist aesthetics 'mainstream' women's fashions may seem homogeneous, this misses the complex decisions, and the creativity, pleasure and the pain, that negotiating a feminine 'look' demands. If, as Partington argues, clothes are a 'complex language', then the ways in which we use this language involves the acquisition of particular cultural knowledge, competences and codes. Competence in using the language of clothes has often been seen as a specifically feminine competence, but it is important to remember that these competences are marked by the accents of class, 'race', ethnicity, age, and so on. This is partly recognised in the ways in which clothes are designed, marketed and mediated for different market segments rather than for a mass-market of women. For example, different 'feminine' looks are sharply distinguished by age and therefore, the relationship between fashion and femininity will be sharply distinguished between, for example, *Just Seventeen, Marie Claire* and *Good Housekeeping*. Nevertheless, most women's magazines, like cinema and novels, are crucial arenas for educating women in what and where to buy clothing and how to use and transform these commodities into a particular look (Winship, 1987, 48). This section thinks about fashion as part of consumer culture and concentrates on how women's magazines and the cinema perform a crucial function in inviting women to consume and educating them in how to put what together. However, as Chapter 3 suggested, women may also gain pleasure from these cultural forms because they offer opportunities to exercise feminine consumer competences and skills.

Chapter 3 explored how cinema has addressed women as consumers and was a site for the dissemination of consumer knowledges and competences. Historical studies of film have emphasised the way in which cinema has acted as a 'shop window': not only have films been used as a showcase for consumer goods, the use of tie-ins allows both the film and the commodities highlighted by them to be displayed together (Eckert 1990, 106). Furthermore, in the 1940s and 1950s, 'cinema chains were built near shopping areas, and the matinee screenings encouraged women to combine shopping with a visit to the cinema' (Stacey 1994, 180). More recently in Hollywood, invitations to consume range from what has become known as 'product placement' (for example, a lingering shot on an AppleMac computer) through the popularisation of particular looks (for example, the *Annie Hall* look; the *Pretty Woman*-style spotty dress) to more general constructions of what is desirable and stylish. Furthermore, merchandising has also become crucial in these processes with items such as *Lion King* lunch boxes and *Malcolm X* baseball caps.

Charlotte Herzog has discussed the ways in which, from 1910 onwards, tie-ins between women's fashions and movies were designed to promote both products and helped educate women in how particular products could 'perform' (1990, 134). Herzog focuses on the ways in which fashion-show sequences were used in Hollywood to allow the female viewer to see how elements of a style were put together. Female viewers 'learn how to transform themselves into a "look" by comparison with another woman who is "looked at"' (p. 159). Hollywood stars have also played a central role in promoting fashion and beauty products. For example, Jackie Stacey notes how 'star styles displayed on the screen were quickly reproduced as a line of clothing in department stores' and the appearance of stars in magazines was also a crucial way of promoting fashionable styles (1994, 182). Critics such as Doane have seen women as being doubly subordinated through being positioned by cinema as both passive spectators and consumers, arguing that women purchase commodities to produce themselves as objects of the 'male gaze'. However, as was argued in both Chapter 3 and Chapter 6, notions of the passive female spectator and the passive female consumer have been questioned by many feminist critics. Stacey's research, discussed in Chapter 3, demonstrated that although Hollywood cinema did construct the female spectator as a consumer, women 'also used commodities connected with stars in ways that do not conform to the needs of the market (both in its marital and economic senses)' (1994, 189). Many of Stacey's respondents enthusiastically recount their investment in star styles and star images, talking about the ways in which they drew on star images in putting together a 'look'. While, this could be seen as the passive reproduction of feminine ideals of the period, Stacey argues that feminine consumption was far more contradictory. For example, by adopting the glamorous and sexy fashions of American stars, Stacey argues that women challenged what was seen as 'restrictive British femininity, be it "the dowdiness of women in wartime Britain, the restrictions of factory regulations about hairstyles or the perceived lack of glamour of motherhood ... the reproduction of self-images through consumption was perceived as a way of producing new forms of "American" feminine identity which were exciting, pleasurable, and in some ways transgressive' (p. 205).

If cinema has played a role in educating women in the knowledges, skills and competences that are necessary to sustain new consumer markets, then it also offers women an opportunity to use these feminine competences in watching a film. Indeed, attention to clothing details in films and fiction have often been thought of as a 'homage to woman's "preoccupations"' (Gaines 1990a, 19). Costume has often been used to support a film's narrative and acts as the 'key to the personality of the wearer' (Gaines 1990b, 184). The ability to 'read' film costume can, therefore, offer an additional source of meaning and pleasure within screen fictions, although as Partington has argued, to the audience skilled in reading clothes, it can also make 'the plot structure somewhat redundant' (1991, 62). Costume is also a crucial mechanism through which 'femininity' is performed in cinema. While narratives which centre on the transformation of a female protagonist are far from new (*Now Voyager* is often cited as a 'classic' example), Charlotte Brunsdon has argued that in recent Hollywood cinema, shopping and trying-on-clothes sequences highlight the ways in which women 'can try on identities and adopt them': for example, in *Pretty Woman* (1990) and *Working Girl* (1989) (1997, 86). These films invite us to distinguish between different femininities and highlight the ways femininity is 'performed', and can therefore be transformed, through the use of commodities. Tess (Melanie Griffith) in *Working Girl*, in order to progress from secretary to executive, needs to effect a transformation in which she takes off the loud and gaudy styles which announce her as both a secretary and working class, and to adopt the simpler and more 'classic', 'power-dressed' style of the executive (Brunsdon, 1997, Entwistle, 1997).

Although this section has concentrated on cinema, other media forms are also resources for learning to construct the feminine self. Indeed, as Brunsdon notes, the emphasis on femininity as a 'performance' is a longstanding feature of women's magazines (magazines are discussed in more detail in Chapter 8). Similarly, breakfast and daytime TV in the UK has shown an increasing fondness for 'make-over' features which again construct a narrative of transformation and offer advice not only on how to realise a new feminine self but also how to switch between feminine selves. The ways in which clothing is mediated, therefore, demonstrates that the *play* with identity, the ability to make ourselves over through fashion, is part of everyday cultural competences.

Fashioning the feminine self

The last two sections have explored the ways in which everyday fashion practices do not simply reproduce femininity but involve the production of a feminine self. Women are educated in consumer competences which suggest that femininity, rather than simply being natural, has to be 'put together'. This is not to argue that films do not work to naturalise femininity and there is no notion of a 'natural' feminine look. Just as some second-wave feminists believed in the possibility of a 'natural' from of female-ness that was 'outside' of fashion, so many narratives of transformation also privilege the idea of revealing a 'natural' feminine self. For example, while *Pretty Woman* centres on the transformation of Vivian (Julia Roberts) from a hooker in 'street clothes' into a 'princess' fit for her prince, Edward, Charlotte Brunsdon argues that 'Vivian is shown to be already "pretty" *before* she gets the accoutrements of expensive femininity' (Brunsdon 1997, 99). She argues that 'the transformation achieved through the series of expensive outfits . . . implicitly uses a model of natural femininity. In the shopping trip Edward's credit card buys for Vivien what she already deserves' (*ibid.*, 100). However, while the notion of a 'natural' femininity – a 'natural' beauty – is a popular one across media forms, it is often contra-dicted by the presentation of the 'natural look' as one look among a range of feminine looks. For example, the fashion and beauty pages in women's magazines present looking 'natural' as some-thing which must be achieved: intensive skin care is demanded for a 'natural' complexion and applying a range of products such as tinted moisturisers, brown mascara and 'barely there' lip colour are demanded for 'a natural look'. Furthermore, as Evans and Thornton argue, what the 'natural look' looks like changes over time (1989, 14). Therefore, the ways in which we are instructed on how to construct our 'natural' feminine selves, means that women are used to seeing the 'natural' as a 'performance'.

The ways in which knowledge about fashion and beauty is mediated does not present women with a single definition of femininity but a range of feminine 'looks'. Furthermore, women are often encouraged not only to select a feminine look, but also to move between feminine looks. As Wilson has argued, from the nineteenth century onwards, fashion has been used to demarcate different roles: as sub-divisions in dress have increased, clothes come to represent 'a socially defined time of day, or occasion, or an individual state of feeling' (1985, 35). The construction of different feminine roles through different clothes was also illus-trated in Partington's work on the New Look: the recognition of the elements which we use to produce different femininities allowed women to produce hybrid forms of dress and femininity. Partington's study also revealed the ways in which working class-women used clothes to articulate an identity which was both gendered and classed. Other critics have noted how fashion can be used to create 'hybrid' identities in which different traditions are spliced together to negotiate new ways of being. For example, young British-Asian women often find themselves caught between two identities, 'British on the streets; Asian at home'. However, by fusing elements of Asian and British dress to create a hybrid style it becomes possible to think of being an Asian woman and being a British woman together and to resist traditional cultural categories which keep these identities apart (Khan 1993, 68).

Recent feminist critics have not only highlighted the ways in which fashion and beauty practices can be used as a form of resistance by women, but also the modes of feminine pleasure produced by these practices. For example, Hilary Radner has noted a shift in the ways in which 'making up' is presented in both the editorial and advertising content of women's magazines. She argues that from the late 1970s onwards, beauty products have been aimed increasingly at the independent woman who wants to gratify herself in an attempt to bring together the 'seemingly contradictory demands of femininity and autonomy' (1989, 304). While women have often been seen to buy into the false promises of beauty products, Radner argues that if women are thought of as 'buying an activity', and 'if a woman takes pleasure in making up, she received the product for which she has paid' (p. 306). Making up, therefore, is considered as a pleasurable feminine practice. Although women are subject to ideas about feminine beauty and feminine grooming, Radner argues that beauty practices are primarily performed for the self because the results of using a face mask, an eye gel or an 'instant beauty' fluid 'are usually imperceptible to anyone but the practitioner herself' (p. 311). The investment of large amounts of money on beauty products 'is pleasurable precisely because it is excessive' (p. 311).

However, while fashion and beauty practices can be thought of as pleasurable feminine practices, consumption cannot only be equated with pleasure and leisure. Joanne Entwistle's analysis of 'power dressing' demonstrates how the idea of 'dressing for success' required 'a new attitude to consumption which sees it as serious labour' (1997, 323). Dress manuals such as John Molloy's *Dress for Success* (1975) advised the aspiring female executive on the science of 'wardrobe engineering'. If a woman wanted to get to the top in business or the professions, these manuals claimed, she needed to abandon buying clothes for aesthetic and emotional reasons, and instead take a scientific approach to fashioning a professional self. As Entwistle argues, power dressing 'was to play an important part in structuring the career woman's everyday experience of herself, serving as a mode of self-presentation that enabled her to *construct* herself and be *recognised* as an executive or business career woman' (1997, 312). Dressing for success was part of a wider discourse in the 1980s through which a new type of feminine identity, 'the career woman', was produced. Power dressing provided the professional working woman 'with a means to *fashion* herself *as* a career woman' and, therefore, produce a new 'feminine' self (p. 315). The idea of 'dressing for success', Entwistle argues, 'advises career women to treat their dress as part of the work they must put in in order to increase their chances of success' (p. 322). In this way, she identifies a new attitude to consumption as labour rather than pleasure, which differs from, for example, consumption as domestic labour or the labour involved in producing the feminine self more generally. Crucially, power dressing is both represented and experienced by women as part of their working lives.

Entwistle's analysis also raises another key point about the ways in which feminine selves are constructed and performed through fashion by emphasising the way in which power dressing didn't just enable women to appear as career women but experience themselves as career women. This point is taken further by Efrat Tseëlon who argues that just because the appearance of femininity is culturally constructed does not mean that women cannot experience femininity as 'real' (1995, 34). Tseëlon notes how writings on fashion and femininity have tended to ignore women's experience of fashion and, drawing on interview data, she explores how 'sartorial identities are related to ... [women's] sense of self' (p. 39). She argues that 'the act of representation modifies the nature of the represented object', that is, the woman herself (p. 3). In this way, women can be thought of as both active in producing a feminine self while their consciousness of themselves is also transformed by this activity. Tseelon's work offers a useful corrective to some of the studies of fashion which simply assume how women experience clothes.

Like Tseëlon, Skeggs examines women's experience of cloth-ing. Skeggs, like Partington, is interested in the ways in which class cuts across the production of gendered selves through fashion but, in the process, also demonstrates the ways in which fashion might not only be a source of resistance, empowerment and pleasure, but also pain. Her study of white, working-class women, introduced in Chapter 6, shows that putting together a particular look not only involves the construction of a gendered self, but also a classed self. The ways in which the women in her study 'perform' femininity through their fashion practices is also crucially an attempt to put together a 'respectable' feminine 'look' which distanced themselves from the signs of 'working-classness'. This is clearly articulated in the way in which one of the women attempts to distance herself from the 'tartiness' which informs representations of working-class women by simulating an 'elegant' and 'classy' look informed by representations of middle-class women (Skeggs 1997, 84–5). Similarly, a number of the women in her study worked on their bodies through exercise to distance themselves from the fat body, the body 'out of control', which is often equated with working-classness. For many of these women, clothing could be used to distance themselves from what they did not want to be. However, any pleasure or sense of empowerment which could be gained from fashion practices was always threatened by the possibility that other people might judge them, a situation which produces, and is produced by, an intense sense of pain and injury.

This chapter has explored the ways in which feminine identities are constructed and negotiated through fashion and beauty practices. Feminist criticism has moved from thinking about the possibility of getting outside of fashion and throwing off a feminine 'mask' to thinking about fashion as a site of struggle over the meaning of gendered identities (Wilson 1985). For this reason, it is crucial to explore how clothing is used to construct and negotiate the meaning of femininity in specific historical contexts. Just as Partington's study offered a way of understanding working-class women's response to the dual feminine images promoted in the post-war period, so Entwistle's study demonstrates how the dressed-for-success, 'enterprising' feminine self was a product of both changing discourses of women and work and the 'enterprise culture' of the 1980s. Skeggs' work also acts as an important reminder that the ability to play freely with identity through clothing, which has been claimed to be a feature of postmodernism, is not a free-for-all. While women can experience fashion as freedom and pleasure, women who are positioned as 'other' do not construct the feminine self from a position in which they feel 'right' and 'legitimate' in what they do: they are aware that they may be judged and found to be 'lacking' in some way.

Notes

1 Indeed, Brownmiller goes much further in her critique of feminine dress. For example, she argues that she will not wear skirts because 'I don't like this artificial gender distinction. Because I don't wish to start shaving my legs again. Because I don't want to return to the expense and aggravation of nylons. Because I will not reacquaint myself with the discomfort of feminine shoes. Because I'm at peace with the freedom and comfort of trousers ... Because I remember resenting the enormous amount of thinking time I used to pour into superficial upkeep concerns, and because the nature of feminine dressing is superficial in essence – even my objections seem superficial as I write them down. But that is the point. To care about feminine fashion, and do it well, is to be obsessively involved in inconsequential details on a serious basis.' (1984, 81).

Further reading

Ash, J. and Wilson, E., eds, *Chic Thrills: A Fashion Reader* (Berkeley and Los Angeles, University of California Press, 1993)

Barnard, M. *Fashion as Communication* (London, Routledge, 1996)

Entwistle, J. 'Power Dressing' and the Construction of the Career Woman, in M. Nava *et al.*, eds, *Buy This Book: Studies in Advertising and Consumption* (London, Routledge, 1997)

Evans, C. and Thornton, M. *Women and Fashion: A New Look* (London, Quartet, 1989)

Gaines, J. and Herzog, C., eds, *Fabrications: Costume and the Female Body* (New York, Routledge, 1990)

Wilson, E. *Adorned in Dreams: Fashion and Modernity* (London, Virago, 1985)

Wright, L. Objectifying Gender: The Stiletto Heel, in J. Attfield and P. Kirkham, eds, *A View from the Interior: Women and Design* (1995 edition), (London, Women's Press, 1995)

8
Youth cultures
and popular music

Debates about youth cultures have traditionally been identified with debates about changes in society. In feminist studies of youth culture, therefore, there is often a concern with the extent to which youth cultures reproduce gender inequalities and 'damaging' modes of femininity or, alternatively, whether youth cultures are sites in which new, more 'progressive' modes of femininity are produced which challenge or resist existing gender relations. While popular music has been seen as an important element of youth cultures, the study of pop has become an increasingly dynamic field in its own right over the past fifteen years. However, questions about gender have been marginalised in the ways in which media and cultural studies has approached both youth culture and popular music. This chapter analyses why many studies of youth and pop have been blind both to questions about gender and to feminist concerns, and examines the work of critics who have made an intervention in these fields.

The chapter tackles four key areas. The first section examines work on youth subcultures within cultural studies. Sections two and three explore the work of feminist critics (in particular, Angela McRobbie) who have analysed how feminine identities are constructed and negotiated in girls' magazines and the extent to which these magazines have changed since the 1960s. Sections four and five examine debates about whether pop songs reproduce gender inequalities or whether women's use of pop – for example, in the activities associated with fandom – might be empowering. The final section considers the relationships between women's music-making and feminism. The chapter as a whole is concerned with the extent to which youth culture and popular music reproduce wider gender inequalities and divisions. Furthermore, it analyses the extent to which youth cultures and popular music offer spaces in which what it means to be a woman can be negotiated and in which 'alternative' feminine identities can be produced.

Youth subcultures, subcultural theory and femininity

The agenda for work on youth subcultures within cultural studies has been heavily influenced by three key books produced at the Centre for Contemporary Cultural Studies in the 1970s: Stuart Hall and Tony Jefferson's edited collection *Resistance Through Rituals* (1976); Paul Willis's *Learning to Labour* (1977); and Dick Hebdige's *Subculture* (1979). In response to earlier work which had assumed that youth shared a common experience and a common youth culture, these critics argued that class differences cut across generational experience to produce different experiences of youth. In particular, they examined how some working-class youths produced their own distinctive youth subcultures. For these critics, while many working-class youths' cultural practices could be understood in relation to their working-class 'parent' culture, some young people produced a distinctive youth subculture which is informed not only by this class culture, but also by a distinctive, and historically specific generational experience: 'Through dress, activities, leisure pursuits and life-style, they may project a different cultural response or "solution" to the problems posed for them by their material and social class position and experience' (Clarke *et al.* 1976, 56–7).

However, there were significant differences in the focus of these studies. For example, Willis's work was also an intervention into debates in the sociology of education and centred on the ways a group of 'lads' in a secondary school drew on their working-class culture to 'resist' attempts to 'school' them, while *Resistance through Rituals* and *Subculture* were more concerned with the history of post-war British 'spectacular' youth subcultures (teds, mods, skinheads, punks, etc.). However, these subcultural theorists shared a common interest in how subcultures were a means through which working-class youth challenged, and attempted to resist, the dominant culture. In this way, an emphasis on class struggle and class politics structured subcultural theories, and questions about sexual politics and gender were marginalised.

All of these critics also created cultural distinctions between members of youth subcultures and the 'mainstream', the majority of young people. For these critics, youth subcultures are valued positively because, it is supposed, they are *actively produced* by young people themselves; they are defined by their distance from *commerce*; they are therefore more '*authentic*'; they are a means by which young people express their *difference*; and they are *deviant, resistant* and *oppositional*. In this way, members of youth subcultures are distinguished (in both senses of the word) from the majority of young people who, it is claimed, implicitly or explicitly, *passively reproduce* what is offered them by the dominant culture; consume a ready-made *commercially produced* youth culture; are therefore '*inauthentic*'; are *homogeneous*; and are '*straight*' and *conformist*. However, a further opposition can be mapped on to these claims: the characteristics associated with youth subcultures are ones that are commonly associated with 'masculinity', and the characteristics associated with the 'mainstream' are ones that are commonly associated with 'femininity'. This is compounded by the ways in which subcultural theories have tended to see youth subcultures as inherently male and masculine (Thornton, 1995).

These subcultural theories are rich, engaging and complex works which have been hugely influential. However, while there have been numerous criticisms of them, this section focuses on feminist responses to subcultural theory and, in particular, on the work of Angela McRobbie who has asked why 'the very term subculture has acquired such masculine overtones' (Garber and McRobbie 1991, 3).[1] First, she argues that it is necessary to explore whether girls are actually absent from youth subcultures or whether they have simply been written out of subcultural histories. Second, if there is lower female participation in subcultures, then it is necessary, she claims, to examine how subcultures work to exclude girls by reproducing gender inequalities. Third, if subcultures are masculine and male-dominated, it is necessary to consider whether young women produce their own distinctively feminine cultural response to their gendered, classed and generational experience.

Girls, of course, are not totally absent from youth subcultures, but they are relatively absent in both subcultural theory and the subcultures themselves. The distinction between the public, masculine sphere and the private, feminine sphere structures access to subcultures. Subcultural theorists in their emphasis on deviant youth have tended to see 'the street' as 'the home' of the subculture. Yet as McRobbie points out, 'the street' has never been seen as a safe or respectable place for women to hang out. In this way, the gendering of space (see Chapter 6) means girls are less likely to participate in many subcultures.

However, subcultures which are located in clubs, and where dance is a central focus of the subculture, may offer more opportunities for girls (Garber and McRobbie 1991). Indeed, this could explain why there is a relatively large female involvement in recent rave, dance and club cultures. However, subcultural theory has underplayed the importance of dance because it is commonly seen as 'trivial' and 'feminine', 'a ritual without resistance' (McRobbie 1991, 197). Yet, in some subcultures, such as rave, where dance 'becomes the motivating force for the whole subculture', feminine competences are given recognition (McRobbie 1994, 168).[2]

If dancing is usually seen as feminine, then so are fashion and style. However, for critics such as Hebdige, 'the style of a subculture is primarily that of its men' (McRobbie 1991, 24). For Hebdige, a key form of subcultural resistance is articulated through the production of a distinctive subcultural style which disrupts and subverts taken-for-granted hegemonic meanings (see Chapter 7). However, although subcultural styles have disrupted 'naturalised' meanings, they have frequently reproduced the meaning of gender differences – 'it is punk girls who wear suspenders after all' (McRobbie 1991, 26). Furthermore, when subcultures did offer an 'escape' from traditional gender roles, these opportunities for escape were mainly for men. For example, Hebdige examines how members of the Bowie subculture challenged 'at a symbolic level the "inevitability", the "naturalness" of class and gender stereotypes' (1979, 89). However, while male participants in this subculture, and the later New Romantics, may have had the opportunity to play with the boundaries of masculinity and femininity, 'gender experimentation, sexual ambiguity and homosexuality among girls are viewed differently' (McRobbie 1991, 27). However, this is not to suggest that female subcultural styles simply reproduce ideas about 'natural' femininity: they are often more contradictory. For example, while some feminists have been appalled by the use of pornographic imagery by punk girls in their ensembles of rubber wear, stockings and suspenders, these aggressive styles could also be seen to mock 'normal' ideas of feminine prettiness and passivity.[3]

One aspect of women's contribution to subcultures that has been frequently neglected, McRobbie argues, is their role in the production and retailing of subcultural styles. The 'mundane act of buying' was ignored by subcultural theorists because shopping was seen as a 'feminine' activity. Indeed, the idea that styles could be bought contradicted the notion that subcultures produced their shocking styles in 'an act of creative defiance' (McRobbie 1994, 136). As McRobbie has noted, it is often women who both produce and sell subcultural clothing and accessories in places such as London's Camden Market and Manchester's Affleck's Palace.

Sarah Thornton's *Club Cultures* offers a further explanation of why youth subcultures are 'masculine' spaces. Thornton notes that the emphasis on resistance, authenticity and 'hipness' in subcultural theory reproduces the ways in which subcultures see themselves in relation to the 'inferior' 'mainstream'. Being a member of a subculture is about 'hipness' and 'coolness', and being 'hip' is a form of what Thornton (drawing on Bourdieu) calls 'subcultural capital'. Subcultural capital is 'objectified or embodied' in having the right look, the right record collection and in being 'in the know', all of which appear to be 'second nature' rather than something that has to be worked at (1995, 11–12). Subcultural capital is obviously distributed along age lines, but after age it 'is aligned most systematically with gender' (p. 13). 'Hip' boys in club cultures gain a sense of distinction from their musical preferences: girls often feel unable to compete in the 'game of "hipness", they will often defend their tastes ... with expressions like "It's crap but I like it"' (p. 13).

The idea that the 'hip' subcultural world is masculine, and the 'unhip', 'mainstream' feminine, is also reaffirmed by the way 'hip' clubbers in Thornton's study imagine their own place in the world in relation to the homogeneous 'others' in the 'Chartpop disco', 'a place where "Sharon and Tracy dance around their handbags"' (p. 99). The imagined activities of respectable working-class women help to confirm the 'hip' clubbers' sense of distinction: 'Sharons and Tracys' were seen to be 'overwhelmingly interested in the sexual and social rather than musical aspects of clubs' (p. 99). This characterisation 'is not primarily a vilification or veneration of girls' sexuality (although that gets brought in), but a position statement made by youth of both genders about girls who are not culturally "one of the boys"' (p. 104). Subcultural knowledges and competences can, in this way, be understood as masculine, although they can be 'acquired' by girls. The ways in which subcultural theory splits the world up into the stylish, resisting subculture and the 'normal' conforming 'mainstream' reproduces rather than analyses these distinctions.

It is, therefore, not surprising that subcultural theory cannot deal with the experience of many young women. When 'youth' is equated with boys, and 'youth subcultures' are equated with 'radical', 'hip' boys, it is unsurprising that when girls mime to Wham, Take That or Eternal on the dance floor, they are seen as irrelevant or worse.

If youth subcultures operate to exclude women, and are often defined and given coherence by a rejection of the feminine, then it is necessary to consider whether there are ways in which 'young girls interact among themselves ... to form a distinctive culture of their own' (Garber and McRobbie 1991, 11). Although McRobbie has addressed this question from a number of angles, there are several themes that run through her analysis of femininity and youth culture. First, she is concerned with how young women negotiate what it means to be a teenage girl and 'win space' for themselves. Second, she has analysed the ways in which the cultural forms and practices of young women reproduce 'traditional' modes of femininity in which girls are prepared for their future roles as wives and mothers. Third, McRobbie has also identified transformations in teenage femininities, which begin to challenge these earlier orthodoxies. Fourth, because girls' cultures are often produced drawing on commercial, mass-produced forms such as girls' magazines, they have been vilified by subcultural theorists. However, McRobbie argues that young women make active use of a range of commercial cultural forms produced for them, and integrate them into a range of cultural practices. Finally, McRobbie notes how teenage girls are subject to spatial controls and family responsibilities that are less likely to effect boys. Therefore, girls' cultures are usually less visible because they are an attempt to 'win space' within the home.

In the mid-1970s, McRobbie drew on these ideas in an attempt to make young women's cultural practices visible by producing an ethnographic study of the lived culture of a group of working-class young women. If Willis's *Learning to Labour* had produced an account of how boys drew on their class background to produce their own distinctive subculture within the school, then McRobbie set out to explore what girls 'actually do' (1991, 35). She demonstrated how the girls in her study were born into a 'culture of femininity' which is transmitted to them by other women in the family and which the girls reworked and used as a cultural resource. The 'culture of femininity' was also informed by the mass-produced commercial culture that catered for teenage girls: magazines such as *Jackie* and teenage fashions. The girls used the 'culture of femininity' to 'win space' for themselves within the school, the youth club and the family home.

For example, the girls drew on the 'culture of femininity' to make the experience of school meaningful to them: they rejected the school's agenda and replaced it with their own by adapting the school uniform to make it fashionable and by reading *Jackie* in class. The girls rejected and resisted the school's attempts to prepare them for working-class female occupations because they had a different sense of their future careers: the 'culture of femininity' placed value on the roles of wife and mother and this was how they understood their future. The ways in which they 'replaced the official ideology of the school with their informal feminine culture' indicates 'the importance of family and domestic life to the girls' (McRobbie 1991, 51). They believed that it was the family, rather than the school, which provided them with 'really useful knowledge' for later life. However, while the girls *produced* their own cultural response in order to resist and oppose the school, they also ended up *reproducing* the roles required of them as working-class women in a capitalist society by seeing marriage and motherhood as a form of 'election'. One of the key mechanisms for securing these girls' consent to the role of wife and mother, McRobbie argues, is the 'ideology of romance' promoted in publications such as *Jackie*. This is the subject of the next section.

Teenage femininities and girls' magazines (1): *Jackie* and its readers

For feminist critics, girls' magazines have been seen as significant because of their power to define and shape teenage femininities.[4] Angela McRobbie has been central in analysing girls' magazines and the shifts in her own work have shaped, and been shaped by, wider transformations in feminist cultural studies. In her early work, as she has recently argued, the opposition between 'feminism' and 'femininity' were central 'framing devices' in staking out this field of study (1996, 172). In some ways, this reproduces the opposition between the subcultural and the mainstream discussed in the previous section: a feminist radical minority culture is opposed to a feminine conformist majority culture. For feminists in the mid-1970s, 'virtually everything in the women's magazine connects with oppression' (p. 172). However,

McRobbie argues, shifts in both feminist theories and girls' magazines in the 1980s and 1990s have broken down the opposition between feminism and femininity: magazines such as *Just Seventeen*, and *More!* have negotiated forms of 'popular feminism' and there is 'a greater degree of fluidity about what femininity means' (McRobbie 1994, 157; see also, Winship 1985) In this way, feminist theories about girls' magazines can be read as a product of their time in the same way that the magazines themselves are.

McRobbie's work from the mid-1970s to early 1980s on the girls' magazine *Jackie* is framed by the opposition between feminist and feminine identities. *Jackie* was the best-selling girls' magazine of the period and McRobbie demonstrated how the ideology of teenage femininity in *Jackie* was organised around romance and produced a damaging form of feminine subjectivity: girls were encouraged to see the pursuit of romance as the most important feature of their lives. The 'code of romance' which is 'concerned with the narrow and restricted world of the emotions' is outlined most forcefully in the stories which are one of the main ingredients of *Jackie* (1991, 95). While, on the one hand, the world of romantic relationships is presented as fun, on the other, it is presented as deadly serious and 'the essence and meaning of life' (p. 96). For McRobbie the messages produced by *Jackie* stories are 'limited and unambiguous': '1. the girl has to fight to get and keep her man; 2. she can never trust another woman unless she is old and "hideous" in which case she does not appear in these stories anyway; 3. despite this, romance, and being a girl, are fun' (p. 101). In this way, McRobbie argues that *Jackie* centres around 'romantic individualism': there are no opportunities for female solidarity because all girls are in competition for the 'right boy' and 'true love'. In *Jackie*, to be a girl is to be immersed in a world of the emotions, in which romance displaces 'all ... traces of adolescent sexuality' (p. 107).

This conservative and conformist femininity, McRobbie argues, is also reproduced in other parts of the magazine. The problem pages are based on values which 'are wholly conservative and endorse uncritically the traditional female role' (p. 110). Fashion and beauty pages are equally problematic: beautification is equated with 'self-improvement' and the conservative, neat and matching fashions suggest that a girl's appearance should 'please both boyfriend and boss alike and threaten the authority of neither' (p. 125). The pop pages are not interested in music but stars, offering their readers yet 'another opportunity to indulge their emotions, but this time on the pop-star figure rather than the boyfriend' (p. 127).

Although McRobbie aimed to validate girls' magazines as worthy of cultural analysis, her aim was not to validate *Jackie* but demonstrate the damage it did to young women. The different parts of the magazine discussed above equated being a woman with entering into the 'world of the personal and the emotions' (p. 131). This extremely narrow definition of teenage femininity, McRobbie argued, made 'it difficult for readers to imagine alternatives' (1981, 115). Once locked into the ideology of romance, girls saw their futures in terms of being wives and mothers, their 'feminine' careers totally at odds with the project of feminism. As McRobbie has herself more recently acknowledged, this 'emphasis on ideology also presupposed some state of purity, knowledge and truth outside ideology, a space which in those early days feminism felt itself to occupy' (1996, 174).

In his critique of McRobbie, Martin Barker picks up on this issue. He argues that critics often seem to 'begin with a model of what ought to happen in stories for girls – the kind of anti-sexist messages they want to put across. Anything that does not conform to that is then accused of doing the opposite' (1989, 135). This has implications for the ways in which critics read *Jackie* and the assumptions they make about how it is read by teenage girls. McRobbie's reading of *Jackie* as a monolithic ideological bloc is achieved by privileging some aspects of the magazine over others, by assuming that different parts of the magazine work together to form a 'unified text' and, in the process, by ironing out contradictions in *Jackie*. Furthermore, Barker argues, there is no singular *Jackie* ideology – even in its romantic fiction – because *Jackie* changed over time. For example, while McRobbie argued that the ideology of 'romantic individualism' creates mistrust between girls, Barker's analysis shows how 'Girls are regularly advised to value their female friendships' (p. 249).

In this early work, McRobbie assumes that girls passively absorb and reproduce *Jackie*'s ideology of adolescent femininity, a problem she readily acknowledges in her later work. This ignores the way the magazine is integrated into girls' collective cultural practices. Elizabeth Frazer, in her study of girls reading *Jackie*, argues that these girls made an active engagement with the magazine and suggests that 'a self-conscious and reflexive approach to texts is a natural approach for teenage girls' (Frazer 1992, 194).[5] However, the arguments about improvements in girls' magazines in the 1980s and 1990s often still assume that *Jackie* was without contradiction, and its readers passive and isolated. In this way, *Jackie* and its readers are envisaged as the 'other' of contemporary magazines and their readers.

McRobbie's critique of *Jackie* is not only underpinned by an opposition between the feminist and the feminine *Jackie* reader, but also between the 'subcultural' and the 'mainstream'. For example, McRobbie criticises *Jackie*'s fashion coverage because it 'settles for mainstream chain-store style' and ignores the more radical subcultural style of punk (1981, 126). Likewise, the pop pages 'concentrate on mainstream show-biz pop music, they are only interested in commercial pop and rarely show pictures of new wave or more experimental bands' (p. 127).[6] In the process, McRobbie not only distinguishes herself from oppressive aspects of 'conventional' femininity, but also uses her 'subcultural capital' to distinguish herself from the sheer 'unhipness' of 'conventional' femininity. Two overlapping value systems are at play in evaluating the 'real and remarkable shifts' in girls' magazines: progress is evaluated not only in terms of the breakdown of the distinction between feminist and feminine identities, but also in the breakdown of the distinction between (masculine) 'subcultural' and (feminine) 'straight' identities. The feminine is doubly-damned.

Teenage femininities and girls' magazines (2): *Just Seventeen* and *More!*

In the 1980s and 1990s McRobbie turned to the new wave of girls' magazines such as *Just Seventeen* and *More!*. During this period, it was not only the magazines themselves that changed: transformations in feminist cultural theory also changed the ways in which feminists approached them. Feminist cultural critics in the 1980s paid increasing attention to questions about pleasure (see Chapter 5), and, in the process, began to admit their own 'guilty' pleasures in the texts which, as feminists, they 'knew' they 'ought' to be criticising. Once feminists admitted to their own pleasures in cultural forms such as women's magazines, McRobbie argues, this broke 'the barrier which divides feminists from "ordinary" women and girls' (1996, 174). Furthermore, if feminist critics had come out of their encounter with girls' magazines relatively unscathed, then this raised big questions about 'the assumed success of ideology' (p. 174). If feminist critics hadn't been dupes of the ideology of teenage femininity, it was arrogant to assume that 'ordinary women' had been.

The major change which characterises girls' magazines in the 1980s is the decline of romance and the rise of pop as the '*conceptual umbrella*' which gives the magazines their identity. (McRobbie 1991, 168). However, during this period the magazines also increasingly introduced their readers 'to the seduction of buying' (1991, 176). In the new magazines, feminine identities are no longer defined through romance but are shown to be constructed through the use of commodities: for example, in the choice between Oasis and Top Shop for clothes, between a Take That or a Blackstreet CD, between Keanu Reeves and Leonardo DiCaprio. The down-side of this process, McRobbie argues, 'is that readers become more strenuously addressed as consumers' (p. 186). Indeed, Helen Pleasance has argued that although these consumer choices offer a sense of freedom, 'the unending logic of consumption secures an even tighter closure than romance, because dissatisfactions can be assuaged more easily; consumable products are meant to have limited appeal, romantic partners are not' (1991, 77).

However, McRobbie also identifies signs of 'progress' in the treatment of pop in *Just Seventeen*. Although the magazine is primarily interested in pop stars rather than their music, *Just Seventeen* does not present pop stars as figures for emotional investment, but instead simply offers a 'profusion of facts' (McRobbie 1991, 171). However, this information overload on the habits and characters of pop stars is presented in an ironic, knowing way, in a manner that knows 'its silly, but its fun'. These facts are accompanied by a 'profusion of visuals' (p. 171). There is an increased emphasis on an explicitly sexual display of the male body in which the reader is invited to make the star a figure of sexual fantasy.

There is also evidence of 'progress' in the fashion and beauty pages. By learning to construct feminine identities through consumer goods, McRobbie argues, girls are encouraged to experiment and be creative. When *Just Seventeen* encourages girls to achieve their own individual style it may reproduce the '*the language of fun and femininity*' found in *Jackie*, but it also '*takes on a new more confident edge*' (p. 182). This new individuality and confidence, she argues, is an advance on the 'conformity' and 'conservatism' of *Jackie*. Girls, influenced by the pop visuals, are encouraged to put together the new, the second-hand and the customised to create their own 'trademark' look. The fashions display a 'spectacular parade of retro, revivalist subcultures which coexist side by side' (p. 179). While the equation of femininity and prettiness has not been displaced, girls are also encouraged to use style to demonstrate personality and a sense of fun. Therefore, while the new magazines subject girls to a 'hard sell', they also produce a space in which femininities appear to be less fixed and more fluid. For McRobbie, there is 'a redefinition of the feminine self. It can be endlessly constructed, reconstructed and customised. No longer lavishing attention on the male partner, the girl is free to lavish attention on herself and she is helped in this task by the world of consumer goods at her disposal' (1994, 165).

However, it is in *Just Seventeen*'s problem pages that McRobbie finds *'the strongest definitions of teenage femininity'* (1991, 165). Girls are treated as if they are entitled to sexual knowledge, problems such as abuse are discussed, lesbianism is treated as a viable option, and girls are encouraged to be independent and assertive. Although McRobbie is wary of the problem page's 'power to define' teenage sexuality, the discourses of sexuality in *Just Seventeen* are influenced by feminism. While the fashion and beauty pages construct a 'consuming self', the problem pages construct a 'responsible' self (p. 183).

By the 1990s, sex had become the new 'conceptual umbrella' underpinning many women's and girls' magazines, partly fuelled by the recognition that 'sex sells'. However, in magazines such as *More!*, McRobbie argues, there is a new 'boldness (even brashness) in the ways in which women's sexual identities are constructed' (1996, 177). Furthermore, sex is increasingly treated in an 'ironic' and 'knowing' way. This creates an increased sense of detachment and a space for 'a degree of critical reflection on the normative practices of both femininity and sexuality endlessly incited, invoked and otherwise presented as imperative' (p. 178). Rather than presenting sexuality as 'natural', the magazines work to denaturalise sex: 'sex is now recognised as something which has to be learnt' (p. 186).

Therefore, while McRobbie is not claiming that these new magazines are beyond criticism, she argues that the sexual, feminine self found in the new girls' magazines is better than the emotional, feminine self found in *Jackie*. 'The emphasis on female sexual pleasure; the demystification of romance and the idea that female sexual technique has to be learnt and that it is not some magical or mystical effect; the wide availability of information; the assumption that knowledge is power; the attention to sexual health and to equality in social relationships, even the question of sometimes liking what is bad for us; all of these were issues endlessly debated in feminism in the mid-1970s onwards' (1996, 186). Therefore, McRobbie argues, in magazines such as *Just Seventeen* and *More!*, there is evidence to suggest that feminism has entered into popular culture: these magazines construct new modes of feminine subjectivity which might not identify themselves as feminist but, none the less, can no longer operate as the 'other' of feminism.[7]

Furthermore, McRobbie argues, 'girls have changed. They do not want to be represented in a humiliating way. They are not dependent on boys for their own sense of identity' (1994, 164). While this begs the question of whether girls ever wanted 'to be represented in a humiliating way', it also reiterates McRobbie's narrative of progress. The debate on girls' magazines is no longer framed by an opposition between feminism and femininity, but between 'new' femininity and 'old' femininity. Therefore, McRobbie's narrative of 'progress' is partially dependent on the *Jackie*-girl of the 1970s who continues to operate as the incontestably bad 'other', trapped in a living hell of romantic dependence. If the new feminist theoretical approaches were brought to bear on the girl culture of the 1970s, and the femininities of the period were studied historically, a more complex and contradictory picture of 'the *Jackie* reader' might emerge, which would also require a rethinking of the current magazines.

By the 1980s, not only did cultural critics increasingly question the distinction between subcultures and commerce, the same period also saw a proliferation of subcultural styles in which, it was argued, everyone could 'play' with style, and mark out their identities through commodities. This situation, it was claimed, undermined the distinction between subcultures and the mainstream: even clothing outlets such as Miss Selfridge and Top Shop appeared to be offering a range of different styles. McRobbie argues that the *Just Seventeen* girl is invited to mix old with new, customise her jeans and rummage through second-hand stalls in constructing her unique stylised self (although caution is needed in generalising from the pages to the activities of the readership). If the processes of stylisation which once characterised youth subcultures have now gone 'mainstream', this would seem to suggest that the value system by which cultural critics judged subcultures as good, and the 'mainstream' as bad, has been dissolved. However, McRobbie's work is still partially dependent on this opposition. For example, she argues: 'In all these style ideas the influence of punk (the standard item is a pair of ripped Levi 501s) and of Madonna, is most startlingly clear. This is a messy unkempt and exaggerated look. The ideal model is a kind of urban ragamuffin' (1991, 179). However, this 'messy unkempt' look may not appeal to readers of different classes in the same way. As one of the young women in Skeggs' study of young, white, working-class women puts it, 'if you were poor or at least not very well off you wouldn't dare look ... scruffy because everybody would know just how little money you had so its really only the very rich who can get away with it. What I mean is its just like another way of maintaining differences between groups. You have to be really rich to be really scruffy or else you'd feel really bad and be dead ashamed of yourself but they're not, they get away with it' (Skeggs 1997, 91).

Looking different for young women is sometimes the result of a privileged position: sometimes looking 'normal' and 'conservative' is not a result of passivity or a lack of inspiration, but is a means of negotiating a safe place in the world.[8]

Love songs and teenybop

A few years ago Mavis Bayton commented that given pop music's importance in women's lives, it was strange, but true, that 'feminist theory has not concerned itself with popular music.' (1992, 51). Although the situation is slightly better today, there is still a dearth of work on women musicians and performers, and on the ways in which women use music (although feminists have made more of an intervention in the study of music video).[9] Feminists' lack of interest in pop, Bayton argues, is partly explained by the way in which rock is seen as a 'masculine' form. However, feminists have also tended to ignore pop which is usually classified as 'feminine'. This disdain for pop needs to be understood in the context of the value system which legitimates 'rock as "serious" music, in contrast to the "light" and seemingly "feminine" frivolity of pop' (p. 52).[10] While feminists may have rejected rock as 'masculinist', much feminist writing on music still accepts the terms of this rock ideology: like girls who invest in 'subcultural capital', feminist critics are not immune to the desire for the feelings of cultural distinction which comes from being 'culturally one of the boys'. There are good reasons for this: pop music criticism is still something of a 'boyzone' and more structured by 'hipness' than most academic fields. For women working in the field, producing feminist work may be hard enough, without having the added burden of being seen to take 'girly music' seriously.

As a result, there has been no parallel debate in pop music studies to the debates about 'women's genres' in relation to film, TV and fiction, discussed in Part II (Bayton 1992, 54). Consequently, there has been little attempt by feminists to challenge the hierarchies that equated 'feminine' pop with 'bad' music. None the less, some critics have discussed love songs and 'teenybop' as 'feminine' musical forms which address a female audience, although much of this work is now dated.[11] However, as Bayton argues, 'romance, female gendered identity, etc. are constructed as much by pop songs as by films; arguably more so' (Bayton 1992, 54), and, for this reason, it is worth returning to these debates and reevaluating them in the light of contemporary feminist criticism. This section examines work on love songs to identify how their feminine concerns, and the ways in which they address the female listener, have been seen as problematic by feminist critics.

The assumptions of mass culture criticism have historically framed the ways in which love songs, like romantic fiction, have been discussed.[12] Love songs were classified as the bad 'other' of whatever type of music the particular critic wanted to identify as more 'authentic' or 'honest' or 'radical': their 'feminine' characteristics (in particular, sentimentality) and female listeners were offered as further 'proof' of their degraded status. Furthermore, second-wave feminist critiques of love songs tended to reproduce many of these assumptions and rejected love songs because of their 'feminine' characteristics. These feminists also distinguished between the 'false emotions' of the love song and the allegedly more 'authentic', and 'sexual', nature of rock. For example, Sheila Rowbotham claimed that, 'Every rock record simply was. The words were subordinate to the rhythm and the music went straight to your cunt and hit the bottom of your spine. They were a great release after all the super-consolation romantic ballads like "Three Coins in the Fountain" ... or the twee coyness of "Love and Marriage".' (1973, 14). Ideas from mass culture theory and second-wave feminism, along with subcultural theory, have structured the ways in which feminist cultural critics have approached love songs. The debate was often organised around the distinction between rock and pop: rock was associated with masculinity, sexuality, authenticity and rebellion, pop with femininity, romance, and the inauthentic and conservative realm of 'show-biz'.

The most oft-cited piece in relation to love songs, and gender and pop more generally, is Simon Frith and Angela McRobbie's 'Rock and Sexuality', first published in 1978. For these critics, rock is a masculine form and pop a feminine one. Although they claim that they do not believe 'that there is some sort of "natural" sexuality which rock expresses' (1990, 373), the idea that rock 'expresses' sexuality and pop 'represses' sexuality structures the article. For example, they claim that 'cock rock' (a dominant mode of rock in the period in which they were writing) 'allows for direct physical and psychological expressions of sexuality; pop in contrast is about romance, about female crushes and emotional affairs. Pop songs aimed at the female audience deny or repress sexuality' (p. 380). Girls learn to 'interpret their sexual feelings in terms of romance' in pop in the same way as they are encouraged to do in cultural forms such as *Jackie* (p. 378).

For Frith and McRobbie, the archetypal form of pop associated with femininity is 'teenybop' – for example, the music of pin-ups such as Donny Osmond, David Cassidy and The Bay City Rollers. Teenybop, they argue, draws on 'older romantic conventions': it transforms male sexuality into 'spiritual yearning' and presents 'female sexuality as serious, diffuse and implying total emotional commitment' (p. 375). Underpinning Frith and McRobbie's argument is the assumption that teenybop performers are presented as vulnerable and gentle in order to encourage girls to buy into the ideology of romance. Pop may offer girls a vision of freedom but only the freedom to be wives, mothers and objects of male desire (p. 381). For these critics, the ideology of romance, which is the 'dominant mode of control in pop music', is 'the icing on the harsh ideology of domesticity' (p. 387).

This argument raises a number of questions. While rock is treated as problematic in terms of its sexual politics and the way it excludes women, it is pop that is treated as musically inferior: rock is 'musically interesting', pop 'mainstream' and 'lightweight' (p. 379). Frith and McRobbie's political objection to romance is entangled with a musical distaste for 'girly' music. Indeed, elsewhere McRobbie has dismissed Bananarama for sounding 'like a group of girls upstairs on the bus home from school' (McRobbie cited in Bradby 1990, 367). In the process, questions about the pleasures that pop love songs offer their listeners are marginalised. If rock is as misogynistic as it is often claimed to be, then the appeal of sentimental chart-pop which draws on traditionally feminine codes and competences, might be totally understandable.

Frith and McRobbie also pay little attention to the diversity of pop's romantic narratives, even at the time they were writing. Unlike many of the narratives found in romantic fiction, pop does not necessarily deal in 'happy ever afters' but offers a wide range of ways of narrating romance and defining what love means. As Simon Frith has more recently argued 'Obsession? Pain? Beautiful feelings? Power? Love songs give private desires a public language, which is why we can use them (and our uses are not necessarily gender divided)' (1990, 424). Furthermore, if romance, like sexuality, is understood as produced through discourse (see Chapter 3), then romance and sexuality need not simply be thought of as polar opposites. Moreover, it becomes possible to explore the ways in which discourses of romance and sexuality are not necessarily mutually exclusive but overlapping in much pop today. For example, Take That's versions of 'Could it be Magic?' and 'Relight my Fire' quite explicitly bring romance and sex together. This is not to suggest that overlapping discourses of romance and sexuality in popular music do not produce gendered 'relations of subordination and domination' (Jackson 1995, 52), but to argue that this may be far more complex and contradictory than is commonly assumed. Furthermore, the ideological effects of popular music cannot simply be deduced from the ways in which different genres of music are assumed to be 'sexed' (Negus, 1996).[13]

None the less, feminist accounts of the female listener have tended to reproduce a distinction between the feminist and the 'ordinary woman/housewife'. For example, Germaine Greer claims that 'the bored housewife whiles away her duller tasks half-consciously intoning the very forgettable words of some pulp lovesong' (1970, 164). In feminist cultural studies, Ros Coward has envisaged 'housewives' as isolated in the private sphere where lyrics 'pass unmediated into our unconsciousness' (1984, 147): 'daytime radio tells women who are isolated and at home, and possibly very fed up, that the choices they made were OK' (p. 150).

Frith and McRobbie produce a more complex argument about the relationship between listening, gender and identification. For these critics, rock and pop have different modes of gendered address which position male and female listeners in different ways. In the 'sexually exclusive', masculine world of rock, the male listener identifies with the rock performer. However, they argue, 'The teenybop performer, by contrast, addresses his female consumer as his object, potentially satisfying his sexual needs and his romantic and emotional demands. The teenybop fan should feel that her idol is addressing himself solely to her; her experience should be as his partner' (Frith and McRobbie 1990, 375). As a result, for these critics, rock is masculine, and the voice of the singer is male, and there is consequently little space for the female listener. In this way, their argument about rock has some similarities with the idea that in cinema the male gaze creates a male spectating position. Although pop deals with more 'feminine' affairs and, therefore, offers more space to the female listener, Frith and McRobbie argue that the 'sexed' voice of the male teenybop performer means that the only position that the female listener can take up is as his object – the passive 'you' when he declares 'I love you'. In a similar vein, Dick Bradley has argued that Elvis Presley's songs invite women 'to identify with the female objects of desire and longing addressed or referred to in the lyrics of the songs' (1992, 139).

There are a number of problems with these ideas. First, even if we accept the idea that the sex of the voice determines the position we take up in relation to it, Frith and McRobbie largely ignore the opportunities that women may have for identification with an active, desiring female voice (Bradby 1990). Second, the idea that the sex of the voice determines how the listener is positioned by a song is extremely questionable. While there have been attempts to develop a more psychoanalytically informed version of this thesis, which draws, for example, on Mulvey's notion of a male gaze, these have also proved problematic. Third, Frith and McRobbie's approach tends to assume a heterosexual listener in much the same way as theories of cinema spectatorship. Finally, Frith and McRobbie assume that the recording determines how we listen to it. This ignores the many ways in which listeners use and appropriate pop music. As with other cultural forms, pop songs are not free to mean anything but, perhaps even more than film, TV and fiction, they provide for an 'ambiguity of response' (Frith 1990, 423). Pop music provides a soundtrack to our lives and, as a result, it may be much more enmeshed with our every-day experiences than many other cultural forms.

Female fandom

The portrait of the 'ordinary' teenage girl or 'housewife', inter-polated by love songs in her bedroom or kitchen, is problematised by studies which examine how women use pop stars and pop music as a cultural resource. Although, as Bayton (1992) has noted, there has been little work on women's consumption of music but there have been some studies of female fandom. Work on fandom has attempted to challenge the ways in which fans are often seen as 'pathological', 'deviant', 'dangerous' and 'other'. For example, Joli Jenson (1992) has argued that while the aficionado of high culture is seen as educated and rational and gains a prestige through their association with high-status objects, the fan is often portrayed as uneducated and emotional, and damned through their association with 'low-status' cultural forms. As a result, for Jenson, 'the real dividing line between aficionado and fan involves issues of status and class' (1992, 21): it is a distinction between those who possess 'legitimate' cultural capital and those who do not. This also can be used to explain distinctions within popular culture: the rock aficionado is often seen as rational and controlled, the pop fan as emotional and out of control.[14] However, as Thornton suggests, popular music's cultural hierarchies are also gendered. For this reason, 'hysteri-cal' pop fans are usually portrayed as female.

Feminist critics have not only challenged these cultural hier-archies, but have also considered how the cultural practices involved in fandom might 'win space' for women, and offer them feelings of empowerment. For example, Ehrenreich *et al.* argue that, in the mid-1960s, Beatles fandom offered American girls the opportunity to negotiate some space for themselves within the constraints of teenage femininity during the period. In an era when 'good girls' were responsible for stopping things 'going too far' with boys, Beatles fandom gave girls the opportunity 'to abandon control – to scream, faint, dash about in mobs' and, in the process, 'to protest the sexual repressiveness, the rigid double standard of female teen culture' (1992, 85). The Beatles gave girls an opportunity to express sexual feelings, an act of rebellion in itself. As Ehrenreich *et al.* argue, 'It was even more rebellious to lay claim to the *active*, desiring side of a sexual attraction: the Beatles were the objects; the girls were their pursuers' (p. 90). In this way, Ehrenreich *et al.* support Frith and McRobbie's claim that attending a teenybop concert 'gives girls the chance to express a collective identity' (Frith and McRobbie 1990, 381).

This theme is taken up by Sheryl Garratt (1990; 1994) in her reflections on being a Bay City Rollers fan in the 1970s. She reflects on how a Rollers concert gave girls a chance to be 'loud' and 'uninhibited'. However, she argues, these feelings of euphoria were not simply induced by the Rollers themselves, but were produced by the practices involved in attending the concert and the experience of 'mass power'. As she recalls, '9 May 1975 was the only time I've been part of such a large group of women . . . all with one purpose, and seen how mindlessly, joyfully powerful that can be. This must be the feeling boys get on the stands at football matches, all cheering for the same team.' (1994, 83). Being a pop fan, Garratt argues, was really an 'obsession . . . with ourselves, about being with your mates on the bus and in each others bedrooms, practising the dancing and making the scrapbooks' (1990, 402). In the 1990s, with the success of boybands such as Take That, East 17 and Boyzone, the demand for both teen idols and the experience of fandom has not diminished. Indeed, the fans are increasingly important in pop videos, not only to 'authenticate' the bands in 'live' performance, but also as an acknowledgement that the other fans are as much a part of the experience as the stars. The despair and dismay fans felt when Take That split up was as much a mourning for the loss of friendships and bonds that fan activities had produced, as the loss of the object of their affections.[15]

The literature on female fandom may contribute little to our understanding of women's use of musical texts and have a tendency uncritically to celebrate the activities of fans, but it does begin to challenge the critical double standard which sees young women's investment in pop as silly and trivial. It also challenges the idea that the teenybop fan sits alone in her bedroom, passively absorbing the ideology of romance. The notions of being girls together and of 'having a laugh' that are involved in fan activities have been taken up in the star image of the girlband, the Spice Girls, with great success. The Spice Girls have, in turn, spawned their own female fans, and their slogan, 'Girl Power', has been interpreted in the British media as heralding the arrival of new forms of female solidarity, a new assertive feminine identity and a form of 'popular feminism'. Indeed, there are obviously some parallels between the new feminine identities McRobbie identifies in young women's magazines and those promoted by the band. However, the Spice Girls also make a very public display of many elements that have been a long standing part of cultures of preteen femininity: the value of female friendships, the fantasies of being powerful or of being someone, the fun of dancing and dressing up. Valerie Walkerdine's analysis of the culture of preteen working-class girls suggests that it is these elements of the Spice Girls which might also be the basis of their appeal. The girls in her study used 'pop songs because they are glamourous and exciting, because they present a model of femininity which is far from the boring school girl' (1997 154). In this way, the Spice Girls could be seen to represent 'the lure of "fame", particularly of singing and dancing [which] offers working-class girls the possibility of a talent from which they have automatically been excluded by virtue of their supposed lack of intelligence or culture' (p. 50).

Feminism, women and the production of pop

Previous sections have considered how many feminists have equated 'feminine' popular music with 'bad' pop. Although there are overlaps, music that is classified as 'feminine' is not necessarily the same as music produced by women. The question of whether music produced by women is, or should be, different to music produced by men has engaged feminists working in this area. Furthermore, feminist critics have questioned whether there could be, or should be, a distinctively feminist music.

Studies of women in the music industry have demonstrated how few women occupy 'key decision-making positions' (Negus 1992, 127). Women tend to be given more feminine, 'nurturing' roles in what Carmen Ashurst-Watson calls 'all those "keep the artist happy departments"' where 'women are used to negotiate artists' emotional needs' (Rose 1994a, 141). Women are also predominant in publicity departments which liaise with journalists in what Parkin has called 'institutionalised flirting' (Negus 1992, 115). If women are excluded from key positions in the record industry, they are also excluded in the 'production' side of pop, a problem compounded by women's 'technophobia'

(Bayton 1990, 242). Furthermore, it has been argued that many popular musical forms are inherently masculine. However, Sara Cohen's study of local music making in Liverpool found that 'women were not simply absent from the music scene but were *actively* excluded' (1991, 208). In this way, Cohen argues, rock is not 'naturally male ... [but] is actively "produced" as male' (1997, 17).[16]

Because most studies of women musicians have been produced by journalists rather than academics, they tend to focus on 'famous women in rock' rather than women's wider involvement in music making (Bayton 1992). However, Bayton's research into women musicians demonstrates how 'feminism has been a major force in getting women into popular music making' (1993, 191). Her interviews with female musicians revealed how feminist discourses informed their attitudes to music making: for example, they shaped working principles in women's bands, image and performance and the subject matter of their songs.

However, as Bayton argues, just as there is no single variety of feminism, so there is no single set of feminist ideas about popular music. Some female musicians tend towards 'folk feminism' (see Chapter 2) in their cultural politics, and claim that some musics are more intrinsically 'female' than others. For example, Bayton argues that 'Some feminists considered all electric music to be "male", because of its loudness and the way in which the panoply of amplification devices distances the performers from the audience' (1993, 185). For these musicians, women's 'femaleness' could be better expressed through the more 'ideologically safe' musical form of folk (pp. 185–6). While this approach to music making is based on the idea that feminist music should express women's *difference*, other feminist musicians demanded the right to be treated as *equal* to men.[17] For these feminists, the idea that women's music should be 'softer' than men's music worked to reproduce stereotypical ideas about femininity. Furthermore, Bayton argues that feminist musicians have debated whether feminist music can also be 'mainstream' music. These issues structure much of the following discussion.

The values of 'folk feminism' have found their way into popular music criticism. This feminist approach celebrates music which expresses women's essential difference and searches for 'authentic' female voices which express their 'femaleness'. While the 'authenticity' of these female voices is often equated with a distance from commerce and/or the media, this often ignores the

ways in which the 'authenticity' of some female musicians – especially singer-songwriters – is a product of the promotional
strategies and the media publicity through which their star
images are created. For example, Joni Mitchell (along with such
as Sinèad O'Connor and Alanis Morissette) has often been seen
as an 'authentic' and 'truthful' female voice, but the idea that she
is 'stripped bare' and 'naked' when she communicates to her
audience is also central to the ways in which she is sold. In this
case, both feminist critic and female singer collude in the idea
that the female singer can reveal 'an "authentic" reality'
(Reynolds and Press 1995, 249). This position rests on the idea
that there is some female 'essence', untainted by culture, and
implies that, underneath the world of 'appearances', all women
are 'essentially' the same.

Simon Reynolds and Joy Press are keen to distance themselves from these essentialist positions which aim to identify an
'authentic female voice'. Instead, they turn to female musicians
who use avant-garde techniques to disrupt and disturb rock's
form. For example, they claim that '[Patti] Smith returns to the
non-sense and glossolalia of Little Richard's awopbopaloobop,
and gives it a Joycean spin: her singing is pure rock 'n' roll holler
and the invocatory babble of a prophetess' (1995, 357). Likewise
they compare the Throwing Muses to Virginia Woolf and Doris
Lessing (p. 370). In this way they validate some female rock
music because it conforms to another aesthetic tradition which is
seen as unproblematically superior. However, they also draw on
the French feminist, Hélène Cixous, to argue that these musicians are working within a feminine aesthetic which preexists,
and therefore ruptures, patriarchal language. In this way,
Reynolds and Press's argument is still underpinned by a notion of
a female essence which somehow pre-exists culture.

Whereas the critics discussed above suggest that feminist
popular music can challenge patriarchy through the use of female
musical languages, other feminist critics have considered the
ways in which women have used music to negotiate the cultural
meanings of femininity. Joanne Gottlieb and Gayle Wald's study
of Riot Grrrl demonstrates how it draws on feminist principles.
Riot grrrl culture, they argue, not only draws on the DIY spirit of
punk 'to blur the boundaries between production and consumption' but operates as a support network for women who want to
make music, attempting 'to use female community as a way of
combating forms of discrimination and abuse that limit women's

power' (1994, 263). Kearney (1997) has also noted how this DIY ethic draws on modes of organisation from radical feminism. These principles are not just promoted through music but also through the fanzines and internet sites which help support the riot grrrl network.

Gottlieb and Wald examine how 'riot grrrls draw upon their experiences of girlhood to emphasise difference *in concert with* female equality' (1994, 266). Riot Grrrl bands work within a musical form which is usually seen as masculine: hard, fast rock. However, while the 'sex and anger' of rock is usually seen as masculine, Gottlieb and Wald argue that it is these very characteristics which can open a space 'for the politicisation of sexuality and female identity' (p. 253). The naming of Riot Grrrl bands – for example, Hole and Dickless – often acts as a form of 'talking back' in which rock's masculine terms are reclaimed and subverted by women.[18] However, riot grrrl bands do not only assert their equality by claiming rock for women, they also use this form to redefine 'girl identity', preferring the more angry 'grrrl'. Through their music and practices, they also assert that it is 'different for girls'.

> By underscoring many traditional paradigms of girl culture – such as the intensity of early female friendships, the centrality of menstruation as a sign of 'womanhood', the importance of secrets and secret-telling as forms of rebellion against parental control, even the early sexual play between girlfriends – and making them foundational to their political social and musical interventions, riot grrrls foster an affirmative mode of public, female self-expression that does not exclude, repress or delegitimise girls' experiences or their specific cultural formations. (Gottlieb and Wald 1994, 266–7)

Gottlieb and Wald show how riot grrrl bands draw on the cultural forms and modes of organisation from both feminism and preteen femininity to negotiate what it means to be a young woman. In this way, they reject the idea that music expresses a female identity and think of music as a space in which feminine identities are constructed and reconstructed. Furthermore, Kearney has argued that whereas second-wave feminists tried to expose gender differences, the riot grrrl scene has been more interested in 'deconstructing' them (1997, 224). However, because riot grrrl bands align themselves with 'independent' music, which is defined in opposition to 'mainstream' music, this 'may preclude the possibility of having a broad cultural or political impact' (Gottlieb and Wald 1994, 271).

While riot grrrl offers a way of negotiating a primarily white mode of feminine identity within rock, female rap acts have used music to reconstruct ideas about black femininity. Hip-hop culture, like rock culture, has often been identified as masculine and misogynist, primarily because of its lyrical content, but also because of media coverage of rap performers. However, like riot grrrls within rock, female rappers have tried to appropriate rap for their own ends. As Tricia Rose argues, 'Black women rappers affirm black female popular pleasure and public presence by privileging black female subjectivity and black female experiences in the public sphere. Public performance also provides a means by which young black women can occupy public space in ways that affirm the centrality of their own voices.' (1994b, 182). For example, Rose argues that women rappers have used music and video as a way of raising awareness of black women's history, to assert the right to define their own sexual identities and to challenge the 'aesthetic hierarchy' which equates feminine beauty and sexual attractiveness with white femininity (p. 168; see also Perry, 1995).

However, the dynamics of 'race' and racism mean that female rappers have had a rather different relationship to both the masculinity of the musical form that they are dealing with, and to feminism, than riot grrrls. Rose argues that to simply create an opposition between 'bad' sexist male rappers and 'good' anti-sexist female rappers misses the contradictory and dialogic character of hip-hop: the themes of women's rap are articulated 'first, in dialogue with male rappers' sexual discourses, and then in dialogue with larger social discourses, including feminism' (1994b, 147). This emphasis on dialogue, rather than opposition, between male and female rappers is necessary because although many male and female rappers may have very different notions of sexual politics, they also need to maintain a solidarity against racism (p. 149). Therefore, while female rap tracks are often 'caustic, witty, and aggressive warnings' to, and about, men (p. 155), female rappers are often loathe to condemn some of the more anti-female antics of their peers because it feeds into a wider process in which black masculinity is seen as 'pathological'. Furthermore, the dialogue that women rappers have with feminism is very different to that of riot grrrls. Although female rappers are often highly critical of sexism and support women's independence and empowerment, Rose argues that they are often loathe to define themselves as feminist because feminism is identified as a white women's movement. Feminism's insistence on 'sisterhood' and sexual politics as the fundamental form of politics, fails to take account of 'the realities of racism [which] link black women to black men' (p. 177).

Once the cultural differences between women are taken into account, it becomes even more problematic to talk about an 'authentic' female voice: indeed, on what grounds would it be possible to decide whether Sporty Spice, Queen Latifah, Courtney Love, kd lang or Mary J. Blige best expressed what it means to be a 'woman'? The work of critics such as Rose, Gottlieb and Wald offers a way of understanding popular music as a site in which gendered identities are negotiated. However, while studies of youth culture have pointed to the ways in which 'mainstream', commercial forms such as *Just Seventeen* have negotiated modes of 'popular feminism', 'mainstream', 'girly' pop has received little critical attention. The exception has been in studies of Madonna which see, in her star image, a new mode of feminine identity which is neither feminist, nor 'traditionally' feminine.[19]

Feminist pop music criticism has largely looked for signs of progress outside of 'feminine' pop. While some feminists have searched for a 'female' music 'outside' of the rock/pop divide, others have seen women's movement into more 'legitimate' musical spheres such as rock as a sign of 'progress' (but see Bradby 1990). With the increasing importance of digitally produced dance musics within youth culture, alongside the increasing recognition given to black musics within popular music criticism, the rock/pop divide is no longer as central to pop music criticism as it once was. However, pop music which is associated with 'feminine' characteristics has still received little serious attention from feminist critics, most of whom, it would seem, still equate good music with 'boys' music'. In this way, feminist critics still wish to be, in Thornton's words, 'culturally one of the boys'.

Notes

1 For examples of criticisms of subcultural theories, Clarke (1990), Middleton (1990), and Thornton (1995).

2 None the less, in some club cultures where dance is central – for example, northern soul in the 1970s and jazz in the 1980s – it is male dancers who are more spectacular, athletic and command more space. For more on dance music cultures, see Reynolds (1997), Pini (1997), Thomas (1993).

3 For more on women and punk, see Roman (1988) and Miles (1997).
4 Work on younger girls' comics has been produced by Barker (1989) and Walkerdine (1990). Also see Walkerdine (1997) for a wider discussion of young girls' culture.
5 Indeed, it is surprising that McRobbie ignores the ways in which collective consumption of the magazine shapes the ways in which it is used as she had noted how the ideology of romance was used as a source of collective resistance in her ethnographic study of the culture of working-class girls (Barker 1989, 248).
6 Lest this give the wrong impression, the *Jackie Annual 1979* includes a feature, 'Girls at the Top' about female pop stars who 'expect to be taken seriously' including bass player Gaye Advert from new wave band The Adverts and commenting on Linda McCartney's musical contribution to an animated film entered in the Cannes Film Festival (p. 53). A pop spread, 'Our Favourite Bad Guys' includes Jean Jaques Burnel of The Stranglers and Johnny Rotten (pp. 48–9).
7 Nor is McRobbie out on a limb in this view: Sheila Rowbotham has recently stated that 12-year-old girls today 'seem remarkably resourceful. Pretty confident. And I think their magazines are rather good, actually.' (Aitkenhead 1997, 4; see also Stuart 1990).
8 As Walkerdine has argued, 'It is much easier to find cultural markers of solidarity and resistance than to engage with the complex and painful intersection of the psychic and the social' (1997, 14).
9 Little attention is given to music video in this chapter as much of the feminist writing that exists is more interested in the visual image rather than the music (Goodwin, 1993). However, for examples of feminist work on video, see Kaplan (1987b), Schwichtenberg (1992) and Stockbridge (1990). Many feminist debates about music video have been preoccupied with Madonna (see, for example, Schwichtenberg 1993). For debates about girls' use of Madonna videos see Lewis (1990). For a recent attempt to bring sound and image together in the feminist analysis of music video, see Whiteley (1997).
10 See also, Bradby (1993) and Cohen (1997).
11 Indeed, critics such as Frith and McRobbie have been keen to distance themselves from the positions they took on rock and pop in the mid-1970s.
12 See, for example, Hayawaka (1957); Hughes (1964); Hoggart (1958); and Harker (1980).
13 For example, Oasis are often characterised as the epitome of a 'laddish' rock tradition, yet not only has Liam Gallagher often been presented in girls' magazines as a teenybop idol, a song such as 'Wonderwall' also fits very neatly with the conventions that Frith and McRobbie ascribe to teenybop. Lyrics such as 'There are many things that I would like to say to you, but I don't know how ... Maybe you're gonna be the one that saves me, For after all, you're my wonderwall' seems to resemble the way Frith and McRobbie claim the teenybop male is presented as being 'soft, romantic, easily hurt, loyal and anxious to find true love' (Frith and McRobbie 1990, 375).
14 Indeed, this distinction between the aficionado and the fan is also interesting in relation to debates about gender, subcultural capital and record collecting (see Straw 1997).
15 I am grateful to Joanne Whitehouse for these insights.
16 Indeed, Cohen shows how the gendered opposition between 'the street' and 'the home' works to exclude women from rock scenes: '"The street", like "the road", is associated with live performance, male activity and rebellion, and with public spaces women are not supposed to frequent' (1997, 30).

17 See Kearney (1997) for a discussion of how these different feminist approaches to music making came into conflict over riot grrrl bands.
18 A similar process has been associated with female rap acts such as Bytches With Problems where derogatory names for women are appropriated and their meanings transformed in the process (Perry 1995; Skeggs 1994).
19 There are numerous writings on Madonna: indeed, the debates about her significance would probably constitute a chapter in themselves. However, many critics have been more concerned with her star image and her videos than with her music. For examples of this criticism, see Schwichtenberg (1993) and Lloyd (1993).

Further reading

Bayton, M. Feminist Musical Practice: Problems and Contradictions, in T. Bennett et al., eds, Rock and Popular Music: Politics, Policies, Institutions (London, Routledge, 1993)
Ehrenreich, B., Hess, E. and Jacobs, G. Beatlemania: Girls Just Want to Have Fun, in L. Lewis, ed., The Adoring Audience: Fan Culture and Popular Media (London, Routledge, 1992)
Gottlieb, J. and Wald, G. Smells Like Teen Spirit: Riot Grrrls, Revolution and Women in Independent Rock, in A. Ross and T. Rose, eds, Microphone Fiends: Youth Music and Youth Culture (New York, Routledge, 1994)
McRobbie, A. Feminism and Youth Culture: From Jackie to Just Seventeen (Basingstoke, Macmillan, 1991)
Rose, T. Black Noise: Rap Music and Black Culture in Contemporary America (New England, Wesleyan University Press, 1994)
Thornton, S. Club Cultures: Music, Media and Subcultural Capital (Cambridge, Polity, 1995)
Whiteley, S., ed., Sexing the Groove: Popular Music and Gender (London, Routledge, 1997)

Part IV

CONCLUSIONS

9

Feminism
in popular culture

This chapter brings together debates about the relationships between feminism and popular culture in the 1980s and 1990s which explored how feminism was envisaged within popular culture. These debates are organised around concepts such as 'backlash', 'post-feminism', 'celebrity feminism' and 'popular feminism', and attempt to get to grips with the question 'where has feminism gone?' As will become clear, there has been considerable disagreement about how feminism has figured within the popular and about how to theorise the relationship between feminism and popular culture in the process.

The chapter returns to some of the major themes that have structured this book. It reflects on what is at stake in feminism's engagement with popular culture, and on how feminists have made distinctions between the 'good' and the 'bad', the 'progressive' and the 'reactionary'. These distinctions also reveal the different ways in which feminists have envisaged the relationships between themselves, 'the popular' and 'ordinary women'. Throughout this book, forms of feminist cultural politics which position themselves as 'outside' and 'against' 'the popular' have been problematised. This chapter examines forms of feminist cultural politics which are premised on an engagement with 'the popular'. From this perspective, a central question is whether feminism can intervene in, and 'make-over', 'the popular'.

Backlash and post-feminism

One response to the question of how feminism was positioned by the media was offered by the 'backlash' thesis. The most well-known exponent of this thesis, Susan Faludi (1992), claimed that during the 1980s, there was a backlash against feminism in both the US and the UK. The backlash, she argues, claims that the equal rights for women, for which feminists had fought, have made women miserable. In response, Faludi claims that it is not feminism that has made women miserable but the backlash itself which aims to turn back the clock and erode the progress brought about by feminism. Faludi illustrates her case with a mass of data which she offers as evidence not only for women's lack of equality but for the existence of the backlash. For Faludi, popular culture has played a major part in promoting the backlash and creates 'false images of womanhood' (1992, 9). She claims that the media is saturated with images of miserable single women, evil career women and happy mothers who are content to turn their backs on the world of work.

Although Faludi claimed that the backlash was not a conspiracy or an 'orchestrated movement', her book none the less makes the backlash appear like a pretty orchestrated attempt to get women back into the home. Although Faludi acknowledges that not all aspects of popular film and TV confirmed the backlash thesis, she often makes these exceptions fit her rule by claiming that more positive TV shows were cancelled, while ignoring the fact that cancellation is the fate of nearly all US TV shows. There is little room for contradiction or struggle within Faludi's seemingly endless list of examples of backlash media texts: nearly everything *can* be read to prove the backlash thesis, but many of these readings are highly questionable. Of course, this begs the question of how, given the backlash is endemic, Faludi's book was ever published and why she received so much, often positive, publicity within the media.

Despite attempts to distance herself from the popular and to criticise it from a feminist position, Faludi herself operates within the popular: like Friedan before her, she is a journalist. If Faludi's own work is an example of a form of 'popular feminism', this suggests there may be more exceptions to disprove her rule. Furthermore, if there are some texts of the period which seem to support the 'backlash thesis' more than others – *Fatal Attraction* (1987) being the most oft-cited example – these films were also often criticised within the media for being attacks on independent, single women.

The backlash thesis is seductive because it seems such a simple and all-encompassing explanation of feminism's 'failure'. This is evident in some of the ways in which the backlash thesis has been reproduced by some feminists working within cultural studies. Indeed, while to some extent, Faludi acknowledges women's power to resist the backlash, Susan Danuta Walters (1995) sees her female students as 'dupes' of the backlash: her students aren't feminists, therefore, she reasons, the backlash must have been successful. Today, she argues, feminists 'experience ourselves as both anachronistic ... and frustrated by the reluctance of our female students to "declare" themselves. If identifying oneself as a feminist carried a certain daring and rebellious cachet in the early 1970s, in the early 1990s it is looked on with either a nasty disdain or (worse, I think) a blasé and tired indifference' (1995, 141). In the rush to blame 'the backlash' for her students' refusal of her feminist identity, Walters does not question why feminism is failing to engage these students. She also ignores the generational politics at play and the fact that young women may not simply want a feminist 'make-over' but may be actively questioning the values of feminism.

Both Faludi and Walters equate the backlash with an era of 'post-feminism' which they characterise as 'anti-feminism' (although Walters also implicates feminist post-structuralism). While there were undoubtedly attacks on women's rights in the 1980s – for example, campaigns centred around 'family values' – to characterise a post-feminist culture as anti-feminist culture overstates the case. Furthermore, the ways in which critics such as Faludi and Walters have used the term post-feminism suggests that 1970s feminism is the 'authentic' and only form of feminism (Brunsdon 1997). Walters takes the students' refusal of her definition of feminism to mean the end of feminism itself. However, Brunsdon argues, post-feminism can be a useful term if it is recognised as a different historical period which does not mean the end of feminism but 'a changed context of debate on feminist issues' which is also marked by a change 'in popularly available understandings of femininity and a woman's place' (1997, 101–2).

These different understandings of post-feminism can be seen in the different ways in which Walters, Faludi and Brunsdon envisage the relationship between the film *Pretty Woman* (1990) and feminism (see also Radner, 1993). *Pretty Woman*, a major box-office hit, is a romantic comedy centring on the relationship between Vivien (Julia Roberts) a prostitute, and Edward (Richard Gere) a millionaire businessman. Edward hires Vivien as his 'companion' for a week and, in the process, each of them 'rescues' the other from their problems, is transformed in the process and falls in love. Both Faludi and Walters read *Pretty Woman* as 'emblematic of the post-feminist genre' which 'offers yet another backlash dystopia' (Walters 1995, 126). Therefore, for these critics, *Pretty Woman* is a 'delusive fiction' (Walters

1995, 127): it is post-feminist because it is *anti*-feminist and, in disavowing feminism, wants to turn the clock back to *pre*-feminism.

However, Brunsdon rejects the idea that the film is post-feminist because it is 'bypassing, ignoring or attacking feminism' but argues that it can be thought of as 'post-feminist' if we think about how *Pretty Woman* actually engages with feminism (1997, 82). Brunsdon is not arguing that *Pretty Woman* can be labelled a 'feminist' film, but that it is informed by 1970s feminism while at the same time disavowing it (p. 83). While Vivien is preoccupied with her appearance and getting her man, she 'also has ideas about her life and being in control which clearly come from feminism' (p. 87). Vivien may make herself desirable for Edward but she is also desiring, a position informed by feminism. In this way, Brunsdon argues, *Pretty Woman* is post-1970s-feminism but it is not anti-feminist. Vivien, alongside the character of Tess in *Working Girl*, is a type of 'girly heroine' whose femininity is partly formed by feminism but is also a rejection of a 1970s feminist identity.

In this way we can think of *Pretty Woman* as neither pro-feminist nor anti-feminist but a product of the post-feminist 1980s where many modes of femininity are articulated in relation to feminism. Brunsdon's argument is valuable because it offers a way out of the impasse of thinking of feminist and feminine identities as simply polar opposites, an impasse that renders each identity inflexible and ultimately historical. Instead, Brunsdon offers a way of thinking about how many contemporary femininities are historical products that are marked by 1970s feminism but do not conform to the feminist 'make-over' that critics like Walters want to effect.

Popular feminism and post-feminism

If feminists such as Faludi defined the 1980s and 1990s as a post-feminist period characterised by backlash, then other feminists have produced a more optimistic reading of the same period. While recognising that this period had contradictory effects on gender relations, some feminists have considered how feminist ideas were taken up in popular forms and practices to produce forms of 'popular feminism'. While there was little consensus about what popular feminism was, or should be, these feminist critics shared the belief that feminism could no longer position itself outside and against popular culture, but, instead, had to see popular culture as a site 'where meanings are contested' (Gamman and Marshment, 1988, 1). This section explores some of these debates and not only looks at the ways in which debates about popular feminism envisaged the relationship between feminism and popular culture, but also at some of the studies of popular forms and practices where elements of a 'popular feminism' were found to exist.

Gamman and Marshment's collection *The Female Gaze* (1988) was an important intervention in these debates and demonstrated an awareness that thinking about the relationship between feminism and popular culture was always going to be a difficult endeavour. The collection raises crucial questions about the grounds upon which forms are categorised as 'feminist' or 'non-feminist'. First, Margaret Marshment (1988) argues that if an increasing number of women in 'masculine' roles are seen as a sign of 'progress', this reproduces the idea that masculine values are fundamental human values. Second, she argues that if feminist texts are seen as those which legitimate 'traditional' feminine traits such as domesticity, motherhood and passivity, this can lead to a position in which femininity is treated uncritically. Finally, if feminist texts are equated with those which use avant-garde representational strategies which seek to abolish gender boundaries, this would suggest that we doomed to never find such examples within the 'popular'. The debates about films such as *Aliens* (1986) and *Terminator II* (1992) illustrate these problems all to well.[1] As Shelagh Young argues 'what constitutes feminist "art" or political practice is very much dependent on how the commentator defines feminism' (1988, 176).

Gamman and Marshment also raise questions about the ways in which feminism is part of popular culture. For example, they question whether feminism 'is a presence at all, or whether, in order to enter the mainstream, feminism is co-opted by being harnessed to other discourses which neutralise its radical potential' (1988, 3). The idea of co-option surfaces in many critiques of the idea of 'popular feminism'. For example, some commentators argue that images of 'liberation', 'freedom' and 'independence' for women now populate many media forms because they *sell*, but, in the process, become detached from feminist discourses which gave them any 'radical' meaning. According to this argument, in advertising the 'liberating' effects of tampons and sanitary towels are sold to a post-feminist generation but have lost any connection to feminist understandings of 'liberation'. The co-option line tends to stress the down-side of feminism's entry into the popular, emphasising how feminism in the process has supposedly been 'made safe' and has done little to disturb or subvert 'traditional' femininity.

Many critics have therefore rejected this co-option model and considered instead how feminist ideas are negotiated within the popular with contradictory effects. Indeed, this is the position taken up by Gamman and Marshment who argue that because popular culture is a site of struggle, it produces spaces where meanings can be contested, 'with results that might not be free of contradictions, but which do signify shifts in regimes of representation. And thus perhaps commonsense notions about women' (1988, 4). This position underpinned the analysis of a whole range of popular forms and practices such as advertising, tv, popular fiction, youth culture, women's magazines, pop music, and film.

While most feminists found 'popular feminism' a contradictory phenomenon, there were more optimistic and pessimistic versions of this work. Feminist concerns, it appeared, were a presence in many popular forms and practices. Many women's magazines and daytime TV shows encouraged women to be assertive, independent and to fight for their rights and they even campaigned around feminist issues such as sexual discrimination, sexual harassment, rape and child care. However, despite this seeming 'progress' many critics were also wary. Some spoke of co-option, noting that feminism would be popular only as long as it sold and arguing that the designer post-feminist 'new woman' which was found in the pages of magazines such as *Elle* 'was a luxury the majority of women can't afford' (Lee 1988, 172). Others noted how popular feminism emphasised individual problems and solutions rather than the notion of collective struggle that had been so fundamental to the feminist project. As Skeggs has argued, individualism can be positive with its emphasis on entitlement, independence and sexual power, but in the process, it 'detaches feminism from the social and the systemic' (1997, 144). Furthermore, she argues, this individualism can work to block change and 'links between [the] individual and collective' (p. 144).

Many feminists working within cultural studies, while disagreeing about whether these changes should be seen as positive or negative, have examined the how the entry of feminism into the popular has produced new forms of femininity that are not 'feminist' but do not conform to 'traditional' forms of feminine subjectivity either. For example, Marshment argues that the heroines of blockbusters such as *Woman of Substance* 'are neither feminist, nor traditionally feminine: in the 1980s neither traditional femininity nor feminism is quite acceptable as a self-definition for many women' (1988, 43). Angela McRobbie's analysis of young women's magazines, discussed in Chapter 8, also analyses new femininities which are formed in relation to feminism but do not identify themselves as 'feminist'. McRobbie suggests that 'We have to look to what emerges between feminism and femininity and we have to attend to the inventiveness of women as they create new social categories' (1994, 8). Analyses such as these attempt to break down the opposition between feminist and feminine identities. However, in the process, there is a tendency to create a new opposition which allows the new femininities (not feminist, but informed by feminism) to be privileged over 'traditional femininity' which operates as a homogeneous, non-contradictory 'other'.

These debates about 'popular feminism' also depend on some problematic assumptions about the relationship between the 'feminist' and the 'popular'. These debates address the problem of what role 'feminists' should take in relation to popular culture. While some reject a position in which the feminist is envisaged as outside and against the popular, this can still produce a tendency to position the 'feminist' as someone who will intervene in, and 'make-over', the popular in their own image. This mode of address lingers in Gammon and Marshment's analysis when they argue that it is necessary for 'feminists to intervene in the mainstream to make our meanings part of "commonsense" – or rather to convert commonsense into "good sense"' (1988, 2). On the one hand, this statement seems to offer an eminently sensible and viable model of feminist cultural politics. However, on the other hand, this reproduces the figure of the feminist as the woman 'in the know' and the popular is still presented as somehow inadequate in itself. This has proved to be a real dilemma for feminist cultural studies. For example, Angela McRobbie has argued that we must refuse 'the lure of believing that if we try hard enough we can reproduce our feminist selves and our feminist theory in our daughters and with our students' (1994, 9). Her work on young women's magazines testifies to her desire to look positively, but not uncritically, at

what emerges 'between feminism and femininity' in these magazines and to identify the existence of something we might call
'popular feminism' in them. However, the model of 'make-over'
and 'recruitment' still lingers on in her work: the positive changes
in women's magazines are, in part, attributed to the intervention
of female magazine professionals who have been familiarised with
feminist cultural studies as students. As McRobbie, puts is, 'I
cannot think of a single women's or girl's magazine whose (full-
time or freelance) staff does not include some of my ex-students'
(1997c, 204). In this way, debates about popular feminism are
often dependent on a 'make-over' politics, while simultaneously
trying to disavow this dependence. There is a real tension here
between wanting to hold on to the identity 'feminist' and wanting
to see how feminism can be made to mean differently for different generations of women.

None of the feminist critics who have explored manifestations of 'popular feminism' would make the case that some form
of feminism is saturating popular culture. Unlike the advocates of
the 'backlash' thesis, debates about popular feminism have never
argued that it was omnipresent. Indeed, debates have often
centred around a limited range of examples. However, the
language of 'co-option' and 'recruitism' has maintained a tension
in thinking about the relationship between feminism and popular
culture. The language of 'co-option' acts as a reminder that the
existence of feminist ideas within the popular should not mean
that these manifestations of popular feminism can be treated
uncritically. Yet, at the same time, it suggests that there is a
better, 'unpopular' form of feminism. The language of
'recruitism' is evidence of a feminism which seeks to transform,
rather than simply analyse, popular culture along more egalitar-
ian lines, without the 'moralistic' tones which have accompanied
some feminist cultural criticism. But at the same time, this position wishes to maintain 'ownership' of feminism, maintaining the
privileged position of the feminist as the 'expert' on women's
issues.

Resignifying feminism

So far this chapter has introduced debates about how femininism
has been represented within popular culture. It is not necessary
to subscribe to the backlash thesis in order to acknowledge that
feminism is still frequently represented as a threat or as ridicu-

lous. However, as Charlotte Brunsdon's conception of post-feminism suggests, we are now living in a historical period that is post second-wave feminism. For this reason, it is not surprising that 'there is some form of feminist discourse' occuring across a range of popular forms (Wicke 1994, 765). For example, many popular prime-time TV dramas, such as *ER* and *Ally McBeal* could only be the product of a historical context that was partly formed by feminism. For many feminist critics, the entry of feminism into the popular has not been unproblematic: feminist themes can be appropriated, losing their radicalism and becoming attached to more conservative agendas. However, this need not necessarily lead to a pessimistic position because these discourses and images 'are also up for grabs, open to feminist reformulation' (Probyn 1993b, 284).

While models of feminist intervention in the popular tend to assume that a feminist 'make-over' of the popular is a good thing, this section explores some examples which question this feminist authority. First, it considers forms of 'popular feminism' which, in different ways, question some of the assumptions and the authority of 'official' forms of feminism (albeit mediated by feminist analysis). Second, it explores a couple of studies which demonstrate why women may choose to make alliances with many feminist concerns but refuse the identity 'feminist'.

The TV sitcom *Roseanne* has received a fair amount of attention from critics interested in the relationship between feminism and the popular. Both Lee (1995) and Rowe (1997) have noted how *Roseanne* is both informed by feminist concerns yet at the same time presents a critique of some of the assumptions of feminism. As Rowe argues, Roseanne exposes 'the gap she sees between the ideas of the Women's Movement of the late 60s and early 70s on the one hand, and the realities of working-class family life two decades later on the other' (1997, 75). Within *Roseanne*, the on-going struggles in which women are engaged are as much a product of class as they are of gender. *Roseanne* shows that the ways in which second-wave feminism defined women's rights and ideas of 'liberation' were dependent on a position of privilege, and a freedom from the pressures of everyday working-class life. Furthermore, *Roseanne* problematises notions of a universal form of female oppression by demonstrating that working-class men and women share a common form of economic oppression. For some critics, 'Roseanne, despite her transgression of the codes of feminine behaviour and appearance, is still the ideal mom, but with the sentimentality removed' (MacDonald 1995, 144). However, Rowe notes how the character Roseanne acknowledges and exposes 'her oppression as a working-class wife and mother, while at the same time finding dignity and fulfilment in these roles' (1995, 47). In this way, Roseanne neither simply celebrates the feminine role of mother nor simply condemns it as the site of women's oppression, and, in so doing, refuses the opposition of feminism and femininity. She instead interrogates what it means to be a working-class wife and mother, trashing notions of the 'perfect mother' who puts everyone elses interest before her own while defending her family from those who would seek to judge them as 'abnormal'.

Oprah Winfrey has identified her talk-show as a form of 'televisual feminism' which aims to 'empower women' (Squire 1997, 99). In many ways, the *Oprah Winfrey Show*, from the 1980s through to the mid-1990s, was a clear example of how feminist concerns have entered 'the mainstream'. As Squire argues, the show is woman-centred (the host, many of the guests and members of the audience are female), it often addresses 'female-identified topics' and discusses 'injustices which are at the heart of much contemporary feminist campaigning like job discrimination, male violence and sexual abuse' (p. 99). However, *Oprah* is not promoted as a 'feminist' show, and, Squire argues, some feminist critics have claimed that it 'is too frivolous to be feminist' (p. 109). However, as Wicke argues, to reject the forms of the celebrity zone where people like Oprah Winfrey operate is to ignore 'its reality and political potential' (1994, 756). For Wicke, critics who see 'celebrity feminism' as the frivolous and ideologically suspect 'other' of academic feminism fail to recognise that 'the energies of the celebrity imaginary are fuelling feminist discourse and political activity as never before' (p. 758). Furthermore, *Oprah* not only creates a televisual space for a form of popular feminism, but one defined by black feminism (Squire 1997, 105). Indeed, she claims, *Oprah* is sometimes 'better able to recognize the shifting and intersecting agendas of class, gender and "race" than is much feminist theory' (p. 107).

Oprah is underpinned by the aim of empowering women. Squire notes that the show does not subscribe to a particular 'brand-name' feminism but meshes together different forms of feminism, 'indicating variously an interest in women's political, economic, and educational advancement; in women getting help for personal and relationship problems; and most generally, in women perceiving a range of individual and social choices as open to them and deciding among them' (Squire 1997, 102). However, Squire questions the effects of the daily repetition of narratives which transform victimisation into empowerment: although these narratives of empowerment might offer hope, she argues that the frequent repetition of stories about how women are disempowered and suffer makes them begin to seem to be less like individual and 'psychological' problems, and more like 'facts ... that demand explanation in other, social terms' (p. 102). A similar point could be made about the 'based on a true story' made-for-TV movie which often focuses on 'social problems' faced by women. While these movies also construct narratives in which the heroine moves from a position of victimisation to one of empowerment, and are often seen as individualising social problems, the cumulative effect of watching these movies can generate a sense of the multiple, everyday and collective ways in which women are disempowered. Many of these movies are also notable because they demonstrate the ways in which gender inequalities intersect with class inequalities. Furthermore, although some of these movies do individualise social problems, some also emphasise that the struggle for change can only be achieved by collective female action.[2] What both *Oprah* and some of these TV movies succeed in doing is producing what Elspeth Probyn calls 'a shock of recognition of being gendered in and amongst women' (1993a, 55), a form of address that 'unpopular' feminisms have not always been able to achieve.[3]

If Oprah Winfrey maintains a connection to the identity 'feminist', and in particular to black feminism, then it is also necessary to consider why the identity feminist may also be refused while many of the 'contents' of feminism are taken on board. Tricia Rose draws on her interviews with black women rappers to argue that while these women are often labelled 'feminist', they were not comfortable with the label and 'perceived feminism as a signifier for a movement that related specifically to white women' (1994b, 176). Therefore, although these women identified with many of the aims of feminism, and, in their work produced a dialogue 'within and against dominant sexual and racial narratives in American culture' (p. 147), they resisted the historical identity feminist. As Rose argues, 'Gender-based alliances across race, especially in a racist society, is a problematic move for black women. This may in part explain black women rapper's hesitancy in being labelled feminists' (p. 177).

This is accentuated by the attacks on male rap for misogyny by white feminists which are read as an attack on black men. This raises real problems for alliances between women in the name of feminism. The label and identity 'feminist' which is experienced as conferring a sense of value for those who call themselves feminists may be an identity to be questioned and resisted.

Skeggs' study of white working-class women in the North of England offers a different way of understanding why feminism may be refused.[4] Skeggs points out that knowledge about feminism is 'textually mediated': the ways in which we position ourselves in relation to feminism and the identity 'feminist' will depend on the knowledge we have about feminism (1997, 140). The texts through which feminism and the feminist is mediated are also historically and geographically specific. The women in her study, largely conducted in the 1980s, positioned themselves in relation to a range of contradictory representations of feminism centring around media presentations of feminist anti-nuclear protesters at Greenham Common; the 'corporate feminism' of Thatcher's Britain; the 'popular feminism' of publications such as *Cosmopolitan* and performers such as Madonna; the women involved in the miners' strike; and the researcher herself (p. 145). Although these representations produced contradictory images of feminism, many of the women refused the identity 'feminist'. Drawing on the 'you can have it all' images of popular feminism which are found in some women's magazines, some of the women equated the identity feminist with a middle-class achiever or as someone 'in control' of her life. Although these women were sympathetic to many feminist ideas and might define themselves as 'strong women', for them, the feminist was someone who occupied a different class position. Furthermore, feminists were sometimes seen as women who had the luxury of putting themselves first, a luxury that they couldn't afford. This is the same luxury that is refused in *Roseanne*: while the show has been criticised for the ways in which, despite Roseanne's resistance to ideas of 'the perfect mom', she ultimately puts her family's needs before her own, this ignores the ways in which Roseanne's welfare is dependent on the family's welfare. From these women's social, cultural and economic location 'feminism is seen to be selfish, a prerogative of the privileged, something that benefits those in different economic, social and cultural circumstances', benefits from which they feel excluded (Skeggs 1997, 153).

However, Skeggs argues that feminism was also used by some
of the women as a framework which enabled them to understand
bad experiences such as domestic violence and to envisage
change (p. 157). Furthermore, 'Although not clearly identifying
or recognising themselves as feminist, the women are involved in
many struggles which could be seen as feminist; over the use of
space, constructing safe areas for the children to play, organizing
campaigns to save a local nursery and challenging sexist behaviour [...] feminist scholars often forget the amount of daily
struggle and resistance in which women are engaged' (pp.
155–6). Once formulated in this way, 'women's struggles' take on
a form which can be claimed for 'feminism' while not recognising
themselves as 'feminist'. While it is possible to see such practices
as post-feminist, and formed in relation to feminism, it is also
important to recognise that these forms of struggle and resistance
may not be directly indebted to feminism and, indeed, may have
existed prior to (second-wave) feminism. Such caution might also
begin to break down the antagonism between feminism and the
popular, the feminist and the 'ordinary woman', because it opens
up questions of how popular practices which might be identified
as feminist, pre-date 1970s feminism.

Skeggs' study also highlights the lived experience of being the
'other woman' of feminist discourse. 'They did not recognize
themselves as the "woman" of much feminist address and they
did not want, yet again, to be positioned as other to it and judged
as lacking ... They rarely gave their consent to feminism because
they were rarely addressed, recruited or asked' (p. 156). This
demonstrates the ways in which the opposition between the feminist and her 'other', the 'ordinary woman', in structuring feminist
discourses produces material effects which severely undermines
the claims of feminism to act on behalf of 'women': 'The subject
of feminism should not be normalized, "othered", made invisible
or made to feel inadequate' (p. 158). The importance of some
forms of 'popular feminism' such as those seen on *Oprah* is not
simply about the size of their audience but the ways in which their
mode of address seeks to include rather than exclude.

Feminism and distinction

Throughout this book I have demonstrated how there has been a
shift in feminist cultural criticism from a situation in which feminists positioned themselves as outside of and against the popular,

to one in which feminists have considered not only how different popular forms and practices may privilege feminine competences that have traditionally been devalued, but also explored how feminism itself has entered the popular. However, to grant legitimacy to forms of popular feminism entails giving up some forms of feminist authority. The tensions produced by this can be seen in the recurring opposition between the 'feminist' and the 'ordinary woman'. The 'feminist' and the 'ordinary woman' are not reflections of pre-existing identities but are the product of the way 'we create groups with words' (Bourdieu cited in Thornton 1995, 101): the activities that feminists attribute to the 'ordinary woman' cannot be equated with actual 'women'. However, as Thornton argues, 'Distinctions are never just assertions of equal difference; they usually entail some claim to authority and presume the inferiority of *others*' (1995, 10). If feminism is predicated on a model where, on the one hand, it claims to 'speak' for women, but, on the other hand, is based on a refusal of these women as inferior to the feminist, then it is necessary to think very carefully about the power relations which sustain feminism's legitimacy. Furthermore, if the historically produced identity 'feminist' positions 'ordinary women' as its inferior other, it is not surprising that feminism should be refused. Indeed, in Bourdieu's (1984) terms, this acts as a refusal of the refusal that feminists have made of them. As Skeggs argues, 'Why should women incur losses on their cultural capital to inhabit a position that they recognize as belonging to others ... who have the power to make negative evaluations of them?' (1997, 57).

There remains in much feminist cultural criticism an underlying 'recruitism' in which the objective of feminist cultural politics is to 'make-over' both 'the popular' and 'the ordinary woman'. This, it has been argued, reproduces power relations between women in which the feminist is seen to have the expertise and the authority to legislate on what is in 'women's interests'. As Ang and Hermes have argued, 'a flexible and pragmatic form of criticism might be more effective than one based on predefined truths, feminist or otherwise' (1996, 129). Indeed, instead of popular culture being the object of a feminist 'make-over', analysing 'the popular' could teach feminists how to 'make-over' feminism.

Notes

1 See Creed (1993) and Penley (1989).
2 For examples, *Ultimate Betrayal* focuses on the needs of sisters to act together to bring a court case against their father who sexually abused them as children. *For their Own Good* shows how class and gender intersect in the workplace. The film centres on a group of women working in a factory with dangerous chemicals whose employers, in an attempt to avoid law-suits against them, force them to choose between having a hysterectomy and losing their job, only to make them redundant a short time later. *With Hostile Intent* shows the need to act together to fight the victimisation of female police officers by their male colleagues. *When He's Not a Stranger* shows that collective action is necessary in order to prosecute a date rapist.
3 For more on gender and made-for-TV movies, see Rapping (1992; 1994).
4 I am aware that in taking the views of the women in Skeggs' study out of the carefully constructed context of her work that I am in danger of making these women act as 'the voice' of 'ordinary women', something that Skeggs herself avoids in her book.

Further reading

Ang, I. and Hermes, J. Gender and/in Media Consumption, in I. Ang, *Living Room Wars: Rethinking Media Audiences for a Postmodern World* (London, Routledge, 1996)
Brunsdon, C. *Screen Tastes: Soap Opera to Satellite Dishes* (London, Routledge, 1997)
Gamman, L. and Marshment, M., eds, *The Female Gaze: Women as Viewers of Popular Culture* (London, Women's Press, 1988)
McRobbie, A. *Postmodernism and Popular Culture* (London, Routledge, 1994)
Skeggs, B. *Formations of Class and Gender* (London, Sage, 1997)
Wicke, J. Celebrity Material: Materialist Feminism and the Culture of Celebrity, *The South Atlantic Quarterly*, 93(4), 1994.

References

Aitkenhead, D. (1997), Fem and Us, *Guardian*, G2, 13 May 1997, pp. 4–5.

Alexander, S. and Taylor, B. (1981), In Defence of 'Patriarchy', in R. Samuel, ed., *People's History and Socialist Theory*, London, Routledge & Kegan Paul.

Amos, V. and Parmar, P. (1997), Challenging Imperial Feminism, in H. S. Mirza, ed., *Black British Feminism: A Reader*, London, Routledge.

Ang, I. (1996), *Living Room Wars: Rethinking Media Audiences for a Postmodern World*, London, Routledge.

Ang, I. (1990), Melodramatic Identifications: Television Fiction and Women's Fantasy, in M. E. Brown, ed., *Television and Women's Culture*, London, Sage.

Ang, I. (1985), *Watching Dallas: Soap Opera and the Melodramatic Imagination*, London, Methuen.

Ang, I. and Hermes, J. (1996), Gender and/in Media Consumption, in I. Ang, *Living Room Wars: Rethinking Media Audiences for a Postmodern World*, London, Routledge.

Appadurai, A. (1986), Introduction: Commodities and the Politics of Value, in A. Appadurai, ed., *The Social Life of Things*, Cambridge, Cambridge University Press.

Assiter, A. (1989), *Pornography, Feminism and the Individual*, London, Pluto.

Attfield, J. (1995), Inside Pram Town: A Case Study of Harlow House Interiors, 1951–61, in J. Attfield and P. Kirkham, eds, *A View from the Interior: Women and Design* (1995 edition), London, Women's Press.

Attfield, J. (1990), The Empty Cocktail Cabinet: Display in the Mid-century British Domestic Interior, in T. Putnam and C. Newton, eds, *Household Choices*, London, Middlesex Polytechnic and Future Publications.

Attfield, J. (1989), FORM/female FOLLOWS FUNCTION/male: Feminist Critiques of Design, in J. A. Walker, *Design History and the History of Design*, London, Pluto.

Aziz, R. (1997), Feminism and the Challenge of Racism: Deviance or Difference?, in H. S. Mirza, ed., *Black British Feminism: A Reader*, London, Routledge.

Barker, M. (1989), *Comics: Ideology, Power and the Critics*, Manchester, Manchester University Press.

Barnard, M. (1996), *Fashion as Communication*, London, Routledge.

Barrett, M. (1988), *Women's Oppression Today: the Marxist/Feminist Encounter* (second edition), London, Verso.

Barrett, M. (1982), Feminism and the Definition of Cultural Politics, in R. Brunt and C. Rowan, eds, *Feminism, Culture and Politics*, London, Lawrence and Wishart.

Barrett, M. and Phillips, A. (1992), Introduction, in M. Barrett and A. Phillips, eds, *Destabilising Theory: Contemporary Feminist Debates*, Cambridge, Polity.

Bayton, M. (1993), Feminist Musical Practice: Problems and Contradictions, in T. Bennett *et al.*, eds, *Rock and Popular Music: Politics, Policies, Institutions*, London, Routledge.

Bayton, M. (1992), Out on the Margins: Feminism and the Study of Popular Music, *Women: A Cultural Review*, 3(1), 51–9.

Bayton, M. (1990), How Women Become Musicians, in S. Frith and A. Goodwin, eds, *On Record: Rock, Pop and the Written Word*, London, Routledge.

Becker. G. *et al.* (1995), Lesbians and Film, in C. K. Creekmur and A. Doty, eds, *Out in Culture: Gay, Lesbian and Queer Essays on Popular Culture*, London, Cassell.

Beechey, V. (1987), *Unequal Work*, London, Verso.

Bennett, T. (1986a), Introduction: Popular Culture and 'the Turn to Gramsci', in T. Bennett, C. Mercer and J. Woollacott, eds, *Popular Culture and Social Relations*, Milton Keynes, Open University Press.

Bennett, T. (1986b), The Politics of the 'Popular' and Popular Culture, in T. Bennett, C. Mercer and J. Woollacott, eds, *Popular Culture and Social Relations*, Milton Keynes, Open University Press.

Bergstrom, J. (1988), Rereading the Work of Claire Johnston, in C. Penley, ed., *Feminism and Film Theory*, New York and London, Routledge.

Blackman, I. (1995), White Girls are Easy, Black Girls are Studs, in L. Pearce and J. Stacey, eds, *Romance Revisited*, London, Lawrence and Wishart.

Blackman, I. and Perry, K. (1990), Skirting the Issue: Lesbian Fashion for the 1990s, *Feminist Review*, 34, 67–78.

Bobo, J. (1988), *The Colour Purple*: Black Women as Cultural Readers, in D. Pribram, ed., *Female Spectators: Looking at Film and Television*, London, Verso.

Bobo, J. and Seiter, E. (1997), Black Feminism and Media Criticism: *The Women of Brewster Place*, in C. Brunsdon, J. D'Acci and L. Spigel, eds, *Feminist Television Criticism: A Reader*, Oxford, Oxford University Press.

Bourdieu, P. (1984), *Distinction: A Social Critique of the Judgement of Taste*, London, Routledge.

Bowlby, R. (1993), *Shopping with Freud*, London, Routledge.

Bowlby, R. (1992), *Still Crazy After all these Years: Women, Writing and Psychoanalysis*, London, Routledge.

Boys, J. (1996), (Mis)Representations of Society? Problems in the Relationship between Architectural Aesthetics and Social Meanings, in J. Palmer and M. Dodson, eds, *Design and Aesthetics: a Reader*, London, Routledge.

Boys, J. (1995), From Alcatraz to the OK Corral: Images of Class and Gender in Housing Design, in J. Attfield and P. Kirkham, eds, *A View from the Interior: Women and Design* (1995 edition), London, Women's Press.

Bradby, B. (1993), Sampling Sexuality: Gender, Technology and the Body in Dance Music, *Popular Music*, 12(2), 155–76.

Bradby, B. (1990), Do-Talk and Don't-Talk: The Division of the Subject in Girl Music, in S. Frith and A. Goodwin, eds, *On Record: Rock, Pop and the Written Word*, London, Routledge.

Bradley, D. (1992), *Understanding Rock 'n' Roll: Popular Music in Britain 1955–1964*, Milton Keynes, Open University Press.

Brantlinger, P. (1990), *Crusoe's Footsteps: Cultural Studies in Britain and America*, London, Routledge.

Breward, C. (1995), *The Culture of Fashion*, Manchester, Manchester University Press.

Brown, M. E. (1994), *Soap Opera and Women's Talk: The Pleasure of Resistance*, London, Sage.

Brownmiller, S. (1984), *Femininity*, New York, Fawcett Columbine.

Brownmiller, S. (1977), *Against Our Will: Men, Women, Rape*, Harmondsworth, Penguin.

Brunsdon, C. (1997), *Screen Tastes: Soap Opera to Satellite Dishes*, London, Routledge.

Brunsdon, C. (1996), A Thief in the Night: Stories of Feminism in the 1970s at CCCS, in D. Morley and K. H. Chen, eds, *Stuart Hall: Critical Dialogues in Cultural Studies*, London, Routledge.

Brunsdon, C. (1995), The Role of Soap Opera in the Development of Feminist Television Scholarship, in R. C. Allen, ed., *To Be Continued . . . : Soap Operas*

Around the World, London, Routledge.

Brunsdon, C. (1993), Identity in Feminist Television Criticism, *Media, Culture and Society*, 15, 309–20.

Brunsdon, C. (1991), Pedagogies of the Feminine: Feminist Teaching and Women's Genres, *Screen*, 32(4), 364–81.

Brunsdon, C. (1989), Text and Audience, in E. Seiter *et al.*, eds, *Remote Control: Television, Audience and Cultural Power*, London, Routledge.

Brunsdon, C. (1981), *Crossroads*: Notes on a Soap Opera, *Screen*, 22(4), 32–7.

Brunsdon, C. (1978), 'It is Well Known that by Nature Women are Inclined to be Rather Personal', in Women's Studies Group, eds, *Women Take Issue*, Centre for Contemporary Cultural Studies, London, Hutchinson.

Brunsdon, C., D'Acci, J. and Spigel, L., eds, (1997), *Feminist Television Criticism: A Reader*, Oxford, Oxford University Press.

Budge, B. (1988), Joan Collins and the Wilder Side of Women, in L. Gamman and M. Marshment, eds, *The Female Gaze: Women as Viewers of Popular Culture*, London, Women's Press.

Butler, J. (1990), *Gender Trouble: Feminism and the Subversion of Identity*, London, Routledge.

Byars, J. (1991), *All that Hollywood Allows: Re-reading Gender in 1950s Melodrama*, London, Routledge.

Carter, E. (1984), Alice in Consumer Wonderland, in A. McRobbie and M. Nava, eds, *Gender and Generation*, Basingstoke, Macmillan.

Chaney, D. (1983), The Department Store as Cultural Form, *Theory, Culture and Society*, 1(3), 22–31

(charles), H. (1995), (Not) Compromising: Inter-Skin Colour Relations, in L. Pearce and J. Stacey, eds, *Romance Revisited*, London, Lawrence and Wishart.

Charles, N. (1995), Food and Family Ideology, in S. Jackson and S. Moores, eds, *The Politics of Domestic Consumption: Critical Readings*, Hemel Hempstead, Prentice Hall/Harvester Wheatsheaf.

Charles, N. and Kerr, M. (1988), *Women, Food and Families*, Manchester, Manchester University Press.

Christian-Smith, L. K. (1988), Romancing the Girl: Adolescent Romance Novels and the Construction of Femininity, in L. G. Roman, L. K. Christian-Smith with E. Ellsworth, eds, *Becoming Feminine: The Politics of Popular Culture*, Lewes and Philadelphia, Falmer Press.

Citron, M. (1988), Women's Film Production: Going Mainstream, in D. Pribram, ed., *Female Spectators: Looking at Film and Television*, London, Verso.

Clarke, A. J. (1997), Tupperware: Suburbia, Sociality and Mass Consumption, in R. Silverstone, ed., *Visions of Suburbia*, London, Routledge.

Clark, D. (1995), Commodity Lesbianism, in C. K. Creekmur and A. Doty, eds, *Out in Culture: Gay, Lesbian and Queer Essays on Popular Culture*, London, Cassell.

Clarke, G. (1990), Defending Ski-Jumpers: A Critique of Theories of Youth Subcultures, in S. Frith and A. Goodwin, eds, *On Record: Rock, Pop and the Written Word*, London, Routledge.

Clarke, J. *et al.* (1976), Subcultures, Cultures and Class: A Theoretical Overview, in S. Hall and T. Jefferson, eds, *Resistance Through Rituals: Youth Cultures in Post-war Britain*, London, Hutchinson.

Cohen, S. (1997), Men Making a Scene: Rock Music and the Production of Gender, in S. Whiteley, ed., *Sexing the Groove: Popular Music and Gender*, London and New York, Routledge.

Cohen, S. (1991), *Rock Culture in Liverpool: Popular Music in the Making*, Oxford, Clarendon.

Collecott, D. (1995), Bryher's *Two Selves* as Lesbian Romance, in L. Pearce and J. Stacey, eds, *Romance Revisited*, London, Lawrence and Wishart.

Cook, P. and Johnston, C. (1988), The Place of Woman in the Cinema of Raoul Walsh, in C. Penley, ed., *Feminism and Film Theory*, New York and London, Routledge.

Coote, A. and Campbell, B. (1987), *Sweet Freedom* (second edition), Oxford, Blackwell.

Coward, R. (1984), *Female Desire: Women's Sexuality Today*, London, Paladin.

Craik, J. (1994), *The Face of Fashion: Cultural Studies in Fashion*, London, Routledge.

Creed, B. (1993), *The Monstrous-Feminine: Film, Feminism, Psychoanalysis*, London, Routledge.

Daly, M. (1988), In Cahoots with J. Caputi, *Websters' First New Intergalatic Wickedary of the English Language*, London, Women's Press.

Daly, M. (1979), *Gyn/Ecology: The Metaethics of Radical Feminism*, London, Women's Press.

Davis, F. (1992), *Fashion, Culture and Identity*, Chicago, Chicago University Press.

De Beauvoir, S. (1972), *The Second Sex*, (translated and edited by H. M. Parshley), Harmondsworth, Penguin.

de Lauretis, T. (1994), *The Practice of Love: Lesbian Sexuality and Perverse Desire*, Bloomington and Indiana, Indiana University Press.

de Lauretis, T. (1988), Aesthetic and Feminist Theory: Rethinking Women's Cinema, in D. Pribram, ed., *Female Spectators: Looking at Film and Television*, London, Verso.

Deming, C. J. (1990), For Television-Centred Television Criticism: Lessons for Feminism, in M. E. Brown, ed., *Television and Women's Culture*, London, Sage.

DeVault, M. (1991), *Feeding the Family: The Social Organisation of Caring as Gendered Work*, Chicago, University of Chicago Press.

Doane, M. A. (1991), *Femme Fatales: Feminism, Film Theory, Psychoanalysis*, New York and London, Routledge.

Doane, M. A. (1987), *The Desire to Desire: The Woman's Film of the 1940s*, Basingstoke, Macmillan.

Dorner, J. (1995), *Fashion in the Forties and Fifties*, London, Allan.

Douglas, A. (1980), Soft-Porn Culture, *The New Republic*, 30 August 1980, 25–9.

Dowling, R. (1993), Femininity, Place and Commodities: A Retail Case Study, *Antipode*, 25(4), 295–319.

Dworkin, A. (1981), *Pornography: Men Possessing Women*, London, Women's Press.

Eckert, C. (1990), Carole Lombard in Macey's Window, in J. Gaines and C. Herzog, eds, *Fabrications: Costume and the Female Body*, New York, Routledge.

Ehrenreich, B., Hess, E. and Jacobs, G. (1992), Beatlemania: Girls Just Want to Have Fun, in L. Lewis, ed., *The Adoring Audience: Fan Culture and Popular Media*, London, Routledge.

Elsaesser, T. (1987), Tales of Sound and Fury: Observations on the Family Melodrama, in C. Gledhill, ed., *Home is Where the Heart is: Studies in Melodrama and the Woman's Film*, London, British Film Institute.

Embree, A. (1970), Media Images 1: Madison Avenue Brainwashing – The Facts, in R. Morgan, ed., *Sisterhood is Powerful: An Anthology of Writing from the Women's Liberation Movement*, New York, Vintage.

Entwistle, J. (1997), 'Power Dressing' and the Construction of the Career Woman, in M. Nava, A. Blake, I. MacRury and B. Richards, eds, *Buy This Book: Studies in Advertising and Consumption*, London, Routledge.

Evans, C. and Thornton, M. (1991), Fashion, Representation, Femininity, *Feminist Review*, 38, 48–66.

Evans, C. and Thornton, M. (1989), *Women and Fashion: A New Look*, London, Quartet.

Evans, S. (1980), *Personal Politics: The Roots of Women's Liberation in the Civil Rights Movement and the Left*, New York, Vintage.

Faludi, S. (1992), *Backlash: The Undeclared War Against Women*, London, Vintage.

Featherstone, M. (1991), *Consumer Culture and Postmodernism*, London, Sage.

Finch, M. (1986), Sex and Address in *Dynasty*, *Screen* 27(6), 24–42.

Firestone, S. (1979), *The Dialectic of Sex: The Case for Feminist Revolution*, London, Women's Press.

Fiske, J. (1989), *Understanding Popular Culture*, London, Unwin Hyman.

Flitterman-Lewis, S. (1992), Psychoanalysis, Film and Television, in R. C. Allen, ed., *Channels of Discourse, Reassembled*, London, Routledge.

Forty, A. (1986), *Objects of Desire: Design and Society since 1750*, London, Thames and Hudson.

Foucault, M. (1981), *The History of Sexuality Vol. I: An Introduction*, Harmondsworth, Penguin.

Foucault, M. (1977), *Discipline and Punish: The Birth of the Prison*, London, Allen Lane.

Fowler, B. (1997), *Pierre Bourdieu and Cultural Theory: Critical Investigations*, London, Sage.

Fowler, B. (1991), *The Alienated Reader: Women and Popular Romantic Literature in the Twentieth Century*, Hemel Hempstead, Harvester Wheatsheaf.

Fox Genovese, E. (1991), *Feminism Without Illusions*, Chapel Hill, University of North Carolina Press.

Franklin S., Lury, C. and Stacey, J. (1991) Feminism and Cultural Studies: Pasts, Presents, Futures, in S. Franklin, C. Lury and J. Stacey, eds, *Off-Centre: Feminism and Cultural Studies*, London, HarperCollins Academic.

Frazer, E. (1992), Teenage Girls Reading *Jackie*, in P. Scannell, P. Schlesinger and C. Sparks, eds, *Culture and Power: A Media, Culture and Society Reader*, London, Sage.

Freeman, J. (1978), *The Politics of Women's Liberation: A Case Study of an Emerging Social Movement and its Relationship to the Policy Process*, London, Longman.

Friedan, B. (1963), *The Feminine Mystique*, New York, Dell.

Frith, S. (1990), Afterthoughts, in S. Frith and A. Goodwin, eds, *On Record: Rock, Pop and the Written Word*, London, Routledge.

Frith, S. (1988), *Music for Pleasure*, Cambridge, Polity.

Frith, S. and McRobbie, A. (1990), Rock and Sexuality, in S. Frith and A. Goodwin, eds, *On Record: Rock, Pop and the Written Word*, London, Routledge.

Gaines, J. (1994), White Privilege and Looking Relations: Race and Gender in Feminist Film Theory, in D. Carson, L. Dittmar and J. R. Welsch, eds, *Multiple Voices in Feminist Film Criticism*, Minneapolis, University of Minnesota Press.

Gaines, J. (1990a), Introduction: Fabricating the Female Body, in J. Gaines and C. Herzog, eds, *Fabrications: Costume and the Female Body*, New York, Routledge.

Gaines, J. (1990b), Costume and Narrative: How Dress Tells the Woman's Story, in J. Gaines and C. Herzog, eds, *Fabrications: Costume and the Female Body*, New York, Routledge.

Gallop, J. (1992), *Around 1981: Academic Feminist Literary Criticism*, London, Routledge.

Gamman, L. and Marshment, M. (1988), Introduction, in L. Gamman and M. Marshment, eds, *The Female Gaze: Women as Viewers of Popular Culture*, London, Women's Press.

Garber, J. and McRobbie, A. (1991), Girls and Subcultures, in A. McRobbie *Feminism and Youth Culture: From Jackie to Just Seventeen*, Basingstoke, Macmillan.

Garber, M. (1992), *Vested Interests: Cross-Dressing and Cultural Anxiety*, New York, Routledge.

Garnham, N. (1987), Concepts of Culture: Public Policy and the Cultural Industries, *Cultural Studies*, 1(1), 23–37.

Garratt, S. (1994), All of Me Loves All of You, in J. Aizlewood, ed., *Love is the Drug*, Harmondsworth, Penguin.

Garratt, S. (1990), Teenage Dreams, in S. Frith and A. Goodwin, eds., *On Record: Rock, Pop and the Written Word*, London, Routledge.

Gelb, J. (1987), Social Movement 'Success': A Comparative Analysis of Feminism in the United States and the United Kingdom, in M. Fainsod Katzenstein and C. McClurg Mueller, eds, *The Women's Movement in the United States and Western Europe*, Philadelphia, Temple University Press.

Geraghty, C. (1991), *Women and Soap Opera: A Study of Prime Time Soap Operas*, Cambridge, Polity.

Giles, J. (1995), 'You Meet 'Em and That's It': Working Class Women's Refusal of Romance Between the Wars in Britain, in L. Pearce and J. Stacey, eds, *Romance Revisited*, London, Lawrence and Wishart.

Gledhill, C. (1988), Pleasurable Negotiations, in D. Pribram, ed., *Female Spectators: Looking at Film and Television*, London, Verso.

Gledhill, C., ed. (1987), *Home is Where the Heart is: Studies in Melodrama and the Woman's Film*, London, British Film Institute.

Glennie, P. (1995), Consumption within Historical Studies, in D. Miller, ed., *Acknowledging Consumption: A Review of New Studies*, London, Routledge.

Goodwin, A. (1993), *Dancing in the Distraction Factory: Music Television and Popular Culture*, London, Routledge.

Gottlieb, J. and Wald, G. (1994), Smells Like Teen Spirit: Riot Grrrls, Revolution and Women in Independent Rock, in A. Ross and T. Rose, eds, *Microphone Fiends: Youth Music and Youth Culture*, New York, Routledge.

Gray, A. (1992), *Video Playtime: The Gendering of Leisure Technology*, London, Routledge.

Greer, G. (1970), *The Female Eunuch*, London, MacGibbon and Kay.

Gregson, N. and Crewe, L. (1997), Performance and Possession: Rethinking the Act of Purchase in the Light of the Car Boot Sale, *Journal of Material Culture*, 2(2), 241–63.

Griffin, S. (1981), *Pornography and Silence*, London, Women's Press.

Gripsrud, J. (1995), *The Dynasty Years: Hollywood Television and Critical Media Studies*, London and New York, Routledge.

Grossberg, L. (1993), The Formation of Cultural Studies: An American in Birmingham, in V. Blundell, J. Shepherd, and I. Taylor, eds, *Relocating Cultural Studies: Developments in Theory and Research*, London, Routledge.

Hall, S. (1992), Cultural Studies and its Theoretical Legacies, in L. Grossberg, C. Nelson and P. A. Treichler, *Cultural Studies*, New York, Routledge.

Hall, S. (1986), Cultural Studies: Two Paradigms, in R. Collins *et al.*, eds, *Media, Culture and Society: A Reader*, London, Sage.

Hall, S. (1981), Notes on Deconstructing 'The Popular', in R. Samuel, ed., *People's History and Socialist Theory*, London, Routledge.

Hall, S. (1980), Encoding/Decoding, in S. Hall, D. Hobson, A. Lowe and P. Willis, eds, *Culture, Media, Language*, London, Hutchinson.

Hall, S., Critcher, C., Jefferson, T., Clarke, J. and Roberts, B. (1978), *Policing the Crisis: Mugging, the State and Law and Order*, London, Macmillan.

Hall, S. and Jefferson, T., eds, (1976), *Resistance Through Rituals: Youth Subcultures in Post-war Britain*, London, Hutchinson.

Harker, D. (1980), *One for the Money: Politics and Popular Song*, London, Hutchinson.

Haskell, M. (1987), *From Reverence to Rape: The Treatment of Women in the Movies* (second edition), Chicago, University of Chicago Press.

Hayawaka, S. I. (1957), Popular Songs vs. The Facts of Life, in B. Rosenberg and D. Manning White, eds, *Mass Culture: The Popular Arts in America*, New York, Free Press.

Hebdige, D. (1989), After the Masses, in S. Hall and M. Jacques, *New Times: The Changing Face of Politics in the 1990s*, London, Lawrence and Wishart.

Hebdige, D. (1988), *Hiding in the Light: On Images and Things*, London, Routledge.

Hebdige, D. (1979), *Subculture: The Meaning of Style*, London, Methuen.

Heide, M. J. (1995), *Television Culture and Women's Lives: thirtysomething and the Contradictions of Gender*, Philadelphia, University of Pennsylvania Press.

Herzog, C. (1990), 'Powder Puff' Promotion: The Fashion-Show-in-the-Film, in J. Gaines and C. Herzog, eds, *Fabrications: Costume and the Female Body*, New York, Routledge.

Hill, J. (1986), *Sex, Class and Realism: British Cinema 1956–63*, London, British Film Institute.

Hobson, D. (1990), Women Audiences and the Workplace, in M. E. Brown, ed., *Television and Women's Culture*, London, Sage.

Hobson, D. (1989), Soap Operas at Work, in E. Seiter *et al.*, eds, *Remote Control: Television, Audience and Cultural Power*, London, Routledge.

Hoggart, R. (1958), *The Uses of Literacy*, Harmondsworth, Penguin.

Hollows, J. and Jancovich, M., eds, (1995), *Approaches to Popular Film*, Manchester, Manchester University Press.

hooks, b. (1992), *Black Looks: Race and Representation*, London, Turnaround.

hooks, b. (1982), *Ain't I a Woman: Black Women and Feminism*, London, Pluto.

Hughes, D. (1964), Recorded Music, in D. Thompson, ed., *Discrimination and Popular Culture*, Harmondsworth, Penguin.

Huyssen, A. (1986), Mass Culture as Woman: Modernism's Other, in T. Modleski, ed., *Studies in Entertainment: Critical Approaches to Mass Culture*, Bloomington and Indianapolis, Indiana University Press.

Jackson, P. (1993), Towards a Cultural Politics of Consumption, in J. Bird *et al.*, eds, *Mapping the Futures: Local Cultures and Global Change*, London, Routledge.

Jackson, S. (1995), Women and Heterosexual Love: Complicity, Resistance and Change, in L. Pearce and J. Stacey, eds, *Romance Revisited*, London, Lawrence and Wishart.

Jackson, S. (1993), Even Sociologists Fall in Love: An Exploration in the Sociology of the Emotions, *Sociology*, 27(2), 201–20.

Jameson, F. (1979), Reification and Utopia in Mass Culture, *Social Text*, 1, 130–48

Jancovich, M. (1995), Screen Theory, in J. Hollows and M. Jancovich, eds, *Approaches to Popular Film*, Manchester, Manchester University Press.

Janus, N. Z. (1996), Research on Sex Roles in Mass Media: Towards a Critical Approach, in H. Baehr and A. Gray, eds, *Turning It On: A Reader in Women and Media*, London, Edward Arnold.

Jenson, J. (1992), Fandom as Pathology: The Consequences of Characterisation, in L. Lewis, ed., *The Adoring Audience: Fan Culture and Popular Media*, London, Routledge.

Johnson, R. (1986), The Story So Far: And Further Transformations?, in D. Punter, ed., *Introduction to Contemporary Cultural Studies*, Harlow, Longman.

Johnston, C. (1988), Dorothy Arzner: Critical Strategies, in C. Penley, ed., *Feminism and Film Theory*, New York and London, Routledge.

Jones, A. R. (1986), Mills and Boon meets Feminism, in J. Radford, ed., *The Progress of Romance: The Politics of Popular Fiction*, London, Routledge & Kegan Paul.

Jordan, G. and Weedon, C. (1995), *Cultural Politics: Class, Gender, Race and the Postmodern World*, Oxford, Blackwell.

Kahn, N. (1993), Asian Women's Dress: From Borqah to Bloggs – Changing Clothes for Changing Times, in J. Ash and E. Wilson, eds, *Chic Thrills: A Fashion Reader*, Berkeley and Los Angeles, University of California Press.

Kaplan, C. (1986), *Sea Changes: Culture and Feminism*, London, Verso.

Kaplan, E. A. (1987a), Mothering, Feminism and Representation: The Maternal in Melodrama and the Woman's Film 1910–40, in C. Gledhill, ed., *Home is Where the Heart is: Studies in Melodrama and the Woman's Film*, London, British Film Institute.

Kaplan, E. A. (1987b), *Rocking Around the Clock: Music Television, Postmodernism and Consumer Culture*, London, Methuen.

Kaplan, E. A. (1983), *Women and Film: Both Sides of the Camera*, New York, Methuen.

Kearney, M. C. (1997), The Missing Links: Riot Grrrl – Feminism – Lesbian Culture, in S. Whiteley, ed., *Sexing the Groove: Popular Music and Gender*, London and New York, Routledge.

Klinger, B. (1994), *Melodrama and Meaning: History, Culture and the Films of Douglas Sirk*, Bloomington and Indianapolis, Indiana University Press.

Knight, P. G. (1997), Naming the Problem: Feminism and the Figuration of Conspiracy, *Cultural Studies*, 11(1), 40–63.

Kuhn, A. (1984), Women's Genres, *Screen*, 25(1), 18–28.

Kuhn, A. (1982), *Women's Pictures: Feminism and Cinema*, London, Routledge & Kegan Paul.

Laermans, R. (1993), Learning to Consume: Early Department Stores, and, the Shaping of Modern Consumer Culture (1860–1914), *Theory, Culture and Society*, 10, 79–102.

LaPlace, M. (1987), Producing and Consuming the Woman's Film: Discursive Struggle in *Now Voyager*, in C. Gledhill, ed., *Home is Where the Heart is: Studies in Melodrama and the Woman's Film*, London, British Film Institute.

Lee, J. (1995), Subversive Sitcoms: *Roseanne* as Inspiration for Feminist Resistance, in G. Dines and J. M. Humez, eds, *Gender, Race and Class in Media: A Text-Reader*, Thousand Oaks, California, Sage.

Lee, J. (1988), Care to Join Me in an Upwardly Mobile Tango? Postmodernism and the 'New Woman', in L. Gamman and M. Marshment, eds, *The Female Gaze: Women as Viewers of Popular Culture*, London, Women's Press.

Lee, M. J. (1993), *Consumer Culture Reborn: The Cultural Politics of Consumption*, London, Routledge.

Leopold, E. (1993), The Manufacture of the Fashion System, in J. Ash and E. Wilson, eds, *Chic Thrills: A Fashion Reader*, Berkeley and Los Angeles, University of California Press.

Lewis, L. A. (1990), Consumer Girl Culture: How Music Video Appeals to Girls, in M. E. Brown, ed., *Television and Women's Culture: The Politics of the Popular*, London, Sage.

Light, A. (1984), Returning to Manderley: Romantic Fiction, Female Sexuality and Class, *Feminist Review*, 16, 7–25.

Lloyd, F., ed., (1993), *Madonna*, London, Batsford.

Lovell, T. (1990), Landscapes and Stories in 1960s British Realism, *Screen*, 31(4), 357–76.

Lunt, P. K. and Livingstone, S. M. (1992), *Mass Consumption and Personal Identity: Everyday Economic Experience*, Milton Keynes, Open University Press.

Lupton, D. (1996), *Food, the Body and the Self*, London, Sage.

Lury, C. (1996), *Consumer Culture*, Cambridge, Polity.

Lury, C. (1995a), The Rights and Wrongs of Culture: Issues of Theory and Methodology, in B. Skeggs, ed., *Feminist Cultural Theory: Process and Production*, Manchester, Manchester University Press.

Lury, C. (1995b), A Public Romance: 'The Charles and Di Story', in L. Pearce and J. Stacey, eds, *Romance Revisited*, London, Lawrence and Wishart.

MacDonald, M. (1995), *Representing Women: Myths of Femininity in the Popular Media*, London, Edward Arnold.

McGuigan, J. (1992), *Cultural Populism*, London, Routledge.

McNeil, P. (1993), 'Put Your Best Foot Forward': The Impact of the Second World War on British Dress, *Journal of Design History*, 6(4), 283–99.

McRobbie, A. (1997a), The Es and the Anti-Es: New Questions for Feminism and Cultural Studies, in M. Ferguson and P. Golding, eds, *Cultural Studies in Question*, London, Sage.

McRobbie, A. (1997b), Bridging the Gap: Feminism, Fashion and Consumption, *Feminist Review*, 55, 73–89.

McRobbie, A. (1997c), *More!*: New Sexualities in Girls' and Women's Magazines, in A. McRobbie, ed., *Back to Reality? Social Experience and Cultural Studies*, Manchester, Manchester University Press.

McRobbie, A. (1996), *More!*: New Sexualities in Girls' and Women's Magazines, in J. Curran, D. Morley and V. Walkerdine, eds, *Cultural Studies and Communication*, London, Edward Arnold.

McRobbie, A. (1994), *Postmodernism and Popular Culture*, London, Routledge.

McRobbie, A. (1991), *Feminism and Youth Culture: From Jackie to Just Seventeen*, Basingstoke, Macmillan.

McRobbie, A. (1981), Just Like a *Jackie* Story, in A. McRobbie and T. McCabe, eds, *Feminism for Girls: An Adventure Story*, London, Routledge & Kegan Paul.

McRobbie, A. and Nava, M., eds, (1984), *Gender and Generation*, Basingstoke, Macmillan.

Madigan, R. and Munro, M. (1990), Ideal Homes: Gender and Domestic Architecture, in T. Putnam and C. Newton, eds, *Household Choices*, London, Middlesex Polytechnic and Future Publications.

Manifesto for New Times (1989), The New Times, in S. Hall and M. Jacques, eds, *New Times: The Changing Face of Politics in the 1990s*, London, Lawrence and Wishart.

Marshment, M. (1988), Substantial Women, in L. Gamman and M. Marshment, eds, *The Female Gaze: Women as Viewers of Popular Culture*, London, Women's Press.

Massey, D. (1994), *Space, Place and Gender*, Cambridge, Polity.

Massey, D. (1993), Power-Geometry and a Progressive Sense of Place, in J. Bird et al., eds, *Mapping the Futures: Local Cultures and Global Change*, London, Routledge.

Maynard, M. (1995), 'The Wishful Feeling about Curves': Fashion, Femininity and the 'New Look' in Australia, *Journal of Design History*, 8(1), 43–59.

Mayne, J. (1993), *Cinema and Spectatorship*, London and New York, Routledge.

Meyerowitz, J., ed., (1994), *Not June Cleaver: Women and Gender in Postwar America 1945–60*, Philadelphia, Temple University Press.

Middleton, R. (1990), *Studying Popular Music*, Milton Keynes, Open University Press.

Miles, C. (1997), Spatial Politics: A Gendered Sense of Place, in S. Redhead with D. Wynne and J. O'Connor, eds, *The Clubcultures Reader: Readings in Popular Cultural Studies*, Oxford, Blackwell.

Mirza, H. S. (1997), Introduction: Mapping a Genealogy of Black British Feminism, in H. S. Mirza, ed., *Black British Feminism: A Reader*, London, Routledge.

Miller, D. (1998), *A Theory of Shopping*, Cambridge, Polity.

Miller, D. (1995), Consumption as the Vanguard of History: A Polemic by way of an Introduction, in D. Miller, ed., *Acknowledging Consumption: A Review of New Studies*, London, Routledge.

Miller, D. (1994), Material Culture and Mass Consumption, (1994 edition), Oxford, Blackwell.

Miller, D. (1990), Appropriating the State on the Council Estate, in T. Putnam and C. Newton, eds, *Household Choices*, London, Middlesex Polytechnic and Future Publications.

Miller, D., Jackson, P., Thrift, N., Holbrook, B. and Rowlands, M. (1998), *Shopping, Place and Identity*, London, Routledge.

Millet, K. (1977), *Sexual Politics*, London, Virago.

Mitchell, J. (1974), *Psychoanalysis and Feminism*, Harmondsworth, Penguin.

Mitchell, J. and Oakley, A. (1976), Introduction, in J. Mitchell and A. Oakley, eds, *The Rights and Wrongs of Women*, Harmondsworth, Penguin.

Modleski, T. (1987), Time and Desire in the Woman's Film, in C. Gledhill, ed., *Home is Where the Heart is: Studies in Melodrama and the Woman's Film*, London, British Film Institute.

Modleski, T. (1984), *Loving with a Vengeance: Mass-produced Fantasies for Women*, London, Routledge.

Moi, T. (1991), Appropriating Bourdieu: Feminist Theory and Bourdieu's Sociology of Culture, *New Literary History*, 22, 1017–49.

Moi, T. (1985), *Sexual/Textual Politics: Feminist Literary Theory*, London, Methuen.

Morgan, R., ed. (1970), *Sisterhood is Powerful: An Anthology of Writings from the Women's Liberation Movement*, New York, Vintage.

Morley, C. (1990), Homemakers and Design Advice in the Postwar Period, in T. Putnam and C. Newton, eds, *Household Choices*, London, Middlesex Polytechnic and Future Publications.

Morley, D. (1995), Theories of Consumption in Media Studies, in D. Miller, ed., *Acknowledging Consumption: A Review of New Studies*, London, Routledge.

Morley, D. (1992), *Television, Audiences and Cultural Studies*, London, Routledge.

Morley, D. (1986), *Family Television*, London, Routledge/Comedia.

Morris, M. (1997), A Question of Cultural Studies, in A. McRobbie, ed., *Back to Reality? Social Experience and Cultural Studies*, Manchester, Manchester University Press.

Morris, M (1988a), *The Pirate's Fiancee: Feminism, Reading, Postmodernism*, London, Verso.

Morris, M. (1988b), Banality in Cultural Studies, *Block*, 14, 14–23.

Mort, F. (1996), *Cultures of Consumption: Masculinities and Social Space in Late Twentieth-century Britain*, London, Routledge.

Mort, F. (1989), The Politics of Consumption, in S. Hall and M. Jacques, eds, *New Times: The Changing Face of Politics in the 1990s*, London, Lawrence and Wishart.

Mort, F. (1988), Boys Own? Masculinity, Style and Popular Culture, in R. Chapman and J. Rutherford, eds, *Male Order: Unwrapping Masculinity*, London, Lawrence and Wishart.

Moss, G. (1989), *Un/Popular Fictions*, London, Virago.

Mulvey, L. (1988a), Visual Pleasure and Narrative Cinema, in C. Penley, ed., *Feminism and Film Theory*, New York and London, Routledge.

Mulvey, L. (1988b), Afterthoughts on 'Visual Pleasure and Narrative Cinema' Inspired by *Duel in the Sun*, in C. Penley, ed., *Feminism and Film Theory*, New York and London, Routledge.

Mulvey, L. (1987), Notes on Sirk and Melodrama, in C. Gledhill, ed., *Home is Where the Heart is: Studies in Melodrama and the Woman's Film*, London, British Film Institute.

Mumford, L. Stempel (1995), *Love and Ideology in the Afternoon: Soap Opera, Women and Television Genre*, Bloomington and Indianapolis, Indiana University Press.

Murcott, A. (1995), 'Its a Pleasure to Cook for Him': Food, Mealtimes and Gender in some South Wales Households, in S. Jackson and S. Moores, eds, *The Politics of Domestic Consumption*, Hemel Hempstead, Prentice Hall/ Harvester Wheatsheaf.

Murphey, T. (1989), The When, Where, and Who of Pop Lyrics: The Listener's Prerogative, *Popular Music*, 8(2), 185–93.

Myers, K. (1986), *Understains: The Sense and Seduction of Advertising*, London, Comedia.

Nava, M. (1996), Modernity's Disavowal: Women, the City and the Department Store, in M. Nava and A. O'Shea, eds, *Modern Times: Reflections on a Century of English Modernity*, London, Routledge.

Nava, M. (1992), *Changing Cultures: Feminism, Youth and Consumption*, London, Sage.

Nava, M. (1987), Consumption and its Contradictions, *Cultural Studies*, 1:2, 204–10.

Negus, K. (1996), *Popular Music in Theory: An Introduction*, Cambridge, Polity.

Negus, K. (1992), *Producing Pop: Culture and Conflict in the Popular Music Industry*, London, Edward Arnold.

Nelson, C., Treichler, P. A. and Grossberg, L. (1992), Cultural Studies: An Introduction, in L. Grossberg, C. Nelson and P. A. Treichler, eds, *Cultural Studies*, New York, Routledge.

Nixon, S. (1993), Looking for the Holy Grail: Publishing and Advertising Strategies for Contemporary Men's Magazines, *Cultural Studies*, 7(3), 467–92.

Nkweto Simmonds, F. (1995), Love in Black and White, in L. Pearce and J. Stacey, eds, *Romance Revisited*, London, Lawrence and Wishart.

Nochimson, M. (1992), *No End to Her: Soap Opera and the Female Subject*, Berkeley, University of California Press.

Partington, A. (1995a), The Designer Housewife in the 1950s, in J. Attfield and P. Kirkham, eds, *A View from the Interior: Women and Design*, (1995 edition),

London, Women's Press.

Partington, A. (1995b), The Days of the New Look: Consumer Culture and Working Class Affluence, in J. Fyrth, ed., *Labour's Promised Land: Culture and Society in Labour Britain, 1945-51*, London, Lawrence and Wishart.

Partington, A. (1993), Popular Fashion and Working Class Affluence, in J. Ash and E. Wilson, eds, *Chic Thrills: A Fashion Reader*, Berkeley and Los Angeles, University of California Press.

Partington, A. (1991), Melodrama's Gendered Audience, in S. Franklin, C. Lury, and J. Stacey, eds, *Off-Centre: Feminism and Cultural Studies*, London, HarperCollins Academic.

Patton, C. (1995), What is a Nice Lesbian Like You Doing in a Film Like This?, in T. Wilton, ed., *Immortal, Invisible: Lesbians and the Moving Image*, London, Routledge.

Penley, C. (1989), *The Future of an Illusion: Film, Feminism and Psychoanalysis*, London, Routledge.

Perry, I. (1995), It's My Thang and I'll Swing it the Way that I Feel!: Sexuality and Black Women Rappers, in G. Dines and J. M. Humez, eds, *Gender, Race and Class in Media: A Text-Reader*, Thousand Oaks, California, Sage.

Perry, K. (1995), The Heart of Whiteness: White Subjectivity and Interracial Relationships, in L. Pearce and J. Stacey, eds, *Romance Revisited*, London, Lawrence and Wishart.

Petro, P. (1994), Feminism and Film History, in D. Carson, L. Dittmar and J. R. Welsch, eds, *Multiple Voices in Feminist Film Criticism*, Minneapolis, University of Minnesota Press.

Pini, M. (1997), Women and the Early British Rave Scene, in A. McRobbie, ed., *Back to Reality? Social Experience and Cultural Studies*, Manchester, Manchester University Press.

Pleasance, H. (1991), Open or Closed: Popular Magazines and Dominant Culture, in S. Franklin, C. Lury, and J. Stacey, eds, *Off-Centre: Feminism and Cultural Studies*, London, HarperCollins Academic.

Press, A. (1990), Class, Gender and the Female Viewer, in M. E. Brown, ed., *Television and Women's Culture*, London, Sage.

Pribram, D. (1988), Introduction, in D. Pribram, ed., *Female Spectators: Looking at Film and Television*, London, Verso.

Probyn, E. (1993a), *Sexing the Self: Gendered Positions in Cultural Studies*, London, Routledge.

Probyn, E. (1993b), Choosing Choice: 'Winking' Images of Sexuality in Popular Culture, in K. Davis and S. Fisher, eds, *Negotiating in the Margins*, New Brunswick, New Jersey, Rutgers University Press.

Purdie, S. (1992), Janice Radway, *Reading the Romance*, in M. Barker and A. Beezer, eds, *Reading into Cultural Studies*, London, Routledge.

Radford, J., ed. (1986), *The Progress of Romance: The Politics of Popular Fiction*, London: Routledge & Kegan Paul.

Radner, H. (1993), Pretty is as Pretty Does: Free Enterprise and the Marriage Plot, in J. Collins *et al.*, eds, *Film Theory Goes to the Movies*, New York, Routledge.

Radner, H. (1989), 'This Time's For Me': Making Up and Feminine Practice, *Cultural Studies*, 3(3), 301–22.

Radway, J. (1987), *Reading the Romance: Women, Patriarchy and Popular Literature*, London, Verso.

Ramazanoglu, C. (1989), *Feminism and the Contradictions of Oppression*, London, Routledge.

Rapping, E. (1994), *Mediations: Forays into the Culture and Gender Wars*, Boston, South End Press.

Rapping, E. (1992), *The Movie of the Week: Private Stories/Public Events*, Minneapolis, University of Minnesota.

Redhead, S. and Street, J. (1989), Have I the Right? Legitimacy, Authenticity and Community in Folk's Politics, *Popular Music*, 8(2), 177–84.

Reynolds, S. (1997), Rave Culture: Living Dream or Living Death?, in S. Redhead with D. Wynne and J. O'Connor, eds, *The Clubcultures Reader: Readings in Popular Cultural Studies*, Oxford, Blackwell.

Reynolds, S. and Press, J. (1995), *The Sex Revolts: Gender, Rebellion and Rock 'n' Roll*, London, Serpent's Tail.

Roach, J. and Felix, P. (1988), Black Looks, in L. Gammon and M. Marshment, eds, *The Female Gaze*, London, Women's Press.

Roman, L. G. (1988), Intimacy, Labour and Class: Ideologies of Feminine Sexuality in the Punk Slam Dance, in L. G. Roman and L. K. Christian-Smith with E. Ellsworth, eds, *Becoming Feminine: The Politics of Popular Culture*, Lewes and Philadelphia, Falmer Press.

Rose, T. (1994a), Contracting Rap: An Interview with Carmen Ashurst-Watson, in A. Ross and T. Rose, eds, *Microphone Fiends: Youth Music and Youth Culture*, New York, Routledge.

Rose, T. (1994b), *Black Noise: Rap Music and Black Culture in Contemporary America*, New England, Wesleyan University Press.

Rosen, M. (1975), *Popcorn Venus: Women, Movies and the American Dream*, London, Peter Owen.

Ross, A. (1989), *No Respect: Intellectuals and Popular Culture*, London, Routledge.

Rowbotham, S. (1996), Introduction: Mapping the Women's Movement, in M. Threlfall, ed., *Mapping the Women's Movement: Feminist Politics and Social Transformation in the North*, London, Verso.

Rowbotham, S. (1981), The Trouble with 'Patriarchy', in R. Samuel, ed., *People's History and Socialist Theory*, London, Routledge & Kegan Paul.

Rowbotham, S. (1973), *Women's Consciousness, Man's World*, Harmondsworth, Penguin.

Rowe, K. (1997), *Roseanne*: Unruly Woman as Domestic Goddess, in C. Brunsdon, J. D'Acci and L. Spigel, eds, *Feminist Television Criticism: A Reader*, Oxford, Oxford University Press.

Rowe, K. (1995), Studying *Roseanne*, in B. Skeggs, ed., *Feminist Cultural Theory: Process and Production*, Manchester, Manchester University Press.

Ryan, J. (1994), Women, Modernity and the City, *Theory, Culture and Society*, 11(4), 35–64.

Schreier, B. (1984), *Mystique and Identity: Women's Fashions of the 1950s*, New York, Chrysler Museum.

Schwichtenberg, C. (1992), Music Video: The Popular Pleasures of Visual Music, in J. Lull, ed., *Popular Music and Communication*, (second edition), London, Sage.

Schwichtenberg, C., ed. (1993), *The Madonna Connection: Representational Politics, Subcultural Identities, and Cultural Theory*, Boulder, Colorado, Westview Press.

Scott, J. W. (1992), 'Experience', in J. Butler and J. W. Scott, eds, *Feminists Theorise the Political*, New York, Routledge.

Segal, L. (1987), *Is the Future Female? Troubled Thoughts on Contemporary Feminism*, London, Virago.

Seiter, E. *et al.*, eds (1989), 'Don't Treat us Like We're so Stupid and Naive': Towards an Ethnography of Soap Opera Viewers, in E. Seiter *et al.*, *Remote Control: Television, Audience and Cultural Power*, London, Routledge.

Shiach, M. (1994), Feminism and Popular Culture, in J. Storey, ed., *Cultural*

Theory and Popular Culture: A Reader, Hemel Hempstead, Harvester Wheatsheaf.

Silverman, K. (1986), Fragments of a Fashionable Discourse, in T. Modleski, ed., *Studies in Entertainment: Critical Approaches to Mass Culture*, Bloomington and Indianapolis, Indiana University Press.

Skeggs, B. (1997), *Formations of Class and Gender*, London, Sage.

Skeggs, B. (1994), Refusing to be Civilised: 'Race', Sexuality and Power, in H. Afsher and M. Maynard, eds, *The Dynamics of Race and Gender*, London, Taylor and Francis.

Snitow, A. Barr (1983), Mass Market Romance: Pornography for Women is Different in A. Barr Snitow *et al.*, eds, *Powers of Desire: The Politics of Sexuality*, New York, Monthly Review Press.

Sparke, P. (1995), *As Long as it's Pink: The Sexual Politics of Taste*, London, Pandora.

Spigel, L. (1997), From Theatre to Space Ship: Metaphors of Suburban Domesticity in Postwar America, in R. Silverstone, ed., *Vision of Suburbia*, London, Routledge.

Squire, C. (1997), Empowering Women? *The Oprah Winfrey Show*, in C. Brunsdon, J. D'Acci and L. Spigel, eds, *Feminist Television Criticism: A Reader*, Oxford, Oxford University Press.

Stacey, J. (1994), *Star Gazing: Hollywood Cinema and Female Spectatorship*, London, Routledge.

Stacey, J. (1993), Untangling Feminist Theory, in D. Richardson and V. Robinson, eds, *Introducing Women's Studies*, London, Macmillan.

Stacey, J. (1988), Desparately Seeking Difference, in L. Gamman and M. Marshment, eds, *The Female Gaze*, London, Women's Press.

Stacey, J. and Pearce, L. (1995), The Heart of the Matter: Feminists Revisit Romance, in L. Pearce and J. Stacey, eds, *Romance Revisited*, London: Lawrence and Wishart.

Steele, V. (1997), Exhibition Review: Christian Dior. The Costume Institute. The Metropolitan Museum of Art, *Fashion Theory*, 1(2), 231–41.

Stein, A. (1995), All Dressed Up but No Place to Go? Style Wars and the New Lesbianism, in C. K. Creekmur and A. Doty, eds, *Out in Culture: Gay, Lesbian and Queer Essays on Popular Culture*, London, Cassell.

Stockbridge, S. (1990), Rock Video: Pleasure and Resistance, in M. E. Brown, ed., *Television and Women's Culture: The Politics of the Popular*, London, Sage.

Straw, W. (1997), Sizing Up Record Collections: Gender and Connoisseurship in Rock Music Culture, in S. Whiteley, ed., *Sexing the Groove: Popular Music and Gender*, London and New York, Routledge.

Stuart, A. (1990), Feminism – Dead or Alive?, in J. Rutherford, ed., *Identity: Community, Culture, Difference*, London, Lawrence and Wishart.

Tasker, Y. (1998), *Working Girls: Gender and Sexuality in Popular Cinema*, London, Routledge.

Tasker, Y. (1991), Having it All: Feminism and the Pleasures of the Popular, in S. Franklin, C. Lury and J. Stacey, eds, *Off-Centre: Feminism and Cultural Studies*, London, HarperCollins Academic.

Taylor, H. (1989a), *Scarlett's Women: Gone With the Wind and its Female Fans*, London, Virago.

Taylor, H. (1989b), Romantic Readers, in H. Carr, ed., *From My Guy to Sci-Fi: Genre and Women's Writing in the Postmodern World*, London, Pandora.

Taylor, I., Evans, K. and Fraser, P. (1996), *A Tale of Two Cities: Global Change, Local Feeling and Everyday Life in the North of England. A Study in Manchester and Sheffield*, London, Routledge.

Taylor, L. (1995), From Psychoanalytic Feminism to Popular Feminism, in J. Hollows and M. Jancovich, eds, *Approaches to Popular Film*, Manchester, Manchester University Press.

Thomas, H., ed. (1993), *Dance, Gender and Culture*, London, Macmillan.

Thornham, S. (1997), *Passionate Detachments: An Introduction to Feminist Film Theory*, London, Arnold.

Thornton, S. (1995), *Club Cultures: Music, Media and Subcultural Capital*, Cambridge, Polity.

Thornton, S. (1994), Moral Panic, The Media and British Rave Culture, in A. Ross and T. Rose, eds, *Microphone Fiends: Youth Music and Youth Culture*, New York, Routledge.

Thurston, C. (1987), *The Romance Revolution: Erotic Novels for Women and the Quest for a New Sexual Identity*, Urbana and Chicago, University of Illinois Press.

Tong, R. (1992), *Feminist Thought: A Comprehensive Introduction*, London, Routledge.

Traub, V. (1995), The Ambiguities of 'Lesbian' Viewing Pleasure: The (Dis)articulations of *Black Widow*, in C. K. Creekmur and A. Doty, eds, *Out in Culture: Gay, Lesbian and Queer Essays on Popular Culture*, London, Cassell.

Tseëlon, E. (1995), *The Masque of Femininity*, London, Sage.

Tuchman, G. (1978), The Symbolic Annihilation of Women by the Mass Media, in G. Tuchman, A. Kaplan Daniels and J. Benet, eds, *Hearth and Home: Images of Women in the Mass Media*, New York, Oxford University Press.

Turim, M. (1990), Designing Women: the Emergence of the New Sweetheart Line, in J. Gaines and C. Herzog, eds, *Fabrications: Costume and the Female Body*, New York, Routledge.

Turner, G. (1990), *British Cultural Studies: An Introduction*, London, Unwin Hyman.

van Zoonen, L. (1994), *Feminist Media Studies*, London, Sage.

Vice, S. (1995), Addicted to Love, in L. Pearce and J. Stacey, eds, *Romance Revisited*, London, Lawrence and Wishart.

Walkerdine, V. (1997), *Daddy's Girl: Young Girls and Popular Culture*, Basingstoke, Macmillan.

Walkerdine, V. (1990), *Schoolgirl Fictions*, London, Verso.

Walley, J. E. (1960), *The Kitchen*, London, Constable.

Walters, S. D. (1995), *Material Girls: Making Sense of Feminist Cultural Theory*, Berkeley, University of California Press.

Walsh, A. (1984), *Women's Film and Female Experience*, New York, Praeger.

Warde, A. (1997), *Consumption, Food and Taste*, London, Sage.

Warde, A. and Hetherington, K. (1994), English Households and Routine Food Practices, *The Sociological Review*, 42(4), 758–78.

Webster, D. (1988), *Looka Yonder! The Imaginary America of Populist Culture*, London, Comedia/Routledge.

Weedon, C. (1987), *Feminist Practice and Poststructuralist Theory*, Oxford, Blackwell.

Weekes, D. (1997), Shades of Blackness: Young Black Female Constructions of Beauty, in H. S. Mirza, ed., *Black British Feminism: A Reader*, London, Routledge.

Weiss, A. (1994), 'A Queer Feeling When I Look at You': Hollywood Stars and Lesbian Spectatorship in the 1930s, in D. Carson, L. Dittmar and J. R. Welsch, eds, *Multiple Voices in Feminist Film Criticism*, Minneapolis, University of Minnesota Press.

Weiss, A. (1992), *Vampires and Violets: Lesbians in the Cinema*, London, Jonathan Cape.

White, P. (1998), Feminism and Film, in J. Hill and C. Church Gibson, eds, *The Oxford Guide to Film Studies*, Oxford, Oxford University Press.

Whiteley, S. (1997), Seduced by the Sign: An Analysis of the Textual Links between Sound and Image in Pop Videos, in S. Whiteley, ed., *Sexing the Groove: Popular Music and Gender*, London, Routledge.

Wicke, J. (1994), Celebrity Material: Materialist Feminism and the Culture of Celebrity, *The South Atlantic Quarterly*, 93(4), 751–78.

Williams, L. (1987), 'Something Else Besides a Mother': *Stella Dallas* and the Maternal Melodrama, in C. Gledhill, ed., *Home is Where the Heart is: Studies in Melodrama and the Woman's Film*, London, British Film Institute.

Williams, R. (1993), Culture is Ordinary, in A. Gray and J. McGuigan, eds, *Studying Culture: An Introductory Reader*, London, Edward Arnold.

Williamson, J. (1993), *Deadline at Dawn: Film Criticism 1980–1990*, London and New York, Marion Boyars.

Willis, P. (1977), *Learning to Labour: How Working Class Kids Get Working Class Jobs*, Farnborough, Saxon House.

Wilson, E. (1993), Fashion and the Postmodern Body, in J. Ash and E. Wilson, eds, *Chic Thrills: A Fashion Reader*, Berkeley and Los Angeles, University of California Press.

Wilson, E. (1990), Deviant Dress, *Feminist Review*, 35, 67–74.

Wilson, E. (1985), *Adorned in Dreams: Fashion and Modernity*, London, Virago.

Wilton, T. (1995), Introduction: On Invisibility and Mortality, in T. Wilton, ed., *Immortal, Invisible: Lesbians and the Moving Image*, London, Routledge.

Winship, J. (1987), *Inside Women's Magazines*, London, Pandora.

Winship, J. (1985), 'A Girl Needs to Get Street-Wise': Magazines for the 1980s, *Feminist Review*, 20, 25–46.

Wolf, N. (1990), *The Beauty Myth*, London, Chatto and Windus.

Women Take Issue Editorial Group (1978), Women's Studies Group: Trying to do Feminist Intellectual Work, in Women's Studies Group, eds, *Women Take Issue*, Centre for Contemporary Cultural Studies, London, Hutchinson.

Wright, L. (1995), Objectifying Gender: The Stiletto Heel, in J. Attfield and P. Kirkham, eds, *A View from the Interior: Women and Design* (1995 edition), London, Women's Press.

Young, L. (1996), *Fear of the Dark: 'Race', Gender and Sexuality in Cinema*, London, Routledge.

Young, S. (1988), Feminism and the Politics of Power: Whose Gaze is it Anyway?, in L. Gamman and M. Marshment, eds, *The Female Gaze: Women as Viewers of Popular Culture*, London, Women's Press.

Index

Note: 'n' after a page reference refers to a note number on that page.

CPSIA information can be obtained at www.ICGtesting.com
Printed in the USA
LVOW05s1039071114

412205LV00008B/31/P